Mobilizing SAP

Business Processes, ROI and Best Practices

Ravi Kalakota
Paul Kurchina

Mivar Press, Inc.

Publisher's Cataloging-in-Publication Data

Kalakota, Ravi.
   Mobilizing sap : business processes, roi, and best practices / Ravi Kalakota and Paul Kurchina
   p. cm.
   Includes bibliographical references and index.
   ISBN 0-9748270-2-9
   1. Management. 2. Mobile communication systems. 3. Information technology. 4. Business
process—Management.
I. Kalakota, Ravi. II. Kurchina, Paul. III. Title.

HF5548.32 2005
658.8'4—dc21

   2004115683

Mivar Press

Published by Mivar Press, Inc.
4080 McGinnis Ferry Road, Suite 603
Alpharetta, GA 30005

Cover design by Graphix Works.

The publisher offers discounts on this book when ordered in quantity for bulk purchases and
special sales. For more information, please contact Corporate and Government Sales at
Mivar Press at contact@mivarpress.com.

Visit Mivar Press, Inc. on the Web: www.mivarpress.com

Printed in the United States of America.
First Printing 2005

Praise for *Mobilizing SAP*

"Extending SAP enterprise applications to mobile workers in the warehouse, factory floor, and supply chain is something every leading company is thinking about. This book presents a practical how-to guide for extracting tangible ROI from mobile process investments."

Rob Douglas, President, Psion Teklogix Americas

"Mobile technology and applications can become fragmented and, quite simply daunting. Kalakota and Kurchina take the mystery out of mobility. In fact, they provide a roadmap that clearly lays out the SAP application piece and how it smoothly fits into mobile applications (operator rounds, warehousing, condition monitoring). To be competitive, we need this, and we intend to execute."

Robert Soeldner, Executive Vice President Operations, TransAlta

"Mobilizing SAP is a practical guide to identify tangible ROI from your mobility investments. It will enable you to craft a complete change in your enterprise communication strategy, while leveraging your existing corporate assets to attain significant operational improvements."

Cindy L. Warner, Vice President Americas SAP CRM, Capgemini

"A timely read that will be of immense help to companies evaluating the possibilities of mobile business...in Mobilizing SAP, Kalakota and Kurchina help steer companies through the maze of mobile technologies while concentrating on practical real-world strategies to streamline business processes improvement enabled by integrated mobile, wireless, and RFID solutions to create a more responsive enterprise."

Donald J. Frieden, President and CEO, SAT Corporation

"Mobilizing SAP examines the second generation of mobile technologies that unlock trapped productivity. By extending the power of SAP applications, companies can deliver information to the point of business activity where it is needed, resulting in a more informed sales force, and better prepared service technicians."

John G. Bruno, Senior Vice President, Corporate Development, and CIO, Symbol Technologies, Inc.

Contents

Foreword by Shai Agassi vii

Preface ix

Acknowledgements xiii

Part I: The Mobile Fundamentals

1. Mobilizing SAP — Why and Why Now? 1

2. The Mobile Business Landscape 27

3. Mobile Technology — Devices, Operating Systems, and
   Network Infrastructure 47

4. Mobile Application Infrastructure 77

Part II: The Mobile Applications

5. Mobilizing Field Service 101

6. Mobilizing Asset Management 127

7. Mobilizing Direct Store Delivery and Route Accounting 151

8. Mobilizing Sales and Marketing 177

9. Mobilizing Supply Chains 199

10. Mobilizing Employee-Facing Processes and Portals 221

11. Radio Frequency Identification and Auto-ID Infrastructure 241

Part III: Creating the Mobile Strategy

12. Creating and Implementing Your Mobile Solution 273

Endnotes 293

Index 298

Foreword
by Shai Agassi
Member of Executive Board, SAP

The long-term mega-trends are clear: Connectivity to SAP applications (ERP, CRM, SCM, PLM, SRM, and xApps) is going wireless, and many transactions are going to be conducted over powerful handheld computers in the hands of mobile workers. The market for mobile enterprise solutions and services is gaining traction and growing steadily.

Mobility is a strategic innovation issue affecting all areas of business. At SAP, we anticipate that mobile breakthroughs like radio frequency identification (RFID) will spearhead the next wave of business process innovation. Compliance to trading networks, enabled by RFID, will drive the adoption of this technology by the market faster than any of its predecessors. Yet many business and IT managers do not understand what is available or how to implement effective mobile solutions that leverage their investments in SAP.

This book addresses this knowledge gap and identifies mobile process improvement opportunities available by leveraging SAP NetWeaver, RFID, SAP Mobile Business, and third-party mobile applications. It is a must-read for SAP customers and those in the partner community who want to learn how mobile solutions can contribute to ROI.

The perspective of this book is rather unique due to the collaboration of a researcher and a practitioner. Kalakota is a leading authority on IT trends and strategy. Kurchina is a well-known visionary who has been an early adopter of SAP NetWeaver technologies. Both authors are highly regarded in the SAP community.

To help solidify the ideas in the book, SAP was pleased to share its NetWeaver Mobile vision, case studies, and best practices with Kalakota and Kurchina. Through real-world examples, the authors illustrate how SAP's NetWeaver Mobile Infrastructure and applications give SAP customers the opportunity to further improve productivity, reduce errors, cut costs, and maximize the return from their investments.

Another unique aspect of this book is the active participation of many hardware, software, and solutions mobile partners who shared their experiences and insights. In short, Kalakota and Kurchina have co-authored an informative reference that shows by example how organizations can leverage mobile solutions to ensure customer success and value.

As this book demonstrates, the promise of the mobile enterprise is exciting, and its commercial viability is no longer a distant dream. SAP has solutions and infrastructure for mobile business that are designed to take business processes to a new plateau, so start mobilizing your business today.

But, we are just at the beginning of the mobile era of business applications. This book details the first step in the evolutionary process of delivering ubiquitous access to enterprise applications. SAP is looking forward to providing our clients with solutions that enable their employees to work wherever they find themselves and with whatever devices they have available to them.

Shai Agassi
Member of Executive Board
SAP

Preface

Doing more with less. That's the goal of managers faced with increasingly tight budgets across a wide spectrum of industries. Instead of making new investments in enterprise applications, managers across the board are looking for new ways to leverage existing investments, and the spotlight is on SAP.

In the last few years, many companies have spent heavily on SAP applications that integrated their business processes, and they have benefited from tangible improvements in cost and efficiency.

Those same companies now sense another opportunity in mobilizing SAP applications. The goal is to reduce the cost of service, optimize the uptime of their assets, augment operational efficiencies, and enhance customer satisfaction through field operations.

New Opportunities, New Tools, New Understanding

Mobile is becoming central to the way we do business. In the span of a few years, mobile process innovations such as mobile field service and mobile asset management have leaped from being a nice-to-have to a need-to-have enterprise capability. In the food and beverage industry, for example, mobile solutions are considered mission-critical in direct store delivery.

Despite the growing importance of mobilizing the enterprise, most managers still don't understand this complex area. Nor is it easy for them to attain this knowledge. Unlike specialists in the area, managers don't pay attention to the constantly changing technology details necessary to implement a mobile solution. What they are keenly interested in is a business process perspective that shows them how mobile initiatives can contribute to their overall business success. At present, that need goes noticeably unmet.

In particular, the need for a better understanding of SAP NetWeaver Mobile, SAP Mobile Infrastructure, and SAP Solutions for Mobile Business is immediate and widespread.

The Focus of This Book

Best-practice firms realize that the real yardstick for measuring technology value is productivity improvement. Keeping this in mind, this book focuses on a variety of business processes that companies are mobilizing, from sales to service. Our objective is to illustrate the different ways organizations are deploying mobile solutions.

In baseball terms, mobile processes are in the first inning. Like the many technologies before it, people have tended to overestimate the speed of implementation of mobile processes and underestimate their impact. We have only glimpsed the changes that an innovation like the mobile Internet will cause. Add to that the potential of RFID and of powerful handheld computers and smart phones, and there will be profound changes in the way business processes operate.

However, as compelling as its advantages are, true enterprise mobility is highly complex, so another focus of this book is the mobile infrastructure that anchors applications, or what it takes to make mobility work in the real world.

We illustrate the importance of interoperability and integration across systems and applications. Mobile devices must work consistently and reliably. Wireless connections must function persistently and securely, while integrating seamlessly with other enterprise networks and information systems. Monitoring and management capabilities must provide visibility and efficient, centralized control of up to thousands of devices across networks and locations.

What Makes This Book Unique?

Despite the changing market dynamics, most books on mobile business offer either simplistic, high-level overviews in which a single solution is made to fit every problem or the kind of detailed technology analysis and software development techniques that only an experienced developer could understand. We have aimed for the middle ground between those two extremes.

Our goal is to fulfill the need for targeted customer education, mobile business case creation, and a solution blueprint. In particular, this book will provide a balanced, practical overview of mobile process innovation for IT managers, line of business managers, and consultants. We hope to equip readers to make intelligent business decisions related to extracting more ROI from their ERP, CRM, SCM, and PLM investments without dragging them into a morass of detail.

Mobilizing SAP opens with a general mobile applications framework that we have developed based on numerous consulting engagements. It then systematically builds on the various elements of the framework. For instance, in the context of a mobile field service solution, it would lead customers through the following questions or situations:

- I want to implement a mobile field service application. What roadmap should I follow?

- Who are the best-practice companies in mobile field service? What are they doing that is unique?

- If I have a limited amount of money for investment, how should the mobile business case be structured to create the most business value?

- With which of my SAP back-office applications should I integrate my field service solution?

Mobilizing SAP demystifies for managers the capabilities of SAP NetWeaver Mobile and SAP Solutions for Mobile Business. This book is a self-help guide devoted to helping readers understand the basics of how to design and execute a mobile solution. Our secondary goal is to provide a hype-free, practical guide to IT managers, corporate decision makers, technical developers, and others involved with deciding how to use mobile data to improve business performance.

Target Audience

The target audience for *Mobilizing SAP* is mostly managers who are looking for ideas on how to create effective mobile solutions that leverage their current investments in SAP. These managers know that they are not interested in the details of the "cool" technology; they want to understand the mobile business value and ROI.

In particular, business and IT executives, project managers, consultants, and students who are involved with implementing mobile data solutions can all learn from *Mobilizing SAP*. Although we hope it will be of interest to those individuals directly engaged in creating mobile strategy or vendors creating mobile technology, it targets a much broader global audience.

We expect this book to become the playbook for mobilizing business processes. We look forward to hearing from our readers regarding their experiences and insights.

Ravi Kalakota
ravi@ebstrategy.com

Paul Kurchina
paul@kurchina.com

Acknowledgements

The authors would like to thank the individuals who helped make this book possible. A book of this scope requires the hard work and support of many. First, without the tireless efforts and extensive contributions of the SAP Mobile Business group, the book simply would not have been published. Within this group, many people with expertise in related topics contributed to the book and offered invaluable sanity checks and feedback including Peter Zencke, Shai Agassi, Howard Beader, Daniel Beringer, David Robbins, Udo Urbanek, Rudiegar Karl, Torsten Wichmann, Michael Spindler, Joachim Schaper, and Manfred Muecke.

While the aforementioned people helped us get this book near the goal line, without E-Business Strategies' editorial and production group, the book never would have made it into the end zone. We would like to thank Marcia Robinson, Brandon Doty, Allison Loudermilk, Tim Geary, and Jennifer Doty.

Many pioneers in the field, experts, advisers, and friends also have generously shared invaluable insights that have made their way into this book, not just over the last year, but over the last decade. To you, we hope that our descriptions of your ideas and concepts do justice to your mobile visions and entrepreneurial efforts. May the next ten years in mobile technology be as exciting as the last ten years have been.

Ravi Kalakota

Paul Kurchina

Chapter One

Mobilizing SAP — Why and Why Now?

Slowly but surely, mobilizing enterprise applications is rising to the top of the strategic priority list within many corporations. Best-practice companies are seeing the competitive advantage in mobilizing their business processes and their existing SAP enterprise applications and implementing new mobile applications. In this chapter, we present an overview of the mobile landscape — evolution, applications, and adoption trends — that allows readers to assess the current state of the market.

Introduction

Often, what looks like the norm today was once considered impossible. Until May 6, 1954, when Roger Bannister ran the mile in 3 minutes, 59.4 seconds, people thought the four-minute mile was beyond human capability. Experts said the heart was liable to burst attempting to supply enough oxygenated blood to the legs. Yet after Bannister, an English neurologist, showed the power of scientific training, more than 300 runners broke the four-minute barrier within two years.

A similar thing has happened in business. The concept of a productive mobile workforce was simply a vision a few years ago. Only a few innovative companies tried, and even fewer succeeded. But as mobile technology steadily improves, what was once considered impossible is now becoming mainstream.

Consider the following: A field service technician is repairing a high-definition television (HDTV) at the customer's location. He uses a personal digital assistant (PDA) to identify the appropriate replacement part, confirm availability at the nearest warehouse, and arrange for a rush site delivery. The result: The problem gets fixed during the repair visit, saving the customer the hassle of being present and taking time off from work for a subsequent repair visit.

In the insurance industry it is quite common to see claims adjusters toting wireless notebook computers in the field so they can link in real time to enterprise systems. These wireless computers enable them to document and process claim requests at the scene of the accident. The result: a remarkable drop in the time — from weeks to minutes — it takes to issue checks to customers.

The healthcare industry has also incorporated mobile technology. At some hospitals, doctors and nurses rely on PDAs to verify and manage patient information, track medical supplies, match medication bar codes with patient wristbands, and write prescriptions. The result: an increase in reporting accuracy and the reallocation of time from administrative tasks to patient care activities.

The semiconductor industry has gotten creative with mobile technologies. Every microprocessor fabrication plant (or fab) must operate in a clean environment, free of dust and stray electronic signals. These requirements make it nearly impossible for employees within clean rooms to rely on traditional tools, such as tethered desktop PCs or paper. To get around the limitations, workers are using PDAs and notebook computers connected to SAP enterprise applications by means of a wireless local area network (WLAN). The result: enhanced communications, reduced errors, and increased productivity.

Based on these applications and others, it is clear that market leaders are taking a new view: Mobile business applications represent the next evolutionary stage in business automation — where the imperative is extending business processes to mobile employees and customers.

The priority is to improve the paper-based workflows outside the organization. For the last four decades, the majority of IT investments have focused on automating and improving the efficiency of individuals and operating units within the "four walls" of an enterprise. Yet mounting margin pressure, cost-cutting, and an increased call for customization are driving businesses like never before to establish tighter integration with their field operations.

This imperative requires architecting a new infrastructure and a set of mobile applications that are largely underdeveloped today. The build out we are talking about encompasses an interdependent web of infrastructure, technology services, application sectors, and marketplaces. Given the breadth and reach of the mobile applications and infrastructure, we are confident that the mobile market will be much larger than any previous business automation cycle.

What's New? What's Different?

As a business strategy, leveraging mobile applications is not new. In 1986, Frito-Lay, the salty snack food maker, pioneered the use of wireless data communications on delivery routes. The handheld technology allowed drivers to take sales replenishment orders, gather in-store competitive intelligence, and manage routes. At the end of the day, the data was uploaded to Frito-Lay's mainframe sales and pricing databases via docking stations connected to a local area network.

In the early 1990s, FedEx introduced a wireless network application to keep track of document and parcel shipments. In February 1993, UPS responded with its delivery information acquisition device (or DIAD, a custom-built electronic data collector). In the logistics industry, this was the beginning of a major exploitation of wireless, Internet, and supporting technologies to achieve a competitive advantage, as well as to improve mobile worker productivity.

The Frito-Lay, FedEx, and UPS examples illustrate that proprietary wireless data applications have been around for a long time. However, the value of wireless data has not been widely recognized in business and IT circles. It has gone unrecognized because of the formidable costs (infrastructure, programming, and integration) involved in developing robust wireless (also known as connected or always-on) and mobile (also known as disconnected or sync-based) solutions in the 1980s and 1990s.

It is often estimated that FedEx and UPS spent several billion dollars each to develop their underlying infrastructure and applications.

Today, cost is no longer a primary barrier to widespread mobile application development. Mobile communications and handheld technology are rapidly reaching commodity status. As a result, the market focus has shifted from technology innovation to business process innovation. In addition, companies are realizing that mobility is a way to extract a greater ROI from the millions they have invested in enterprise resource planning (ERP), customer relationship management (CRM), supply chain management (SCM), and product lifecycle management (PLM) applications.

Today, leveraging enterprise application investments and realizing an additional ROI are core themes at many companies. Often the value of enterprise applications is not fully captured because they are only available to users with a PC. Bridging the chasm between the mobile workforce and the tethered applications is the goal of mobile applications.

Improving workforce productivity, cutting costs by leveraging existing investments, creating ease of use, and collecting data in real time are four powerful reasons why many public and private sector firms are investing in the mobile enterprise. A clear, detailed roadmap for investing in diverse mobile applications is desperately needed to achieve these goals. That is precisely the focus of this book.

Creating New Business Value

As mobile technology matures, the industry is migrating from a technology-driven (This is cool!) phase to a value-driven (What's the business value anyway?) phase. Evidence of this trend can be seen in the form of:

- **Migration from consumer-facing portals to mission-critical enterprise applications.** In the next three years, companies will realize most of their ROI from the mobile Internet in mundane enterprise processes (productivity improvements and streamlined operations) rather than glamorous consumer-facing applications.

- **Migration from task automation to business process management.** Mobile technologies (WiFi-enabled laptops, handheld computers, PDAs, tablet PCs, smart phones, and peripherals — cameras, scanners, and RFID tags) are transforming field processes from being excessively dependent on pen, paper, and clipboard to being more digitized, real-time processes.

- **Migration from visionary ideas to practical execution.** Mobile infrastructure (3G networks, devices, middleware) is finally in place and is widely available. The expertise among the ecosystem (carriers, infrastructure providers, application enablers, consultants, and IT departments) is coming together to convince and educate skeptical management to invest, implement, and integrate.

Advances in mobile technology coupled with process innovation are beginning to shift the competitive balance across the corporate spectrum and forcing companies to re-examine how they do business.

For instance, UPS has taken advantage of mobile technology to accelerate package delivery and pickup. Progressive Insurance has seized on mobile technology to transform how it prices policies and processes claims. Allscripts is using mobile technology to eliminate errors in medical prescription writing. Wal-Mart is using RFID technology to streamline information flow in its supply chains.

All sorts of industries, such as retail, utilities, manufacturing, and distribution, are finding that the convergence of mobile technology and the Internet gives them an opportunity to create new business value. That value, however, is not well understood because people are looking at it from the wrong angle — from a technology perspective rather than a business value perspective. This is beginning to change. More and more firms are beginning to take a process integration approach to mobile.

Figure 1.1 illustrates the shift taking place as companies switch from a technology innovation focus to a process integration focus for mobile business. Let's take a closer look at the business process impact of mobility.

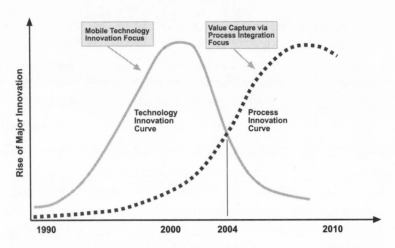

Figure 1.1: Migration from Technology Innovation to Process Integration

Mobile Applications Centered on Processes

Mobile enterprise solutions are as varied as the vast number of companies, processes, and industries out there. Yet a common thread runs through successful mobile implementations: the ability to extend business processes and enterprise applications to handheld devices.

The best ROI for mobile investments often occurs when organizations streamline processes. Successful companies constantly fine-tune the processes that make their businesses go faster. They integrate mobile technologies into their enterprise systems and streamline business processes through the value chain from sales through service.

In a post-PC era, mobile technology is starting to have a great impact on business processes thanks to the convergence of several trends: more powerful devices available at lower prices, higher bandwidth available from carriers and WiFi innovations, the steady advance of application platforms, and the business need to leverage existing investments.

The road to a process-centric model has not been particularly smooth as the next section discusses. We had to endure a period where the applications were proprietary and narrow in their focus.

First Generation: Task-Centric Mobile Applications

In the late 1990s, the entire world began to move from proprietary wireless networks to standards-based infrastructures such as GSM (global system for mobile communication), GPRS (general packet radio service), SMS (simple message service), and WAP (Wireless Application Protocol). This change, coupled with the dramatic innovation in Internet technologies, fostered a movement towards the mobile Internet and the mobile Web.[1]

To leverage the mobile Internet, corporations began to enable specific business tasks on phones and PDAs. They connected their back-end infrastructure with focused mobile tasks like contact management, e-mail, e-commerce, inventory checking, and content downloading.

The first-generation applications were relatively simple. They essentially were software programs that took Web information and displayed it in a special format for the small screens available on mobile telephones and handheld computers such as the Palm III.

Unfortunately, many first-generation solutions didn't account for the fact that the wireless networks of the late 1990s were not ready for prime time. Connectivity was poor, and data transmission crawled at the snail pace of 9.6 kilobits per second. Just imagine downloading a Web page at that speed. You would have to wait several minutes for each download. The typical WAP device also had a limited user interface and little memory, which made it unsuitable for mission-critical enterprise work.

The overhyped WAP, the killer technology of the mobile Internet, flopped miserably. Companies had to write off the millions that they sunk into WAP infrastructure and applications. A good example of this can be seen in the mobile banking and brokerage sector where banks in Europe and North America rushed to develop mobile banking solutions that had extremely poor adoption.

The first-generation mobile process solutions were long on vision and short on business value. Mobilizing an enterprise's mission-critical applications with limited risk and cost and nonproprietary applications was neither practical nor easily done as Figure 1.2 shows.

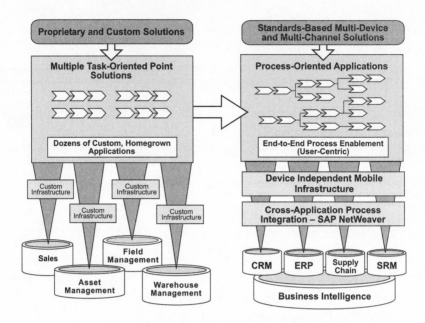

Figure 1.2: From First-Generation to Second-Generation Mobile Solutions

However, as connectivity, hardware, and software steadily improves, the problems that plagued the first-generation solutions are getting fixed, yielding the way for a new generation of mobile applications.

Second Generation: Process-Centric Mobile Solutions

After years of false starts, task-oriented proprietary applications have become more prevalent and viable, but are stepping aside for mobile solutions that are more process-oriented. The mobile applications landscape is maturing and is poised to enter a new growth phase.

The catalyst for all this activity? The standardization of wireless technology, platforms, and applications. With standardization, companies are finally able to move from prototype to production-quality mobile enterprise solutions and thereby realize their intrinsic value.

Powerful handheld devices available in various form factors (display sizes and keyboard layouts) with improved price/performance ratios characterize this second generation.

Unfortunately, despite the benefits, mobile solutions are not widely understood by executives and decision makers. Even those that get it are skeptical due to the unrealistic expectations that earlier vendors and the media set when they overhyped the first-generation mobile solutions.

To help business and IT executives understand the new genre of mobile solutions, the next section

- Provides detailed business scenarios based on priorities (field service, field sales, and asset management) that illustrate value creation in a real-world setting.

- Demonstrates how companies that keep their expectations in check, know what they are trying to achieve, and are prepared to act in logical steps can gain significant ROI.

As the economy improves, we expect mobile enterprise solutions to become the focal point for IT departments and management teams as they help companies streamline business processes beyond the desktop.

Let's look at the specific ways mobile enterprise applications are creating business value.

Seven Ways Business Value Is Being Created

For thousands of companies, SAP's ERP, CRM, SCM, and PLM software constitutes a standard, critical piece of their IT infrastructure. But it is not the only important piece of the puzzle, and in many cases, it is underutilized.

An increasing number of mobile employees is the reason behind this underutilization. These employees often are denied access to the core systems from the field, creating a productivity paradox.

Best-practice SAP customers are beginning to attack the productivity paradox and squeeze significant additional value out of their SAP investments by integrating SAP functions and processes with mobile processes that span their extended enterprise.

Mobile Asset Management	Allows field service engineers to access relevant business processes anywhere, anytime to solve maintenance issues.
Mobile Sales Support	Supports salespeople who need to perform revenue-generating tasks quickly and productively.
Mobile Field Service	Enables field service engineers and technicians to react quickly to customer problems.
Mobile Supply Chain Management	Keeps mobile employees and partners fully integrated with supply chain and direct store delivery (DSD) operations.
Mobile Procurement	Empowers mobile staff to manage the entire procurement function, from price comparison to ordering.
Mobile HR (Time and Travel)	Gives mobile employees access to HR functionality such as time and travel management.
Mobile Executive Intelligence	Keeps executives and managers fully informed about key performance indicators.

Table 1.1: Proven Mobile Strategies That Create Business Value

In this section, we will examine seven ways market leaders are using mobile technology to save money or make money. Table 1.1 lists these seven strategies for achieving a greater ROI. Each strategy, however, aims to correct three widespread problems:

- Lack of accurate, up-to-date data from the field;

- Inability of workers to gain access to the right information when needed; and

- Improving tracking, maintenance, and service of corporate assets.

Let's look at each mobile strategy in greater detail.

Mobile Asset Management (MAM)

Large companies have lots of assets. When these assets break down, the asset management process springs into action. Mobile asset management, or MAM, allows field service and plant maintenance technicians, auditors, and warehouse personnel to access relevant business processes anywhere and anytime.

MAM empowers workers to reconcile assets, change asset statuses, capture asset location, and perform regulatory compliance checks while they are inside or outside of the office. Field technicians can collect timely information about an asset's condition to update back-end systems. Often, these employees depend on bar code readers on their handheld devices to reconcile lost assets with current inventory, decreasing revenue leakage from unused, expensive parts and equipment.

While performing inventory checks, field personnel can capture and compare the location of the asset to its listed status in the back-end system. Field personnel can verify or change the asset status accordingly, for example, if the asset is returned to the warehouse or scrapped. Inventory information is updated instantly to ensure the timely exchange of data. Management can track the location of items to machines, job orders, and users at all times for complete visibility and analysis to improve asset control and reduce costly, excess inventory.

Bopack Systems, a Belgian bar code and labeling machine company, provides us with a good example. The company is using SAP's MAM applications to improve its reaction time for servicing repair requests and to expedite its billing process. In the past, service technicians completed service order confirmations by hand, and the central office then manually processed the paperwork. Errors predictably increased each time a new employee began filling out forms.

Today, after mobilizing its business process, Bopack sends service orders directly to technicians via their mobile devices. Once they receive the order, technicians complete the repairs and return the service confirmation at once to the central office. Since updates are more accurate and occur right away, Bopack is able to track projects more efficiently and can send out a bill as soon as a machine has been serviced.

Mobile Sales Support

Most organizations try to support revenue-generating goals any way they can. It would be hard to find a company that is not interested in more productive mobile salespeople. Mobile sales solutions provide salespeople the ability to access their CRM system, which includes marketing materials, interactive sales tools, sales performance data, and inventory information.

Mobile sales is a customizable SAP application that enables salespeople to access their contacts, call reports, forecasts, and more on their handheld

PDAs. Salespeople can view and modify key customer information —
tasks, accounts, contacts, and opportunities — anytime, anywhere.

In more sophisticated implementations, salespeople can retrieve time-
critical information, not only from these systems, but also from a variety
of other sources, including inventory, product, and pricing information
from ERP systems.

Colgate-Palmolive developed a mobile sales solution in the record time
of three months. Initially focused on the fast-growing Chinese market,
Colgate-Palmolive's solution enabled mobile sales order entry through
PDAs. The company's salesforce accesses time-critical information from
CRM systems and a variety of other sources, including inventory, product,
and pricing information from ERP systems.

Mobile Field Service

Mobile field service solutions help service engineers and technicians
react quickly to customer needs. Providing customers with enhanced
service at all touch points requires extending integrated processes to
employees like field service technicians who typically don't work on
company grounds.

Using a mobile device, the field service technician logs all of his activities
during the service call. The technician can view a list of all visits, and
for each visit either perform the necessary activities — diagnosis, repair,
invoice issuing, or cash collection — or update the customer's status
with a reason code indicating why the service could not be performed,
such as the customer wasn't there. Customers benefit from this real-
time exchange of information as evidenced by the decreasing call-to-
resolution time.

Let's look at a typical example. Messer Griesheim GmbH, an industrial
gas company with production in more than 30 countries, has developed
a customized mobile service solution. Using mobile devices, the truck
drivers scan the bar code on each container of gas, thereby keeping better
track of the containers that have been delivered to or returned by the
customer.

The solution eliminates stacks of paperwork. Customers receive their
gas orders more quickly. The company's delivery and billing departments

now have more accurate records, can better assess customer needs, and can complete the billing cycle faster.

Mobile Supply Chain Management

Mobile solutions are increasing the velocity of supply chains. Supply chains typically have two activity streams: upstream or inbound activities and downstream or outbound activities. Mobile solutions are beginning to have a dramatic impact on the downstream distribution side.

Take, for instance, consumer packaged goods (CPG) manufacturers of products like soft drinks, snacks, dairy, and meats. With vendor-managed inventory (VMI) becoming more prevalent, manufacturers and their distributors are under intense pressure to improve product availability on the store shelf. In order to deliver the right product at the right time, more firms are implementing direct store delivery (DSD) models.

How does DSD work? Using the capability for high-rate order taking, sales and delivery professionals can enter orders into mobile devices and then seamlessly upload the orders into a main order log and back-end system. The orders are then released to the warehouse for picking, packing, and loading and dispatched onto the trucks in order to be delivered according to customer-specified periodic delivery cycles. Handheld route accounting functionality allows the driver to check materials out of the warehouse, make deliveries, return to the warehouse to check in returned materials and collected payments, and, finally, balance and settle materials and payments.

Mobile Procurement

Mobile procurement capabilities give field technicians access to their company's online supply catalog, where they can search through the service parts inventory, compare pricing and product features, and order the parts they need based on up-to-date inventory information. The technicians also benefit from the convenience of one-click purchasing features when ordering parts within predefined online catalogs.

Let's look at a typical example in the telecom industry. Bell Canada has successfully completed the implementation of a mobile procurement solution to automate the procurement requirements of its 4,000 field technicians. With the new solution, technicians instantly can access workflow tools and more than 55,000 online catalog items, regardless of location or device, in both connected and disconnected environments.

As a result of its mobile procurement initiative, Bell Canada maintains more accurate records of spare parts databases through the tracking of inventory levels. The telecom provider has already seen a huge reduction in paper-based administration and manual data entry. Its ultimate goal is to cut its emergency parts orders and overall parts inventory, saving millions of dollars.

Mobile HR Services — Time and Travel

Productivity multipliers are yet another hat that mobile solutions can wear. In a typical organization, employees are away from their desks as much as 50% of the time, and time spent walking to and from meetings or traveling to see customers is wasted without access to key information.

Mobile HR services empower employees to interact directly with the applications used to track time-and-billing stats, payroll, and other HR information. Typically, these initiatives depend on mobile Internet access (so the employee can log on to the system from anywhere) and on single sign-on, so employees do not have to memorize multiple passwords to use the application.

Take for instance, a typical consulting scenario. At the start of a meeting, a consultant can click his handheld to start a time tracker. At the end of the meeting, the consultant can click again to automatically update the HR database. Consultants are able to reduce paperwork by entering time and billing information practically anytime, anywhere.

Delivering the information employees want when they want it makes them more productive. Improving white-collar employee productivity in today's "leaner" organizations is a universal priority. This is forcing many companies to improve administrative processes such as read and review documents, update and assign tasks, monitor projects, generate reports, and participate in workflows.

Mobile Executive Intelligence

Intelligence is enabled by dashboards (or mobile portals) that provide a simple way for executives to monitor key performance metrics from across the business. Executives view portals as a window into business processes that span many systems. Mobilizing portals is likely to return a higher ROI than portal experiences that simply present information.

To deploy an executive dashboard, organizations must not only provide basic database reporting, but also support drilldown into different systems integrated into the portal and bring together key documents from the entire business. Enterprise-wide search across many content repositories and the ability to collaborate on key issues are essential to the dashboard.

While the ROI from the mobile executive dashboard is difficult to quantify, the qualitative improvement in executives' ability to drive tactical strategy and day-to-day operations is often enormously valuable to a company. Figure 1.3 displays the other parties that benefit from mobile process solutions.

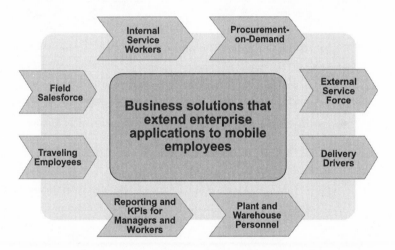

Figure 1.3: Mobile Employees Beyond Enterprises' Traditional Reach

Where Are We in the Mobile Adoption Cycle?

Mobile enterprise applications have slowly migrated from being the sole domain of innovative companies to being the solution of choice for the mainstream marketplace. Let's take a deep breath and perhaps a more academic look at where we are in the adoption cycle.

In order to understand the mobile adoption cycle and the maturity of the mobile technology category, it's useful to reference one of the more popular conceptual models in technology marketing called the technology adoption lifecycle model (see Figure 1.4).

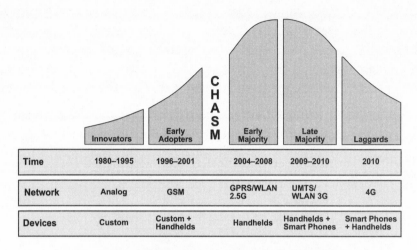

	Innovators	Early Adopters	CHASM	Early Majority	Late Majority	Laggards
Time	1980–1995	1996–2001		2004–2008	2009–2010	2010
Network	Analog	GSM		GPRS/WLAN 2.5G	UMTS/ WLAN 3G	4G
Devices	Custom	Custom + Handhelds		Handhelds	Handhelds + Smart Phones	Smart Phones + Handhelds

Figure 1.4: The Mobile Technology Adoption Curve

Everett Rogers, a sociologist, first presented this model in his 1962 book titled *Diffusion of Innovations*. He developed the concept by studying the adoption rates of hybrid seed among Iowa farmers in the 1940s.

Rogers' initial work in the agribusiness space was later adapted for the technology marketplace rather cleverly by Geoffrey Moore in his 1991 book *Crossing the Chasm*. Moore examined the adoption of a new technology by plotting its lifecycle on an XY chart showing the passage of time along the X-axis and the propensity to buy along the Y-axis.

The resulting chart resembled a bell curve: the fewest buyers at the beginning and the end, the most in the middle. Moore divided the bell curve into five segments, each representing a different type of buyer. The types of buyers, from left to right and early to late, are described as follows:

- Innovators are tech-savvy buyers with a vision. Innovators are often creative types who build solutions from early experimental technology. They love to try new things and believe that following conventional wisdom is the wrong thing to do. The lack of features or functionality does not bother these intrepid users, and they usually do not overly concern themselves with the business case or ROI of an investment. They just do it.

- Early adopters, meanwhile, prefer to understand the practical applications of a technology and are motivated by competitive and market pressures. Unlike innovators, they tend not to be technology people. For instance, in the air parcel industry, FedEx is considered an innovator, whereas UPS is more of an early adopter. Early adopters are willing to take risks and to experiment with technology before it is fully proven.

- Early majority buyers are the first mainstream buyers. They are pragmatic, more risk-averse than early adopters, and prefer to buy a proven solution to an articulated problem. They don't want to be the pioneers, but they also don't want to be left behind.

- Late majority buyers are similar to early majority buyers, except that they tend be very conservative. They also like to wait until there are best practices and proven industry standards before they purchase any technology. Find a person who is getting a cell phone for the first time and you have identified a late majority individual.

- Laggards avoid new technology whenever possible. They can eventually be persuaded to buy if the technology is embedded or has become completely uncontroversial. This segment is also made up of people who are so skeptical that no matter what the evidence is they refuse to change. These are people that may never buy.

Everybody knows each of these kinds of buyers. But wait a minute. If we're talking about *Crossing the Chasm*, then where's the chasm? As Figure 1.4 illustrates, it's the gap between the innovators and early adopters on one side and the early majority on the other. In our world, it's that point at which the experimentation and faith stop; when everything works, business cases are proven, and the deployments begin.

What Caused the Mobile Chasm Effect?

In the early years, the only people using mobile technology were early adopters and technology evangelists. As it becomes more popular with mainstream users, manufacturers (mobile vendors) have to face the challenge of usability. If you have tech-savvy people adopting a technology when it's new, you usually don't need to have simple installation techniques or easy-to-use devices. They will figure it all out.

When technology hits the mainstream, there has to be a greater focus on usability because people dislike spending time with a user interface that's confusing. For instance, the average salesperson wants a handheld device and wants to be able to use it quickly. A lack of usability causes a disruption in the market, which leads to an adoption problem.

As we start crossing the chasm from early adopters to mainstream users, companies expect a minimum level of quality and security for the products they buy. They understand that implementing a new technology without disrupting existing business requires substantial homework and confidence that the real-world issues have been addressed. In the case of mobile applications, vendors have not adequately addressed security or worker productivity or proven cost versus benefit, resulting in a market adoption problem.

Effective marketing and positioning based upon a clear understanding of the customer need, how the technology addresses it, and how well vendors understand the competitive pressures the customer is experiencing are the keys for a technology to cross the chasm.

Applying this reasoning to the mobile category, we believe mobile technology crossed the chasm in 2004. In our view, the chasm period lasted several years from 2001–04. To survive, most vendors, particularly those offering mobile infrastructure products, have adjusted and figured out where their customers' true pain lies and have learned how to address it while differentiating their offerings from others.

Why SAP Mobile Business?

The pace of mobile technology's diffusion creates interesting timing problems for managers who are looking at investing in technology; it also creates difficult vendor selection problems.

Managers are asking: Which mobile vendor do I pick? Who will survive the trauma of new technology innovation cycles? Does this vendor have enough financial strength to be around for a while? Is the vendor solving a tactical or a broader strategic problem?

Picking the wrong vendor to execute a great strategy leads to certain failure — a "B" strategy with an "A" vendor has a better chance of success than an "A" strategy with a "C" vendor.

To understand SAP's position in the mobile enterprise applications space, it is important to understand where we are with respect to the ups and downs of the technology innovation cycle. This will gives us a better understanding of why more companies are choosing SAP NetWeaver Mobile Business to mobilize their enterprise application investments.

The Mobile Innovation Curve

New technologies rarely change the world overnight. As we discussed earlier, the adoption of technology is seldom smooth or predictable. That's why picking a successful vendor is such a high-risk gamble. It doesn't have to be, however, if you understand the dynamics of the innovation curve.

The innovation curve typically begins with an inflection point such as a breakthrough technology. The development of the mobile Internet was a trigger point. This point represented the breakthrough convergence of the Internet and the mobile networks (code division multiple access or CDMA, GSM, and GPRS).

The financial markets and venture capitalists saw opportunity in the convergence. In the late 1990s, many analysts predicted that consumer mobile applications were the next big frontier. The resulting flood of new investment in this area funded many start-ups. This point in the lifecycle of mobile enterprise applications corresponds to the "slope of hype" in Figure 1.5.

When you examine the mobile supplier curve carefully, it resembles a classic technology hype cycle. The first phase of the cycle for a new technology like mobile is an incredible frenzy to be associated with the concept. This we call the slope of hype.

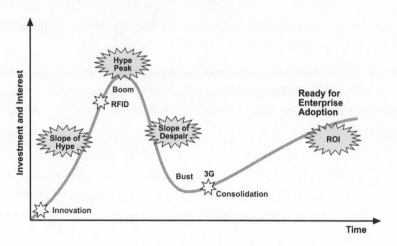

Figure 1.5: The Mobile Supplier Curve

Then comes the hard part: making the technology work takes time and proves more difficult that anyone thought. Start-up companies run out of money and perish and established public companies languish as Wall Street gets bored and loses interest in the sector. This phase we refer to as the "slope of despair."

Phase three is the rebirth and production phase in which the benefits from the technology start to kick in as advertised — just not as quickly as anyone thought. Investors and customers come back to the technology, but with a more studied approach, and a few mega-winners emerge. This last phase we call the "slope of ROI."

The Slope of Hype and the Tragedy of the Commons

In the early battle for dominance in the mobile enterprise applications arena, mobile start-ups tried to deal a powerful blow to the established world. On one side were the large enterprise software companies such as SAP. On the other side were the mobile start-ups anxious to demonstrate how they could surround SAP applications with their revolutionary mobile solutions.

Egged on by venture capitalists, industry analysts, media, and pundits, the start-ups invested heavily in marketing and proceeded to overhype the value of their technologies. Too many start-ups were formed during this period, and they all were chasing the same customers — the innovators and early adopters. The result at the top of this boom is what's known in economics as the "the tragedy of the commons."

The tragedy of the commons concept initially appeared as an essay in *Science* in 1968 by Garrett Hardin, a professor in the University of California system. He wrote that the tragedy occurs because people pursue their goals with the means available to them. Nothing belongs to anyone, yet everything belongs to everyone; thus, when people make use of things, they use what everyone else also owns.

Fishing in coastal waters is an example of this economic phenomenon. Fishermen have every reason to abide by government rules; otherwise, excess fishing may lead to low reserves. Yet these fishermen break the rules. The reason? There is a positive component to their breaking the rules: The more they fish, the more they earn. But there is a negative component as well. As every fisherman thinks alike, all of them tend to fish more, and such excess fishing depletes the reserves, affecting the ecological system, not to mention the livelihood of the fishermen.

What is the common resource in business for suppliers? Customers. Most mobile enterprise software companies in their eagerness to capture market share went fishing for customers in 1999–2001 as fast as they could. They called this the Get-Big-Fast market share strategy. The customers they went after were the early adopters. Just like fish in the ocean, there were not enough early adopters to satisfy the appetite of these companies, resulting in a market bust.

The bottom line is that overinvestment breeds confusion and converts the once promising boom into a resounding bust. The mobile suppliers in a variety of categories like mobile middleware have gone through a withering boom-bust cycle. The curve really hit bottom in 2003, with many technology suppliers going out of business, selling their assets at rock-bottom prices, or merging with stronger players.

The Boom-Bust Cycle in the Mobile Middleware Sector

The mobile middleware segment or wireless application gateway (WAG) ably illustrates the volatile boom-bust cycle. Companies in the WAG segment aimed to serve businesses by providing software infrastructure to support enterprise mobility via cell phones, PDAs, and pagers. At the peak, there were hundreds of start-ups rushing to lock in customers as fast as possible. Sales cycles became longer with too many vendors chasing too few opportunities.

In most crowded markets, when the sales cycles get longer companies tend to run out of money. Longer sales cycles and lack of funding lead to the slope of despair where many of these start-ups, such as Brience, Covigo, 724 Solutions, Isovia, Aether Systems, AvantGo, NetMorf, 2Roam, and Wireless Knowledge, perished or were acquired. This "death spiral" invariably leads to a prolonged downturn where a hundred vendors are reduced to a paltry few.

The death spiral also freezes customers as they are not sure which start-up vendor will survive the shakeout. This boom-bust cycle creates a great opportunity for vendors like SAP who have seen these cycles in different areas: client/server, e-commerce, e-business, and so on.

The Consolidation Phase — SAP Solutions for Mobile

On the other hand, companies like SAP, due to their financial strength, are able to keep developing the necessary mobile infrastructure technology. We are just at the point of consolidation for mobile enterprise applications. There are few financially viable mobile enterprise applications companies left.

What most start-ups don't realize is that mobilizing business processes in large corporations is far more complex than meets the eye, both in terms of technology and business process change. The complexity stems from two variables: multi-channel technology and process changes.

- Technology Change. Because previous cycles in business automation focused on automating internal, not multi-channel business processes, mobile business generally requires brand-new applications and infrastructure. Mobile enterprise solutions that depend on the integration of information across the physical, tele, Web, and mobile channels need a robust infrastructure and applications layer before they are viable.

- Process Change. A growing appreciation has developed that 1) business processes do not change as fast as the technology enabling those changes, and 2) the rate of integration and adoption — even if companies deliver major value (which we believe mobile does) — will be gradual because it requires systems and individuals to act in fundamentally new ways.

Anticipating the complexity of developing a cross-enterprise mobile infrastructure, SAP has steadily improved features and functionality with every version of its mobile engine. Now it is poised to attack the market with SAP NetWeaver Mobile, which is the technical foundation for enterprise mobility within SAP NetWeaver. It provides the technology that powers SAP solutions for mobile business.

The bottom line: Best-practice companies everywhere have an interesting choice: do they go with a trusted partner like SAP who understands what it takes to mobilize enterprise applications or do they put the success of their company in the hands of a start-up or a small company. Given the mission-critical nature of mobile applications, the answer is becoming more obvious. Companies are choosing SAP's solutions for mobile business to streamline their business processes further.

The Case for Investing in Mobile Business

The case for investing in mobile business is founded on the following seven premises:

- **Companies are ready to automate business processes and relationships outside their four walls.** For the last four decades, virtually all IT advancements have concentrated on automating business processes internal to the enterprise (for example, general ledger, manufacturing, human resources). With their IT infrastructure firmly in place, businesses now are looking to automate outside their four walls to tightly couple core business processes with mobile employees and customers.

- **Mobile business ties together the process chain** and involves much more than viewing and entering information into a handheld device. It requires connecting each of the myriad components that comprise the transaction lifecycle, ranging from customer information and contracts, to work order processing, product data, and settlement.

- **The driver of this next stage of automation is not technology** per se, but the changing way in which businesses operate and compete. Mounting competition for customers and shortened product lifecycles are forcing companies to couple their business processes with mobile workers in new ways to improve efficiency, lower costs, and speed time to market.

- **Mobile business revolves around Web-based enterprise applications integrated and delivered via handhelds.** This is evident when you consider the following: 1) enterprise applications are the core engines that automate complex business processes, 2) the Web is the most efficient vehicle for the widespread automation of customer and employee relationships, and 3) mobile technology is the best way to integrate large numbers of mobile workers. Hence, demand for integrated software that streamlines employee and customer relationships with the aid of the wireless infrastructure.

- **Very little of the infrastructure and applications needed to automate business processes and relationships outside the enterprise are in place today.** The mobile infrastructure build out represents an interdependent web of infrastructure, services, software, and applications. Each piece of this technology puzzle drives and depends on the others for success and represents a powerful, multiyear trend.

- **Mobile business will involve larger user populations and transactions volumes and is of much higher strategic value than previous business automation cycles.** In each of the four major automation cycles — mainframe, PCs, client-server, and Web — that preceded mobile business, the successor stage involved more users and larger transaction volumes, and was of a greater strategic value than the preceding stage, giving rise to significant productivity improvements as a result.

- Today, we are in the early stages of a mobile infrastructure build out that is unfolding in three interlocking steps: 1) the ERP bolt-on — handheld extensions of back-office and front-office applications, 2) stand-alone applications for point tasks, and 3) interconnected cross-enterprise solutions. Each phase will produce a discrete set of benefits, beginning with operational cost savings, moving to productivity improvements, and culminating in a set of longer-term benefits, including better capacity utilization, enhanced revenues, and inventory management.

We believe mobile business is in the midst of an investment cycle that will produce tremendous growth and value creation over the next several years. The pressure to invest in mobile will grow steadily as best-practice organizations (innovators and early adopters) begin to realize the value of mobilizing their business processes. Their adoption of mobile will put their competition at a sharp disadvantage, forcing them either to follow quickly or to find themselves at a competitive disadvantage.

Summary

"Any sufficiently advanced technology is indistinguishable from magic."

— Arthur C. Clarke, science fiction author and futurist

After years of hype and false starts, high-speed wireless Internet access is having a huge effect on what mobile employees see and do remotely. E-mail and task-oriented applications increasingly are becoming the norm on devices like Research in Motion's (RIM's) BlackBerry, and the practice of mobilizing enterprise applications is becoming more prevalent. Now, CEOs, CIOs, and managers need to figure out how to make the most of the emerging mobile ecosystem.

The purpose of this chapter was to provide a high-level overview of what has happened in the mobile marketplace. Our goal was to help readers gain a better understanding of the drivers, significance of, and investment opportunities embedded within mobile business, with an emphasis on SAP software and its partner ecosystem.

As the chapter illustrated, the challenges of today's business world are now forcing many organizations to focus more explicitly on their mobile processes (processes that extend beyond their four walls). Improving customer service, cutting out cost inefficiencies, being more proactive and less reactive, and complying with new regulations all push business processes and their effective management to the top of the priority list.

Mobile applications, by driving ROI, are becoming must-have solutions. We are beginning to see demand pick up for solutions like mobile sales, mobile field service, and mobile asset management. As the infrastructure is established, the focus is definitely shifting from technology platforms to applications.

The success of mobile applications ultimately depends on teams' abilities to execute mobile infrastructure projects effectively. However, as an enterprise buyer, surveying and understanding the crowded mobile infrastructure market can be a daunting task. Many different types of vendors, including enterprise application vendors, mobile middleware vendors, and point solution vendors, all seem to have similar approaches and messages.

Making the right infrastructure decisions that create long-term value is a key theme of this book. Without a scalable infrastructure, it would be extremely difficult to implement, deploy, and enhance multiple mobile applications. However, before we talk about mobile infrastructure, it is prudent to set the stage for organizing the different aspects of innovation in the mobile landscape into a mutually exclusive and collectively exhaustive framework.

In the next chapter, we present one such framework that helps managers better understand the distinct areas that make up the mobile landscape.

Chapter Two

The Mobile Business Landscape

WiFi, 3G, Windows Mobile, disconnected infrastructure, Mobile Linux, field sales, field service, mobile asset management, RFID, and BlackBerry — how do these terms fit together? In this chapter, we organize the mobile business landscape. The framework provides a context for understanding the diverse applications. Gaining this understanding is a prerequisite for readers wishing to take their second key step of mobile business projects: analyzing the many opportunities available to them.

Introduction

In March 1990, Motorola marketed a combination wristwatch and pager with the tag line "It's not science fiction anymore."[1] It has taken another fifteen years before this "toy" could be integrated with back-end enterprise applications.

The future has arrived. Mobile solutions are shifting gears from "toys" to "tools." This shift means that business requirements drive implementation, a phenomenon that we explored in Chapter 1 when we discussed the evolution from first-generation to second-generation mobile solutions.

Key characteristics of second-generation mobile solutions include the following:

- A focus on enabling business processes, not just tasks.

- More standardized packaged applications, not customized point solutions.

- An emphasis on mission-critical production systems, not prototypes.

- Proven ROI obtained through process improvement at the employee and enterprise levels.

- A desire to unlock the value of enterprise application investments in an exponential, nonlinear manner.

Now that you understand the mobile market dynamics, it's time to dig deeper and ask what's in it for your organization. Determining mobility's practical applications is difficult without an understanding of the changing business landscape. The first step toward a comprehensive understanding of the mobile environment is to look beneath its surface activity and apparent chaos for patterns. The next step is to categorize these patterns based on the appropriate analytic framework.

As you read this chapter, we encourage you to ask yourself the following questions when thinking about launching mobile solutions:

- What key issues — cost, quality, throughput, productivity, or velocity — affect my business the most?

- What are the performance gaps where improvements are needed?

- How do these business issues coincide with mobility? (In other words, will mobility increase the real-time nature of processes?)

- Which solutions will produce a return on my investment?

- What kinds of mobile solutions can be implemented today?

- How can I extend solutions and plan for evolution as the mobile market matures?

A disciplined approach is the only way companies can fully realize the benefits of mobility.

The Mobile Landscape

Your workforce likely sees mobility everywhere in their personal lives (sports events, ticket verification; restaurants, order taking; car rentals, rapid returns). You can safely assume that they've wondered why similar tasks can't be mobilized in corporations.

It does not take a genius to realize that mobile workplace applications will be instrumental in the quest to attain the next level of productivity gains. To move from vision to reality, however, a sound strategy is required. Such a strategy usually begins by articulating and structuring the opportunity landscape.

Figure 2.1 supports the notion that the mobile landscape can be organized systematically. The components of the mobile business framework presented in the figure are mutually exclusive and exhaustive enough to capture literally every activity taking place in the mobile landscape. A description of each of the major components follows Figure 2.1.

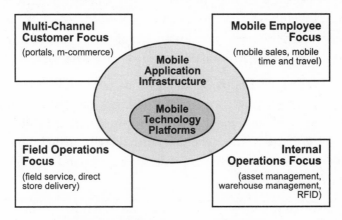

Figure 2.1: Mobile Business Framework

Mobile Technology Platforms. These platforms encompass software (Palm OS or Windows Mobile), hardware (PDAs, notebooks, or smart phones), and network infrastructure (3G or WiFi). Platforms provide the foundation upon which applications can be developed.

Mobile Application Infrastructure. Technology by itself is not enough. You need a layer of functionality that envelops the core technology platforms to enable, deliver, and manage mobile applications and services. Historically, the lack of a robust mobile infrastructure layer has made developing applications very frustrating; however, emerging products like SAP Mobile Infrastructure tackle the issue of multimode application development for multiple hardware devices and network connectivity.

30   Mobilizing SAP

Multi-Channel Customer Focus. The mobile Internet has to be put into the context of how technology fits into everyday customer tasks and lifestyles. Companies can use the mobile Internet to help customers complete transactions more easily. The mobile Internet can also become an important new channel for commerce, but it is not yet clear which tasks, activities, and transactions are a good fit for mobile commerce.

Field Operations Focus. Many enterprises share a common problem: They have made large investments in business applications that are inaccessible once their users leave their desks. Companies are adding wireless access to existing applications in order to leverage their technology investments and increase the productivity of their mobile workforce. Productivity improvements will occur when a company's employees, distributors, and business partners share and access information and perform transactions anytime, anywhere.

Internal Operations Focus. In many industries, the business pace has accelerated so much that a company's fortunes can rise and fall on its ability to monitor and manage the supply chain. Mobile Internet technology enhances supply chain and distribution operations by improving the flow of information, orders, products, and payments among the various players.

Employee Focus. Companies can use the extended Web to develop and deliver new products and services for employees. For example, a wireless portal could complement the enterprise portals to distribute content directly to employees on the go. Companies are using the mobile Internet to change their business process velocity and set new performance standards.

Using this framework, executives can systematically analyze their current operation to determine what new opportunities and risks mobile strategies provide. At a minimum, these executives will understand the business opportunities mobility makes available to them and the risks associated with both pursuing and not pursuing them.

Based on this assessment, executives can realistically determine what, if any, mobile investments they should make, so a longer look at each component is warranted.

Mobile Technology Platforms

Currently, the underlying hardware and software platforms of the mobile Internet are up for grabs, with several different options that IT groups have to wade through carefully.

To build mobile applications, a good grasp of the technology components is helpful:

- Network infrastructure — 2G, 2.5G, 3G, 4G, and WiFi

- Mobile devices — PDAs, smart phones, notebooks, and rugged devices

- Handheld operating systems — Microsoft's Windows Mobile, Palm OS, Symbian, and mobile Linux

- Third-party runtime engines — Java, J2ME, and QUALCOMM BREW

- Peripherals — printers, scanners, readers, and cameras

A brief discussion about each component should illustrate the complex decisions that IT departments frequently face.

The handheld or handset market, which has been dominated globally by a few firms such as Nokia, Motorola, Ericsson, Palm, Symbol, Intermec, Psion Teklogix, and Kyocera, is characterized by fierce competition. Key handset issues that differentiate the various players include battery life, small-screen usability, network connectivity (GSM, UMTS, and WiFi), and ruggedness.

The engineering and performance objectives of portable handheld hardware platforms differ markedly from those of desktop platforms. Established operating systems such as Windows, Unix, and Linux are designed for desktops with ever-increasing processing and storage capabilities; thus, they are unsuitable for portable appliances, which require a smaller, more lightweight, and more flexible operating system. New client-side software platforms must address the unique needs of portable devices and provide a variety of new features, such as connectivity with other devices.

Currently, the operating system segment for handhelds and smart phones is made up of five entities: PalmSource with Palm OS, Microsoft with Windows Mobile, Symbian, mobile Linux, and, to a more limited degree, Research In Motion.

To handle scenarios such as when a company has to deploy the same application on multiple operating systems and handheld devices, a new virtual machine (VM) layer is emerging. Both, QUALCOMM BREW (Binary Runtime Environment for Wireless) and Sun Microsystems are vying for dominance in this important category. Sun is creating a mobile version of the Java environment, a micro Java (J2ME), developed specifically for small devices with small screens.

Is your head spinning with all these choices? We have not even covered the different network connectivity options or peripheral devices! We leave that for the next chapter where we delve into these in more detail.

Mobile Application Infrastructure

A mobile application infrastructure is the foundation on which mobile applications and services can be developed. In the e-business world, this infrastructure is equivalent to the Web servers, Internet service providers, and application service providers that act as the base for building and deploying robust Web applications.

Three general categories of companies make their living through mobile application infrastructures:

- Mobile application platform companies: carrier-class platforms (such as Openwave for mobile operators) and enterprise-class platforms (such as SAP Mobile Infrastructure for corporations).

- Mobile Internet service providers (MISPs): general wireless carriers (Vodafone or Verizon), specialized data carriers, and WiFi hotspot providers.

- Mobile application enablers: data and transaction security, data synchronization, billing and payment service systems, and application integration providers.

Mobile Application Servers

Mobile application providers sell software platforms of prefabricated components that extend companies' business-critical applications to their mobile sales, service, and executive personnel.

Extending e-business functionality to an increasing selection of mobile devices calls for a single common application infrastructure or platform. For example, most applications are designed for viewing with a standard desktop PC. Small-screen wireless devices, such as mobile phones and PDAs, require optimizing the applications for quick viewing and data retrieval. Often, information must be completely reformatted for the best possible user experience.

Successful mobile application platforms provide users access to their business software with no loss in transaction capability and with a consistent user experience based on the type of device and connection speed. Mobile platform designs should be capable of the following:

- **Supporting multiple mobile devices.** The platform should be capable of delivering Web-based content and applications to multiple mobile devices employing diverse technological platforms. It should also be capable of adapting Web-based content and applications to fit the variety of mobile device specifications, capabilities, and formats with their different screen sizes, colors, and markup languages.

- **Optimizing content and applications based on varying connection speeds.** The application platform should optimize the amount and format of content for delivery based on the connection speed of the device requesting the information. It should also integrate effortlessly with the companies' existing Web infrastructures, reducing the need to recreate existing functionality and content solely for wireless delivery. Lastly, the platform should be compatible with existing security standards.

- **Cost-effectively supporting a growing number of applications and increasing capacity.** The application platform should be scalable to support additional applications and increased capacity as businesses expand the scope of wireless delivery to their mobile employees, customers, suppliers, and business affiliates.

• **Enabling companies to develop, maintain, and manage wireless capabilities easily.** The application platform should allow programmers to develop, maintain, and manage wireless delivery capabilities easily as they introduce additional applications and devices or change the format of existing content and applications.

The mobile application platform's primary assignment is to provide middleware for mobile computing. Wireless capabilities do require specialized middleware, and middleware vendors such as SAP are addressing these unique requirements. The features and functionality of middleware products generally includes the ability to support different networks and multiple devices and their form factors, as well as the data security, compression, and synchronization required.

Mobile Internet Service Providers

Mobile Internet service providers (MISPs) are the gateways to the Internet. Wireless carriers such as Vodafone, Cingular, Nextel, Sprint PCS, and Verizon are the MISPs for mobile phone Internet access.

The MISP business model is similar to the traditional Internet service provider (ISP) model. ISPs, such as AOL, MSN, and EarthLink, grant customers access to the Internet over the public switched telephone network (PSTN) for a monthly fee.

Several network independent MISPs — GoAmerica, OmniSky, Boingo Wireless, and Palm.net — specialized in offering wireless Internet access to handheld devices, which they provided over AT&T's and Verizon's networks. Other than WiFi service providers, almost all of these players have gone out of business or exited it as the market moves to 3G services.

Today, the dominant mobile Internet access method is coming from the large telecom players. The wireless access industry is maturing and consolidating around a few players.

Mobile Application Enablers

Mobile application enablers encompass data and transaction security services such as VeriSign, data synchronization services such as Intellisync, and micro-database providers such as Sybase.

A diverse array of businesses dedicated to mobile strategy consulting, implementation, and integration also fall into this category. Other ancillary services of mobile application enablers range from content conversion to project management. These firms run the gamut from full-service consultancies, to niche service providers, to large system integrators.

Mobile computing requires a significant systems integration effort since there is no single development standard for mobile devices. For example, a company's field force uses Symbol devices; its warehouse people prefer Psion Teklogix devices; the salespeople don't go anywhere without their BlackBerries; and the employees use a mix of everything, from Palms and BlackBerries, to Pocket PCs, wireless cell phones, and more. Enterprises must find a way to communicate and secure all of them.

See Chapter 4 for more detail on mobile application infrastructure.

Multi-Channel Customer Focus

Say you are an established company with customers. What can you do with the mobile channel? As customers become more mobile, companies have to figure out new ways of interacting with them. The success of customer-facing mobile initiatives depends on how well companies can extend existing business processes to multiple mobile channels in ways that create value for the customer.

Multi-channel applications are classified according to their purpose:

- Channel presence — information-only marketing channels that inform customers about products and services.

- Channel extension — transaction-capable interactions, a combination of marketing and sales, that can support existing customer outreach strategies.

- M-commerce applications — new services available only in mobile channels such as payment using mobile phones or location-specific coupon retrieval and redemption using handheld devices.

- Channel synchronization — fusion of a portfolio of channels (brick, Web, and mobile) into an integrated offering.

Channel Presence — Information Only

Many companies will use their mobile channel to increase their customers' understanding of their products and services primarily for marketing purposes. Other applications of channel presence include sending digital coupons, providing customer service, and receiving feedback.

These solutions use a transcoding process to make their Web site content quickly accessible from a mobile device. Transcoding converts a company's HTML Web pages into WML (Wireless Markup Language), a content format for the mobile world. Transcoders allow a company to have a quick brochureware channel presence by first reading the firm's Web site and then automating the content.

The quality of transcoding services can vary significantly. Transcoding allows marketing groups to leverage existing Web site material without the time and expense incurred when creating additional content.

Channel Extension — Mobile Channels for Existing Customers

Instead of using the mobile channel to generate sales, some retailers and financial institutions use it as part of a channel extension strategy to support their existing offline and online channels. Apple is an example of such a strategy. The firm offers Web site access for users of HP devices and cell phones. Other popular Web sites, such as Amazon.com, Google, and Yahoo!, are scrambling to deliver their content to Web-savvy consumers through Web-enabled cell phones, two-way pagers, and PDAs.

M-Commerce Applications

M-commerce is defined as the ability to purchase, track, and receive goods and services securely via mobile technology. As companies move from informational to transactional services, specialized m-commerce applications with unique mobile channel capabilities are cropping up.

These capabilities include:

- M-ticketing — for flights and other travel, as well as tickets to movies, concerts, and other performances.

- M-shopping — "personalized shopping" that can be combined with location-based applications.

- M-banking — allowing customers to check bank balances and transfer funds from anywhere and on any device.

- M-trading — buying and selling stocks, bonds, and currencies while on the go and from the most convenient wireless device.

For firms to succeed in each of these m-commerce areas, the top priority in application design must be creating an exceptional customer experience; one that is intuitive, informative, personalized, pleasant, secure, and reliable.

Channel Synchronization — Integrating Offline, Online, and Mobile

Eventually, companies will need to integrate their mobile, brick, and Web business channels. For instance, banks want their on-the-go customers to be able to complete their banking interactions from any channel. Mobile channels are not replacements of existing channels; they are complements for providing more customer convenience.

However, with every channel innovation comes the mistaken belief that existing channels will be displaced by the innovation. Over time, companies perceive the new channels as complements rather than replacements for the existing ones; thus, companies have to undertake the significant task of multi-channel integration.

Field Operations Focus

Fast-moving companies must respond immediately to real-time business changes. Mobile solutions enable these organizations to respond faster to supply chain disruptions by proactively adjusting plans or alerting key personnel about critical events as they occur.

Field operations applications include:

- Field force automation — field service dispatch,

- Direct store delivery, and

- Mobile sales.

Field Force Automation

Mobile two-way radio communications have been around for many years and have proven to be an effective way of delegating work to field technicians and resolving problems. Field force automation, also known as field service dispatch, is one of the most popular mobile computing applications.

In traditional service dispatch, requests are received at a central location where a supervisor decides which representative will take the call. This approach has numerous flaws: It lacks responsiveness; it cannot handle schedule changes on the fly; and it creates delays when technicians order parts from the field electronically, but the transaction must be completed at the office.

Companies that are fed up with traditional service dispatch are embracing mobile data solutions to increase efficiency. AT&T MediaOne, the broadband company that later became part of Comcast Corporation, replaced its paper-based system for responding to service calls with a wireless system that included two-way messaging and a workforce management solution. Time-critical activities, service requests, and up-to-the-minute work assignments can be automatically dispatched to its 1,200 field personnel to ensure timely responses and efficient scheduling. The system led to a 25% productivity gain through improved logistics and fewer canceled appointments.

Direct Store Delivery

In the consumer products, beverage, retail, and grocery industries, direct store delivery (DSD) is a well-established business process. In this process, suppliers' personnel deliver products to each store location and store shelf, directly bypassing the stockroom. Mobile DSD solutions enable drivers to manage DSD, expedite presales orders, reconcile inventory orders, and track product delivery and stock levels.

Mobile DSD solutions increase productivity by streamlining the process and eliminating unnecessary paperwork. For instance, on delivery, each product is scanned, quantities tracked for store acceptance, and information uploaded. Upon order completion, drivers will print a customer receipt via wireless communication with a mobile printer. When finished with deliveries for the day, the mobile DSD solution helps drivers synchronize data with back-end systems for accounting and warehouse inventory functions.

Best-practice companies like Pepsi and Coca-Cola have found that mobile DSD solutions help them improve logistical performance and better monitor, analyze, and integrate data in near real time from sales to settlement.

Mobile Sales

Today's customers want instant information, competitive prices, and faster service when it comes to order status, promotions, and pricing requests. This is pushing salesforces to become even more responsive or risk losing business.

Whether they are on the road or in the office, sales personnel are demanding better communication with back-end systems for scheduling, order entry, sales leads, invoicing, inventory tracking, order fulfillment, and other support information.

Mobile solutions that address the complexities of integrating field sales with back-end systems (for example, user interface, security, and connectivity) are beginning to emerge as investment focus areas for many companies. Mobile sales solutions just might mean the difference between winning and losing business in today's fast-paced marketplace.

Internal Operations Focus

Typical internal operations applications include:

- Mobile asset management,

- Mobile ordering applications (procurement),

- Fulfillment and delivery management (supply chain execution), and

- Asset tracking and visibility (supply chain measurement).

Mobile Asset Management

Companies in industries like manufacturing, utilities, oil and gas, construction, and transportation have large quantities of fixed assets (tools, machinery, and facilities). Maintaining, servicing, and tracking their equipment and assets in a manner that maximizes value can be a daunting task.

Mobile asset management (MAM) solutions help the technicians in these industries perform their daily operations in the field. With the help of a handheld device, these mobile workers can view and update inspection and maintenance data at the point of work and automatically communicate the asset information back to the enterprise.

Take, for instance, the bulk and specialty chemicals industry. When a pump breaks, maintenance workers often travel through football-field-size plants by foot or bicycle to inspect the problem and then travel back to the control room and storage room to arrange for repairs that could take hours. Every minute of downtime for a pump is a potential loss of revenues. The best-practice firms are equipping engineers with handheld computers to report problems and arrange for repair equipment to be brought to the point of the problem.

Minimizing downtime in the course of plant maintenance and in break and fix scenarios is the objective in the utilities industry. Many utility companies such as TransAlta have implemented asset management solutions that enable technicians to collect and access asset information at the point of work, regardless of wireless network availability. The business objective is to improve the integrity of asset data and perform enhanced predictive and preventive maintenance.

Mobile Ordering Applications

Mobile ordering solutions basically extend e-procurement applications and enable customers to place orders on handheld devices. Wesco Distribution, a leading distributor of electrical products, uses mobility to transform its order-to-cash cycle. Wesco's customers are highly mobile and need to order supplies from remote locations. Wesco created a wireless application that lets customers order products from just about anywhere via a handheld device. A key business objective of the new application is to ease some of the pressure on Wesco's busy call center.[2]

The application helps customers save time, manage their businesses, and eliminate order errors. These solutions also include retail reorder applications that use handheld devices to scan item information and either store it locally or transmit it to a central server where it is matched against a replenishment plan. If a certain threshold is met, orders are automatically placed to the suppliers.

Several vendors, including Symbol and Intermec, have been offering a variety of mobile reorder systems for years. Their offerings include simple portable bar code readers and more sophisticated portable data terminals, or PDTs. These tools will read information from assorted devices and automatically transmit this information through wireless local area or wide area networks.

Fulfillment and Delivery Management

Delivery management is a critical function of any supply chain and was one of the first business functions to take advantage of mobile technology. Everyone is familiar with the FedEx or UPS delivery person writing on a tablet. The tablet is a wireless delivery automation platform that integrates the field activities with the company's back office. These drivers use the latest handheld devices to capture critical information and publish it immediately over the Internet. As delivery information is collected, customers can track their order throughout the fulfillment cycle.

This technology alone has helped improve productivity, shorten billing cycles, eliminate proof-of-delivery issues, and improve customer service — all by taking an error-prone, paper-based process that once spanned several days and reducing it to a few minutes.

McKesson, the world's largest healthcare distributor, uses mobile technology to improve its delivery process and electronically confirm every delivery. Approximately 800 of the company's 2,800 truckers use Symbol handheld devices running Palm OS to save the company and its customers time and money. Every package is bar code imprinted and scanned before and upon delivery. McKesson's customers can use the handheld scanners to place orders and obtain instant order confirmation and detailed status. The McKesson example highlights how mobile solutions are rapidly becoming a major presence in the delivery side of the supply chain.

Asset Tracking and Visibility

Imagine a supply chain where raw materials from China become component parts in Taiwan for a product made in Singapore that is then shipped to San Francisco where it is finally assembled and sent to a customer in New York. The manufacturing supply chain has been characterized by global materials movement for decades.

As the world economy transitions to global outsourcing, monitoring highly mobile, geographically dispersed assets takes on increasing importance. Not knowing where products and materials are at any given time along the supply chain is costly. The issues of supply process delays and waste have taken on new urgency with the advent of real-time commerce and increased customer intolerance for fulfillment errors.

Employee Focus: Enterprise Wireless Applications

Last but not least, we have the mobile applications that strive to boost employee productivity. This category includes applications for managing mobile employee access to business information and applications. Employee applications can be broken down into four major segments:

- Messaging solutions,

- Enterprise application extension models,

- Sales or enterprise information portals, and

- Legacy application extension models.

Messaging Solutions

Messaging has become a major application both in the mobile world and in the fixed internet. Messaging applications, such as those pioneered by PalmPilot and the BlackBerry pager, give workers wireless access to corporate e-mail, calendars, and address books while providing a high level of security.

A personal information management (PIM) and messaging application connects all leading mobile devices to existing enterprise messaging and information systems, such as Lotus Notes and Microsoft Exchange. These applications enable users to retrieve and respond to inbox messages, compose new ones, and access and modify contact, task, and scheduling information from anywhere, at any time, and with any device.

Enterprise Application Extension Models

Point solutions extend enterprise applications for easy access. Consider JetBlue Airways' curbside check-in application: The handheld system, which consists of a wireless local area network, portable data terminals, and portable receipt/ticket printer, gives JetBlue's staff access to passenger and flight information via a real-time connection to its reservation system. The line-busting application allows JetBlue staff to check in passengers, print boarding passes, and check luggage virtually anywhere inside or outside the terminal.

The value of this solution for travelers is that it reduces the stress of flying during peak travel times like Christmas. For the company, the value lies in improving on-time operational efficiency by getting passengers, especially late ones, checked in and to the plane immediately.

Business Portals

Business portals give employees a single entry point into their business applications. For example, time and expense entry applications are used by professional service firms whose consultants record information in the field and send it in electronically. All manual, paper-based record entry processes are eliminated, saving time, reducing entry errors, and permitting faster billing and reimbursement. Business portals are designed to overcome such problems by aggregating information from a variety of sources. They compile information from the firm's e-mail systems, front-office applications, legacy applications, and Web-based content and deliver only the most relevant information to the user.

Legacy Extension Models

Most large firms have legacy applications and other focused applications that they have accumulated over the years. Providing access to these applications may become necessary in many industries. One way to do this is through middleware technology that unites disparate computer systems.

Middleware addresses the inefficiencies resulting from the ad hoc buildup of legacy systems over time and distance. Left unchecked, incompatible systems can create "islands of data," with a seriously limited ability to automate work processes and optimize business operations. As companies seek to capitalize on the potential of mobility, using middleware applications to integrate data, business processes, and legacy systems becomes critical.

The SAP Mobile Business Framework

The general landscape framework we have described fits well with the SAP mobile business framework (see Figure 2.2). SAP NetWeaver is the equivalent of our mobile application infrastructure layer.

The different applications that are in SAP mobile business map directly into the framework we presented in this chapter. SAP defines mobile business as the extension of enterprise applications beyond traditional corporate boundaries. To accomplish this extension, SAP is innovating along two fronts: infrastructure and applications.

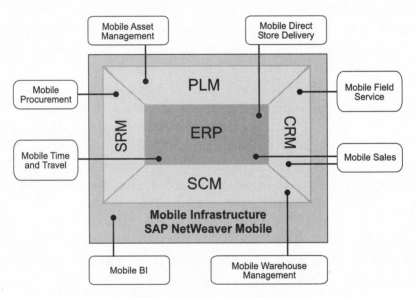

Figure 2.2: SAP's Solutions for Mobile Business

On the infrastructure side, SAP's solution for complete enterprise mobility is SAP Mobile Infrastructure, a technology foundation that is powered by SAP NetWeaver, the company's open integration and application platform that drives lower cost of ownership across heterogeneous IT landscapes. SAP Mobile Infrastructure's goal is twofold:

- Deliver the power of business-critical enterprise systems to all popular mobile devices in both connected and disconnected computing environments.

- Support cross-device — smart phones, PDAs, notebooks, and other mobile devices — scenarios that enable seamless information exchange.

On the application side, SAP's solution includes a set of mobile applications that satisfy customers' need for 24x7 access to corporate data and business processes. SAP's mobile solutions work closely with its enterprise resource planning (ERP), customer relationship management (CRM), supply chain management (SCM), and product lifecycle management (PLM) applications. Whether business is being conducted on the shop floor, at a customer site, or on the road in the middle of nowhere, these applications can minimize integration costs.

Summary

"If you don't know where you're going, you'll end up someplace else."

— Yogi Berra

Mobile business is in its infancy. Until now, no real frameworks for systematically thinking about opportunities or problems existed. Both the business models that support implementation and the competitive landscape are still in flux. By methodically approaching the problem, it becomes clear that the mobile landscape is a complex puzzle that accommodates the development of multiple business solutions.

As we developed the mobile framework, it became clear that mobile solutions extend the value of enterprise application and e-business investments. In one sense, the current transformation is simply the movement of e-business to a mobile environment.

The mobile business is not yet a reality; it is still a developing concept, as are the business applications that support it. In summary, mobile business solutions must take into account the following factors:

- Key enablers — advances in infrastructure, software, and hardware technologies,

- Source of innovation — new application concepts and designs, and

- Arbitrators of success — consumer preferences and marketplace dynamics.

Mobile solution innovations, while exciting in themselves, are significant because they enable the creation of rapid payback or ROI. The relationship between a business problem, the evolution of infrastructure, and the usefulness of an application, however, is not a simple one.

User preferences, corporate capabilities, and process dynamics make mobility even more complex. However, process dynamics will ultimately determine which mobile solutions are successful and which are relegated to the dustbin of history.

Chapter Three

Mobile Technology — Devices, Operating Systems, and Network Infrastructure

The vision is clear: Enterprise application access is going wireless, and devices are becoming more portable. Once you accept this long-term vision, the next question is how do I get there. Unfortunately, managers face a slew of acronyms, slang, and technical terms in figuring out their hardware, software, and operating system options. In this chapter, we define the terms and trends in each area to minimize confusion.

Introduction

It began in January 1975. *Popular Electronics* published a cover story on a computer kit called Altair 8800 that sold for less than $400. It didn't look anything like the machines of today. There was no monitor, no keyboard, and no mouse. The Altair 8800 was a simple box with switches and small lights, designed for scientific calculations. It appealed mainly to hobbyists.[1]

The Altair 8800 was typical of first-generation technology. Many industry executives did not see a need for it. In 1977, Ken Olson, founder, president, and chairman of Digital Equipment, was quoted as saying, "There is no reason anyone would want a computer in their home."

Even consumers did not see any need for it. If someone said a computer would be great for calculations and accounting, people would laugh and answer, "This would never replace the HP-35 four-function calculator."

Or if someone said this would be great for word processing, people would respond, "This will never replace a typewriter." Clearly, the most troublesome aspect was not the technology per se but gauging the scale and speed of user acceptance.

Few could have foreseen what was to come. From that ordinary start in 1975, the PC industry has exploded into a $500 billion annual business. Over the next thirty years, the PC became an integral part of life — word processor and accounting, messaging, and entertainment center. The PC industry's fortunes sway the direction of the global economy. How did this industry become this influential this fast? There are four reasons: Customers found creative uses for the PC. PC software steadily improved in its price/performance ratio. The processor speed followed Moore's Law, doubling roughly every eighteen months or so. Lastly, the Internet greatly increased PC use.

The evolution and adoption of mobile technology in transforming business processes will follow a similar path. There will be intense skepticism followed by grudging adoption. As the prices of mobile devices drop, reliability improves, and the applications get better, demand will explode. Consider this: Today, more than 200 million households worldwide have access to the Web. There are already well over 1 billion cell phone users. Camera phones are the rage everywhere. Handheld sales are beginning to eclipse PC sales. It's only a matter of time before mobile devices become omnipresent in the enterprise.

The mobile economy is inevitable. It is estimated that 20% of the world's population has mobile phones, a number slated to rise to 27% by 2007.[2] However, few business visionaries can predict the shape and form of mobile innovation. Though the future cannot be foreseen, it is possible to generate insight about the mobile economy by developing plausible scenarios based on patterns. Scenarios are relevant to the problem of planning and creating business strategies constructed from various elements — an understanding of current conditions, an identification of the forces for change, and a vision of the future.

The software, hardware, and economic forces shaping the mobile business landscape vary widely. Together they have helped to foster a new business world of extreme workforce connectedness, ultraquick supply chains, and real-time business processes. Few have bothered to analyze the forces underlying mobile business or to relate them to process models.

This chapter attempts to fill this void by identifying a set of trends and directions emerging in the mobile landscape. For clarity, Figure 3.1 groups these trends under broader themes: hardware and device innovation, operating system innovation, and wireless network infrastructure innovation. As these three trends collide, two outcomes are clear: many opportunities for users, software providers, and hardware manufacturers, and much confusion over how the marketplace is evolving.

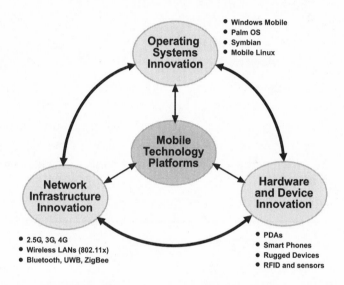

Figure 3.1: The Innovation Circle

Mobile Hardware and Device Trends

When the first walkie-talkie was invented in the late 1930s and early 1940s, its inventors, Al Gross and Donald Hings, could never have imagined that a little black box stuffed with wires would one day become the basis of a worldwide communications revolution. But the basic concept behind the walkie-talkie, communicating with people over a radio link, has been the foundation of all mobile communications.

As people have become increasingly mobile, the need for wireless handheld computers to retrieve, store, and manage information has grown rapidly. It has become increasingly important to both professionals and individuals to have personal and professional information such as addresses, calendars, to-do lists, customer information, and other reference information close at hand and easily managed.

The turning point for this industry occurred in the early 1990s with the invention of the pen-based PDA, which provided consumers a more useful electronic option for organizing information. It even allowed users to synchronize the information they stored in their handheld devices with the information they kept on their PCs. As these products have evolved, they have become less expensive, more intuitive, and easier to operate. Mobile employees, not surprisingly, are using them much more.[3]

In addition, professionals, field workers, and individual consumers increasingly need to communicate while on the go. In an effort to reduce the number of devices that they need to carry to stay connected to critical information, users have begun to adopt a new class of converged handheld devices that provide the combined functionality of cell phones and traditional PDAs.[4] In addition, manufacturers are incorporating information capabilities into a wide range of other devices, including location-aware devices and other consumer products such as wristwatches and game devices.

While most mobile information devices historically have been purchased by individuals, continued pressure to raise productivity is causing enterprises to seek new ways to enable professionals and other workers to be more connected and efficient in both traditional and nontraditional work settings. IT managers are playing a larger role in purchase decisions by setting standards for mobile computing within their organizations. Direct enterprise purchases of mobile devices also are expected to rise, driven in part by great interest in mobile e-mail.

Categories of mobile handheld computing and communications devices include PDAs, smart phones, rugged devices, and tablet PCs.

Personal Digital Assistant (PDA)

The PDA market has progressed greatly in the last decade. Early offerings included AT&T's EO Personal Communicator; Hewlett-Packard's 95LX,

100LX, and 200LX DOS-based palmtop computers; Sharp's pocket-sized Wizard organizers; Motorola's Envoy; and Apple's Newton MessagePad.

Today, the PDA market is focused on two categories of customers: 1) consumers, mainly entry-level, or digital media enthusiasts and 2) business professionals and enterprise users. Products designed for both types of customers incorporate standard software such as address book, date book, clock, to-do list, memo pad, notepad, and calculator. Other features that can be found on PDAs include:

- Wireless communication capabilities, such as Bluetooth, WiFi, CDMA, and GSM or GPRS, that enable messaging, e-mail, and Web browsing;

- Multimedia features, allowing users to capture and view photos and video clips and listen to MP3 music;

- An infrared port for exchanging information between devices;

- A secure digital/multimedia card, or SD/MMC, slot for stamp-sized expansion cards for storage, content, and input/output devices;

- Data synchronization technology (for example, Palm's HotSync) enabling the device to synchronize with desktop applications such as Microsoft Outlook; and

- Productivity software that allows users to create, view, and edit Microsoft Word, Excel, and PowerPoint presentations.

Continuous advances in miniaturization, volume efficiencies, encryption, and wireless networking will make PDAs a cheap, safe prospect for a variety of mobile applications.

In 2004, the PDA market is showing signs of transition as the number of players consolidate. Sony, Sharp, and Toshiba have announced withdrawals of their PDA product line from the U.S. market. According to IDC, worldwide sales of conventional PDAs without phone functions slipped 18% in 2003.[5] The interesting fact is that while the sales of basic PDAs are slowing, the sales of smart phones are speeding up.

Smart Phone Devices

Smart phone handsets are typically mobile phones with better graphics and some Internet browsing and PDA-type capabilities. Smart phones require careful integration of several features: voice, personal information management, or PIM, and messaging. They offer constant access to corporate e-mail as you travel.

Typically, smart phones don't require full PDA capabilities, but the screen size must be large enough to allow calendar and e-mail functions. Examples include Nokia's 3650, Sony Ericsson's P900, or Palm's Treo.[6] In effect, a smart phone has to strike a balance between a wireless handset — easily portable and pocketable — and a PDA, with a focus on PIM, messaging, and browsing.

Smart phones have begun integrating location-aware capabilities. They are attempting to replace global positioning system (GPS) devices, using a technology called assisted GPS, which determines location by triangulation of cell towers instead of satellites.

Size and cost disadvantages mean that smart phones are still not in a position to target the mass consumer market. These two issues are less important to managers, and we expect the smart phone footprint to widen in small businesses and large enterprises in particular, as there is a strong market for data- and voice-centric devices.

Rugged Handheld Devices

The convenience of a PDA, tablet PC, or notebook can also pose a problem: It is very easy to accidentally drop these devices, get them wet, or otherwise put them in harm's way.

To combat these hazards, companies have developed ruggedized notebooks and PDAs. Rugged devices are built to take a beating and keep on ticking. The core components are often enclosed in aluminum or magnesium casing (instead of molded plastic); the keyboard and ports are sealed against dirt, rain, and drinks; and internal devices (like hard disk drives) are shock mounted to absorb vibration.

Ruggedized notebooks are subjected to what is known in the industry as Military Standard 810E (MIL-STD-810E). Among other things, the standard requires the notebook to survive a 3-foot drop onto concrete.

The standard also tests for survivability of prolonged vibration, extreme and sudden temperatures changes, excessive heat, and water spraying.

Before you get too excited about giving your mobile workforce ruggedized notebooks, you should know that they cost about twice as much as an everyday notebook. If your environment is a rough-and-tumble one, you can rest assured that your investment will have a rapid payback. Intermec, Symbol, and Panasonic are the leaders in rugged PDAs.

Critical Requirements for Choosing Hardware Platforms

Organizations now have a new dilemma: choosing which device to select for deployment. Not only is there a wide range of device choices, but the features are ever expanding: voice; data, bar code, and radio frequency identification (RFID) scanning; global positioning systems (GPSs); and signature, video, and image capture are now standard features or options for many devices.

The possibilities are so great that the hardware selection should be driven by the ability to create value. The business value of IT lies in its ability to support business processes more reliably and quickly and at a lower cost. Therefore, the selection and deployment of the underlying device infrastructure to support processes are major issues. Table 3.1 illustrates some important requirements to keep in mind as you think about selecting a device to anchor your mobile business processes.

One or Multiple Devices	Many work styles and business processes will best be met by wirelessly connecting a variety of devices.
Cost of Ownership	Enterprises must consider the total cost of ownership (TCO) in aggregate for each type of worker.
Mobile Remote Management	Device management is required to control TCO, which is driven by a larger software stack on devices that cost much more than the initial hardware.
Security	Onboard, session, and personal firewalls must be considered for thick and thin implementations.
Battery Life	Each mobile worker's workday must be taken into account when selecting devices.
Ongoing Support and Maintenance	Bear in mind the cost of providing "cradle to grave" care of mobile devices, including software distribution.

Table 3.1: Critical Requirements for Selecting Mobile Devices

Mobile Operating Systems

An operating system is defined as the software that controls the operation of a computer and directs the processing of programs (by assigning storage space in memory and controlling input and output functions).

Operating systems are responsible for the following important functions: user interface support; job management (controls the order and time in which programs are run); task management (the simultaneous running of different programs); data management (keeps track of all data required by the programs); and security.

As in the world of personal computers, the basic building block and cornerstone for mobile software is the operating system. Think of the operating system as the foundation for the phone and PDA software onto which the other layers, such as the user interface and the actual applications, can be stacked.

In the Beginning — A Proprietary World

In its early years, the mobile handset industry took a fragmented approach to software. The majority of phones depended on proprietary software from each vendor, with each handset maker using its own operating systems and user interfaces on which its applications ran. In fact, some vendors such as Motorola have even supported a variety of proprietary, internally developed operating systems for their different phone platforms.

Over time, however, the industry has started to awaken to the benefits of adopting a more standardized approach that would bring the industry simpler and potentially more cost-efficient offerings.

Standardization Emerges

Given the very large unit numbers and total revenues involved in the PDA and handset industry, the quest to develop the leading software solutions for this global market has attracted several powerful and innovative contenders, one of whom is, of course, Microsoft.

Microsoft Windows Mobile

Microsoft has sought to extend its reach beyond its PC empire by establishing its Windows Mobile software as a major offering. Microsoft Mobile includes Windows CE for sub-PC computers, Pocket PC for handheld devices, and Smartphone and Pocket PC Phone Edition for voice-enabled handhelds or communication devices.

Symbian OS

Microsoft's aggressive entry into mobile software prompted the formation of Symbian OS. In 1998, Psion, the U.K.-based manufacturer of PDAs, agreed to spin off the software platform (then called EPOC) it was using for its PDAs into a separate company (Symbian) in return for substantial financial backing from Nokia, Ericsson, and Motorola. The three companies agreed to take equal financial stakes in Symbian and use the Symbian OS in future data-enabled phones. Panasonic, Samsung, and Siemens have since become stakeholders. Motorola has recently exited.

PalmSource

A third force in the world of mobile operating systems sprang from the success of the PalmPilot PDAs in the late 1990s. Palm initially focused on its own handsets but later began to license its operating system to others such as Kyocera in the wireless handsets area. Palm has steadily improved its operating system over the years. The release of Palm OS 5 in 2002 provided features such as support for a broad range of screen resolutions, dynamic input area, improved network communication, and Bluetooth. The next generation of Palm OS (called Cobalt) provided integrated telephony features, support for WiFi and Bluetooth, and a better user interface. Palm is increasingly concentrating on supporting smart phones.

Mobile and Embedded Linux

Just to make it interesting, yet another force has emerged in the form of Linux for PDA and smart phone devices. Linux, conceived by Linus Torvalds and developed by a legion of volunteers, has a huge and growing following. The open-source nature of Linux offers developers flexibility and choice. Unburdened by runtime royalties, companies and developers can freely modify Linux to fit their applications.

Mobile Linux has garnered much attention, notably in Asia, with Sharp and Motorola championing Linux/Java-based platforms. Sharp introduced its Zaurus PDA in 2002. In August 2003, Motorola launched its embedded Linux-based A760 high-end smart phone in the Asia-Pacific region. The launch was closely watched by those who see a new trend: open-source operating systems for portable devices. Motorola's developers relied on tools from both MontaVista Software and Metrowerks.[7]

The market for mobile Linux in PDAs and smart phones is still in the innovator phase. We expect it will be several years before it becomes viable for enterprise adoption.

Reviewing Table 3.2 should give readers a better idea of the pros and cons of the mobile operating systems currently on the market.

	Attributes	Potential Issues
Microsoft Mobile	▪ Familiar user interface ▪ Common platform across handhelds, phones, desktops, and servers ▪ Integration with existing desktop applications	▪ Limited experience with mobile voice devices ▪ Limited customization ability ▪ Some vendor and carrier unwillingness to embrace Microsoft
PalmSource	▪ Intuitive user interface ▪ Developed for mobile devices ▪ Range of available applications	▪ Had tremendous market share that has eroded as the company struggled ▪ Limited penetration into the enterprise application space
Symbian OS	▪ Tailored for mobile devices ▪ Easily customized user interface ▪ Supported by multiple vendors; early lead in consumer segment ▪ Integration with desktop applications	▪ Possibly perceived as led by Nokia ▪ Limited corporate or enterprise profile
Mobile Linux	▪ Eliminates royalty payments ▪ Broad developer community ▪ Easily customized	▪ Not originally optimized for mobile devices (memory footprint, battery life) ▪ Limited applications currently available

Table 3.2: Mobile Operating Systems Available

Functionality of Mobile Operating Systems

In the early days of mobile devices, proprietary operating systems were designed to support basic telephony protocols and to run a simple user interface and a few elementary, proprietary applications.

In the last few years, the need for a new generation of operating systems has emerged as the functionality of mobile devices has accelerated. In addition to providing a flexible, scalable foundation for more complex functions and applications, crucial factors for developing today's operating systems remain power management and memory, given the small size of mobile devices. The operating system also needs to ensure even higher levels of reliability and robustness.

Feature	Definition
Kernel	Core software that resides in memory and performs basic and essential operating system tasks.
Input/ouput, storage, and power management	Software that performs critical functions such as data management, communications, power management, pen input, graphics, and other capabilities.
User interface management	Enables users to interact with the handheld device in a consistent, simple, and efficient manner using common input methods such as buttons, a stylus, a keyboard, or voice.
Basic applications	Personal information management applications including datebook, address book, to-do list, memo pad, calculator, and expense management functions.
Application programming interfaces (APIs)	APIs allow licensees, application developers, and other technology providers to develop solutions.
Data synchronization technology	Allows mobile information devices to synchronize information with PCs or enterprise databases.
Desktop software	Helps users to manage their mobile data on their desktop computers and synchronizes this data with handheld devices using synchronization software.

Table 3.3: Elements of a Mobile Operating System

Modern operating systems also have to support the leading 2G, 2.5G, and 3G communications standards and wide area network (WAN) protocols (TCP, IPv4/6); integrated applications for contact management, phone applications, and messaging (SMS and manufacturing message service, or MMS); and some security and multimedia functions and support for multiple user interfaces.

Some operating systems such as Symbian and Linux offer application programming interfaces (APIs) for functions such as location-based services and 3-D graphics, as well as support for Java and C++. Table 3.3 summarizes the main features of a typical mobile operating system.

Third-Party Application Execution Add-ons

Let's consider the following scenario: You want to deploy a field service application that extends SAP and runs on mobile Linux devices, Windows Mobile devices, and PalmSource devices. Your requirements are simple. You don't want to be tied to any operating system or hardware vendor. Enter application execution environments.

Application Execution Environments

PDAs and cell phones have evolved to become a computer in the hand, capable of running different productivity and business applications. This capability is constrained, however, by demands for PDAs and phones to be small, inexpensive, light, and power efficient. These constraints, in turn, have restricted device processing power and memory (storage).

As mobile devices have become more sophisticated and capable of supporting multiple applications, the difficulty of building into the operating system the features necessary to support applications like SAP CRM or ERP has grown. Ideally, applications should scale perfectly with the various PDA and phone models, efficiently use the underlying hardware resources, and provide a consistent user experience.

Operating systems are not the best solution for enabling different applications and wireless data; a complete application execution environment that supports all hardware devices is. Essentially, the application execution environment connects the low-level functions of the mobile device (access to which is enabled by the operating systems) and the higher-level applications (like SAP) written by third parties.

QUALCOMM's BREW platform and Sun Microsystem's Java technology (implemented on mobile phones as J2ME) are two popular application execution environments.[8] The benefit of these environments is clear:

streamlined, efficient software development. With BREW and J2ME, porting applications from device to device almost becomes a trivial task. Time to market is vastly reduced, and new applications work consistently from one hardware model to another.

Both BREW and Java technologies offer a method for executing software applications on a mobile device. To better understand the value of application execution environments, let's look at the differences between server-side execution and client-side processing.

Server-Side Execution

The historic approach to delivering applications to PDAs and phones has been to shift processing power to back-end servers in the operator's network or to a corporate server farm via the Internet (known as server-side execution.) Portals and games using WAP browsers exemplify this strategy.

Content and applications are generated by remote servers, sent through the network, and displayed on the phone's browser. The user then keys in responses to choices displayed on the device screen, which are sent back through the network to the server for processing and response.

The weaknesses of the browser-based server-side approach are clear: high latency and limited interactivity on the mobile device. This makes the most exciting, graphic-rich interactive games impossible — and these represent the bulk of gaming activity on other (non-wireless) handheld platforms.

In effect, with a browser-based solution that requires server-side processing, the mobile phone becomes an unnecessary performance bottleneck and prevents the best applications from being developed because of its inability to process information locally.

Client-Side Execution

Decreases in the size, power consumption, and cost of silicon chips have enabled a second approach: putting more processing power on the mobile device. This opens up a new range of applications based on local, or client-side, processing.

Client-side processing is expected to be the predominant growth area for new mobile wireless applications, rendering today's slow server-side approaches virtually irrelevant for many new applications. Rather than only using the mobile phone's browser to run and interact with applications, the device becomes a true platform for software applications that can offer a startling array of new consumer data services provided by the network operator.

Advantages of Client-Side Processing

Advantages of Java technologies and BREW's client-side processing technology include the following:

- **True real-time processing.** With client-side processing, a new range of applications (such as action games) will be developed because of the BREW platform's ability to download and run applications locally on the phone. Even on circuit-switched networks, applications start immediately since they reside on the phone, with no need to wait for a data call to be initiated. BREW extends this advantage by offering true real-time processing.

- **Fast interactivity with information.** With client-side execution, customers can download a database of travel information about a specific locale to their devices in just a few seconds, then search the database or interact with maps quickly and as often as needed. The locally stored information can also be used to enhance position information for personalized location-based services. All customers enjoy equally fast application response times regardless of network bandwidth. BREW enhances client-side execution by tightly integrating with the phone's basic telephony functions. It's simple for a developer to write applications that take advantage of BREW's telephony management features, so an application can be automatically suspended and then resumed in the event of an incoming call or SMS message.

The battle between Sun's Java and mobile Java (J2ME) and Microsoft's Windows Mobile to be the development platform of choice is likely to be the event to watch over the next few years. Like two prizefighters, we expect these two companies to engage in some serious combat to gain market share.

Network and Connectivity Infrastructure Innovation

Wireless bandwidth is increasing for local and wide area connectivity that supports the higher data transfer demands of business applications such as e-mail with attachments, browsing the Web, multimedia downloads, and interactive applications.

To prepare for the inevitable tidal wave of wireless data traffic, different aspects of the infrastructure urgently need upgrades. These bandwidth improvements are taking place in three areas: in the network, in the home or office, and on your body.

As a result, major trends associated with the development of a wireless data infrastructure include:

- High-speed, always-on mobile Internet connectivity via GPRS (2.5G), 3G, or 4G networks. These wide area networks (WANs) cover states, countries, or even planets with a large number of towers.

- High-speed mobile connectivity via 802.11 a/b/g wireless local area networks (WLANs). These WLANs connect devices in a building, campus, or home.

- Metropolitan area networks (MANs) that join devices over citywide or countywide distances using a handful of towers.

- Personal area networks (PANs) that connect devices over a short distance.

Table 3.4 summarizes the different types of wireless networks. Some devices, such as the rugged Intermec Pocket PC, incorporate Bluetooth, WLAN, and WAN wireless connectivity into one device.

Network Type	Range	Standards	Applications
Wide area	National	GSM, CDMA2000, WCDMA, FLASH-OFDM	Mobile voice and data services, rural Internet access
Metropolitan	<30 miles	802.16 (WiMax), 802.20	Cell site back-haul, campus networks, rural Internet access
Local	<300 feet	802.11x, ZigBee	Internet access, device-to-device communications
Personal	<30 feet	Bluetooth (1.0 and 2.0), ZigBee, Ultrawideband, Wireless USB	Cable or wire replacement

Table 3.4: Wireless Network Types

Wireless Networks: 2.5G, 3G, and 4G

As mobile telephones began to appear everywhere in the early 1990s, their technology actually went through two major generations. First-generation (1G) mobile phones used analog transceivers designed purely for voice calls. These devices were far more advanced than two-way radios and brought users the first widespread wireless access to the traditional telephone network.

Second-generation (2G) mobile phones used digital technology. Transmissions between the base station and the handset relied on one of several different types of digital radio frequency (RF) signaling. Digital voice compression made it possible to fit three or more users on an RF channel that previously could carry only one.[9]

In order for the mobile infrastructure to reach a mass market, networks began to switch from voice to data transmission and communication. Today, the mobile data infrastructure is made up of three generations of technology, called 2G, 2.5G (GPRS), and 3G (third generation). In the near term, the focus is on GPRS, which promises better connect times, quicker downloads, and cheaper rollout.

For several years, the spotlight has been trained on the more glamorous 3G technologies that promise broadband Internet access. Depending on the geography, 3G is one to five years away. Japan and Asia lead, Europe follows, and the United States is last.

In the United States too many fragmented standards and too many carriers have led to basic connectivity that isn't very good. It is quite normal for cell phone conversations to end abruptly and for callers to have to redial. This intermittent connectivity simply would not do in a connected data environment. To improve infrastructure quality, the U.S. companies will require a leapfrog effort, adopting new global standards and solving the base connectivity problem. Only then can they begin to think about adding next-generation services on top.

Why is there so much interest in 3G? Both the phones and the network were designed for voice traffic only. However, the widespread use of laptop computers and other mobile data devices created a demand for a high-capacity wireless network for data transmission. This high-capacity wireless network represents 3G and the convergence of two powerful forces: wideband radio communications and Internet protocol (IP)–based services.

The current market trend is to help operators migrate their technologies to 3G systems, supporting higher bandwidth and greater functionality. The carriers have a vested interest in pursuing high-bandwidth network infrastructure since it will permit them to offer voice service for free, while data services help them to attract and retain new subscribers. The infrastructure firms — Lucent, Nokia, Nortel, Ericsson, QUALCOMM, and others — are actively transforming the wireless voice networks into Internet data-ready, always-on, always-connected networks.

The Capabilities of 3G

There's more to 3G wireless technology than data capacity and new kinds of digital signaling. Its other innovations include the following:

- **Wireless packet switching instead of circuit switching.** 3G systems break data up into self-contained packets (similar to the Internet) instead of establishing a continuous connection that dedicates a circuit for each call. Each packet contains a destination address and a sequence number for independent routing and reassembly into a complete message.

- **An always-on connection that's always there.** Handsets will maintain constant contact with their networks but will exchange packets of information only when needed. This always-on characteristic works well for intermittent data transmission and shortens the time required to set up a new connection.

- **Bandwidth on demand.** Data capacity that can be flexibly shared between users makes better use of the RF spectrum and the network infrastructure. With 3G systems, one user can send or receive several hundred thousand bits per second, while another may only exchange several hundred.

In many cases, the deployment of 3G technology will allow operators to retain much of their existing investment in current 2G mobile technology. 3G can also be deployed incrementally, permitting operators to control the pace of subscriber migration. Wireless operators are expanding the coverage, reliability, and data capacity in their CDMA/1xRTT and GSM/ GPRS phone networks, as well as adding specific data services such as wireless e-mail.

What's Next? 3.5G and 4G

Just when we are talking about finally getting 3G, the next wave of innovation is coming in the form of 3.5G and 4G. 3.5G is an upgrade of 3G, which uses technologies like High Speed Downlink Packet Access (HSDPA) and time division duplex (TDD) and proprietary technologies like FLASH-OFDM.

The 4G mobile communications format is expected to become commercially available around 2010. Samsung Electronics and others are working on 4G.

Wireless LANS: WiFi (802.11 a/b/g)

WiFi — short for wireless fidelity — is a family of wireless local area network (WLAN) technologies based on the IEEE's (the Institute of Electrical and Electronics Engineers) 802.11 standard.

WiFi allows users to surf the Internet at high speeds without physically plugging their computer into anything, as long as they are within a few hundred feet of a central access point (or hotspot). WiFi hotspots have popped up all over — airports, college campuses, hotels, restaurants, gas stations, and bookstores — making access to the Internet easier and easier. Sensing demand, manufacturers are equipping many new laptops, PDAs, and even phones with built-in 802.11 support.

How does WiFi work? WiFi uses 802.11 technology to replace the cable in a network connection, allowing surfers to access the Internet up to about 300 feet from a central access point, without using wires. The number 802.11 refers to a family of specifications developed by the IEEE, which includes three air interface specifications: 802.11a, 802.11b, and 802.11g, as well as several enhancements.

Table 3.5 compares the differences between the three 802.11 air interfaces. Though 802.11g is relatively new, we believe the market will broadly embrace it because it provides backward compatibility with the large amount of "b" equipment already deployed, supports higher data rates, and offers better coverage of the 2.4GHz (gigahertz) frequencies.

WiFi's Limitations and Issues

Though WiFi equipment manufacturers tout maximum data rates of up to 11 Mbps (million bits per second) for 802.11b and 54 Mbps for 802.11g and 802.11a, the actual data rate experienced is dependent on a number of factors:

- **System overhead.** System overhead (data exchanged between the device and the access point that is necessary to maintain the connection) consumes roughly one-fifth to one-third of the gross bandwidth.

- **Wired backhaul.** Internet access will be only as fast as the access point's connection to the Internet. For example, most hotspots are connected to the Internet through a T1, DSL (digital subscriber line), or cable modem connection. Those services typically support Internet access that is no faster than 3 Mbps (1.5 Mbps for a T1). Therefore, an 802.11g hotspot connected to the Internet by cable modem or DSL will provide Internet access at 3 Mbps, not 54 Mbps.

- **Shared connection.** Like other wireless systems, users share the available bandwidth. Because access points typically contain only one radio, all users are restricted to the speed of the slowest user. (If a user with an 802.11b laptop connects to a "g" hotspot, all the other users on that access point will be able to connect at only "b" speeds rather than "g" speeds.)

- **Distance and interference.** Data rates also are affected by distance and interference levels. As a user moves further away from the wireless access point or as interference increases (someone nearby turns on a microwave oven, chats on a cordless phone, opens a garage door, or uses a Bluetooth device) the data rate will decline.

	802.11a	802.11b	802.11g
Popularity	New technology	Widely adopted; readily available verywhere	New technology with rapid growth expected
Speed	Up to 54 Mbps (nearly five times faster than 802.11b)	Up to 11 Mbps (note: cable modem service typically averages no more than 4-5 Mbps	Up to 54 Mbps (nearly five times faster than 802.11b)
Relative Cost	Expensive	Inexpensive	Relatively inexpensive
Frequency	Uncrowded 5 GHz band can coexist with 2.4 GHz networks without interference	More crowded 2.4 GHz band; some conflict may occur with other 2.4 GHz devices like cordless phones and microwave ovens	More crowded 2.4 GHz band; conflict may occur with other 2.4 GHz devices like cordless phones and microwave ovens
Range	Shorter range than 802.11b and 802.11g; 25-75 feet indoors	Good range; 100-150 feet indoors, depending on construction, building, materials, and room layout	Good range; 100-150 feet indoors, depending on construction, building, materials, and room layout
Public Access	None at this time	The number of public "hotspots" is growing rapidly, allowing wireless connectivity in many airports, hotels, college campuses, public areas, and restaurants	Compatible with current 802.11b hotspots (at 11 Mbps); most 802.11b hotspots will quickly convert to 802.11g
Compatibility	Incompatible with 802.11b or 802.11g	Widest adoption	Interoperates with 802.11b networks (at 11 Mbps); incompatible with 802.11a

Table 3.5: Comparing 802.11a, 802.11b, and 802.11g

WiFi's Security Issues

Security has posed an obstacle to the adoption of wireless networking, albeit to a lesser extent than in the past. Since data is transferred over radio waves, it is vulnerable to unauthorized interception. To complicate matters, the Wired Equivalent Privacy (WEP) encryption scheme used in early 802.11b systems is easily compromised.

To cut security risks, the IEEE and WiFi Alliance have collaborated on developing the WiFi Protected Access (WPA) standard, which is replacing WEP. The development has been formalized into the 802.11i standard.

WPA offers several added benefits over WEP, such as checking for proper permission and passwords before allowing network access and supporting stronger encryption. Security is even more of an issue when accessing open networks such as the ones found at coffee shops, airports, and hotels since security features are often turned off to simplify access to the network.

WiFi's Mobility Issues

Unlike 3G networks, WiFi is limited in its ability to offer true mobility. If a corporate WiFi network is correctly engineered, it is possible for users to move between access points without having to log in again. Several enterprise hardware makers sell solutions that treat wireless access points as another network node, which simplifies deployment and management.

Beyond WiFi? WiMax

Unlike WiFi's 150-foot range, WiMax technology (IEEE 802.16) will have a range of miles, spanning entire metropolitan areas and transferring data, voice, and video at faster speeds than broadband (DSL). WiMax offers a way to bring the Internet to entire communities without having to invest billions of dollars to install phone or cable networks.

Intel, one of the biggest backers of the technology, shipped its first WiMax chips to equipment manufacturers in 2004. Full-scale deployment of WiMax is expected to begin in 2007. Intel is conducting about 50 WiMax tests around the United States with a variety of partners to see how equipment from different WiMax suppliers works together and how WiMax service reacts to trees, buildings, and different weather conditions.[10]

Personal Area Networks: Bluetooth, ZigBee, and Ultrawideband

The ability to link peripheral devices such as printers or scanners to PCs has existed for years. More recently, it's become possible to link peripherals to a cell phone. With both cell phones and PCs, the more peripherals that are connected, the more wires are running everywhere, creating a "cable jungle."

The innovative Bluetooth attempts to solve the cable jungle problem.[11] Bluetooth is a low-cost, low-power, short-range radio technology originally developed as a cable replacement to connect devices such as mobile phone handsets, headsets, scanners, and portable computers.

The main advantage of Bluetooth is that it can vastly simplify communications for consumers, taking mobility one step further into home and office markets. Using Bluetooth, data can be transmitted without any wires or cables. By enabling standardized wireless communications between devices, Bluetooth has created a close-range wireless personal area network (PAN).

Bluetooth is suitable for short-range connections among a range of mobile devices, such as those between a mobile phone and a notebook PC or a mobile phone and a headset or LAN access points and laptops or palmtops.

Bluetooth-enabled devices work in the following manner: With Bluetooth, the cell phone acts as a modem. The laptop user opens an application requiring Bluetooth to dial up a network connection. The laptop scans the environment for any Bluetooth-enabled devices by transmitting a series of inquiry packets. The cell phone then replies with a frequency hop synchronization (FHS) packet. The FHS packet contains all the information the laptop needs to create a connection to the cell phone, including both major and minor cell phone device classes. The major device class tells the laptop that it has found a phone; the minor class says that the type of phone is cellular. Every Bluetooth-enabled device in the PAN that is scanning for inquiries will respond with an FHS packet. As a result, the laptop compiles a list of enabled devices. With the link established, information can flow freely over the connection.

Bluetooth technology can lead to increasingly beneficial scenarios. For example, the biggest disadvantage of today's digital camera technology is having to transfer images from expensive memory cards to a computer hard drive or other storage media before printing them. Bluetooth enables users to print the photos directly from their digital camera onto a Bluetooth-enabled printer, or transfer them for printing to a computer equipped with a Bluetooth player or recorder. Apple has taken an avid interest in Bluetooth technology. It's available for Apple computers, keyboards, printers, and even computer mice.

In the home networking arena, another interesting innovation to monitor is called ultrawideband (UWB). UWB is a short-distance, high-speed wireless standard that combines the advantages of both Bluetooth and high-speed LANs (IEEE's 802.11x). Low-power and roughly 40 times the data transmission speed of WiFi, this wireless technology is finally ready to debut in the living room.[12]

ZigBee is the last of the personal area networks. ZigBee is designed to build low-cost networks for lighting, HVAC, and other sensor networks. ZigBee's value proposition is simple: As sensors spread throughout homes and buildings, and as controlling computers become cheaper, there needs to be an easy (and low-cost) way to move information from device to device. The ZigBee wireless protocol provides a mesh-based network, with intelligence to route signals from device to device, at around $1 to $5 per unit. Each ZigBee radio has a range of about 200 meters and contains the smarts to route signals to any other device it can see.[13]

Other Trends of Interest

Alvin Toffler, the futurist, once said, "The future always comes too fast and in the wrong order." The wireless industry supports his statement. Even as 3G and WiFi networks are being switched on around the world, innovation is driving the next wave.

The mobile landscape continues to change as mobile office employees search for additional features and devices to work more efficiently and productively. We thought it would be useful to acknowledge these trends.

- **Miniaturization.** Handheld computing demands increasing functionality in more compact, power-efficient packages. The trend toward miniaturization in microelectronics is occurring simultaneously in handset, screen display, data storage, and power supply technologies.

- **Cars as mobile platforms.** New customer interaction channels are emerging in the form of "smart" things — cars, appliances, and toys. For instance, telematics brings the Web into the car. The automobile, the largest mobile device, is becoming viable as a distribution channel for information, transaction, and entertainment services.

- **Peripheral innovation.** Camera phones, Web cams, portable printers, global positioning systems (GPSs), and handheld credit card readers are changing certain tasks and activities in ways both mundane and profound.

Miniaturization Trends

In the world of wireless, smaller is better in four areas: handsets, screen displays, data storage, and power supply technologies. The key to miniaturization has been the development of extremely compact, power-efficient electronic devices and components — the building blocks of mobile hardware of all kinds.

Handset miniaturization. Mobile phones have dramatically slimmed down since the mid-1980s. In 1986, a cell phone weighed almost two pounds (800 grams). By 1997, the weight was down to an eighth of a pound (50 grams). The handset is currently constrained by several factors, including processing capability, input methodology, and screen form factor. Next-generation phones will have fatter clients, such as Java Virtual Machine (JVM), which enable these devices to do limited "processing." In essence, such devices could lessen data traffic over a network, since basic formatting and logic can be done on the device itself. In order for many PDAs to succeed in the data application market, they must decrease in size and increase their computational ability.

System-on-a-chip. Three long-running miniaturization trends typify the microchip industry. The first trend is feature size, or the width of the wires that provide connections inside the microchip. Feature size continues to shrink. Depending on the type of chip, the features in the newest generation will be 0.13 microns (a micron is one millionth of a meter), down from 0.25 microns. The second trend is the shift to 300-millimeter wafers. Traditionally, chips are cut from 200-millimeter platters of pure silicon, each yielding 100 chips. The shift to the larger size — moving from salad-plate to dinner-plate dimensions — will enable makers to extract 225 chips from each wafer. The third trend is the shift from aluminum to copper as the principal metal for the wires inside the chips.[14]

Flat-panel displays. The same trend toward ultracompact size shows up again in flat-panel display technology. Today's displays — cathode-ray tubes or flat panels — are invariably rigid, glass-encased devices. There is tremendous demand for very small, high-resolution displays for use in head-mounted displays and other mobile applications. For example, the U.S. firm Kopin manufactures a 320 x 240 pixel liquid crystal display (one-fourth the pixel count of a desktop VGA resolution monitor) that measures only 0.24 inches diagonally. Colorado MicroDisplay has developed a liquid-crystal-on-silicon (LCOS) display, which supports a full 800 x 600 pixels in a unit measuring 0.47 inches diagonally.

Scientists are working on new approaches to displaying information that uses, for example, chemical polymers rather than electronic transistors. This means that screens could be printed on flexible pieces of plastic that could be rolled up and stuck in a back pocket. It might also be possible to mount a computer display on a curved surface, or even on existing objects like walls or cars. While they are still in the laboratory stages, these new display technologies might one day allow for astonishing portability.

Rechargeable micro-fuel cells. Japanese wireless operator NTT DoCoMo recently announced that it has co-developed a prototype of a rechargeable micro-fuel cell to power handsets used to access its 3G network. DoCoMo's partner was Fujitsu Laboratories. DoCoMo's rival KDDI Corporation said it too would develop methanol-based fuel-cell power systems for mobile phones with Toshiba and Hitachi.

Fuel cells could significantly extend the amount of time that the 3G phones could be used between charges. The fuel cell generates power by combining hydrogen and methanol, which produces a chemical reaction. The fuel cell has a relatively small footprint (152 x 57 x 16 millimeters) and weighs less than half a pound (190 grams).[15] This is a major innovation as it solves one of the most troublesome problem in mobile computing — long-lasting battery life.

Data storage. Devices used in business may need to store a large amount of data. Disk drives have gone from the large "disk packs" used with mainframe computers in the 1960s and 1970s to the 8-inch- and 5.25-inch-diameter drives in early personal computers, to the 3.5-inch or less drives used in portable computers. At each stage, the size of the drive itself has not only shrunk, but the densities at which data can be stored have increased. The smaller drives store more information than their larger predecessors. Continuing this trend, IBM's Microdisk, the world's smallest and lightest hard disk drive, can store up to 1 gigabyte of data on a disk the size of a matchbox. Weighing only 20 grams (less than a standard AA battery), the Microdisk can hold more than 200 times the data or images held by a standard floppy disk. The Microdisk can be used in most digital cameras, PDAs, laptops, or PC systems with PCMCIA card slots.

Due to the advances driven by digital camera adoption, smaller cards with increasing storage volume are available for PDAs and smart phones. For example, postage stamp–sized Secure Digital (SD) and MultiMediaCards (MMCs) can now store several gigabytes of data. Large storage capacity is central to reducing the need for printed material. In the mid-1990s, external Flash storage cards cost more than $10 per megabyte (for example, a 4MB CompactFlash card sold for about $160 in 1996). Today, these same storage cards can be purchased for less than $0.50 per megabyte. Ready access to up-to-the-minute data can save costs by avoiding additional customer visits and speed up business processes. The microstorage industry bears watching.

Next-generation technological devices should include three core design features: compact form, high performance, and low power consumption. The power supply is the heart of any electronic system. In space-constrained devices, the size of the power supply and power consumption becomes a crucial issue. Users expect electronic devices to work for long periods without recharging. Several firms are working to develop ultra-low-power devices that could run for months on the tiniest of batteries.

Telematics: Cars as Mobile Channels

Automobile manufacturers are beginning to offer wireless services to drivers. Most in-vehicle communication capabilities are still basic. Usually, they consist of a built-in phone linking the driver to a service center operator who provides the driver with emergency assistance, directions, or other basic travel information. Carmakers will increasingly bring wireless capabilities — downloading music, returning e-mail, and on-the-road shopping — to their vehicles. Why? The time drivers spend in their cars makes them a large and captive audience.

Telematics is the basic technology behind products such as GM Onstar, Ford RESCU, and Mercedes-Benz TeleAid. The term originated in the European automotive industry to describe automotive communications technologies. Mercedes-Benz was one of the first companies to use the term, and customers quickly responded. Telematics refers to a complete solution — from the system's and the car's hardware and software to the service center's support.

How does a telematics system work? The heart of the system is the telematics communications unit (TCU), located in the car and connected (wirelessly) to a central service center. The TCU serves as the telematics system's central, fully integrated platform. It communicates location-specific information to a central service center, which delivers support services to a driver via the cell phone. The TCU also connects to the engine control unit, the car's onboard computer, which enables enhanced services such as remote engine diagnostics and automatic airbag notification.[16]

General Motors has announced that for the 2006 model year, 3 million GM vehicles in North America will be equipped with OnStar's in-vehicle safety and communications system, up from 1.4 million in 2004 and 2.2 million in the 2005 model years. The growth in the global in-vehicle information system (IVIS) market can be attributed to several factors. First, a large number of new entrants from the automotive and wireless industries are positioning themselves in the market. In addition, IVIS development has benefited significantly from recent advances in intelligent transportation system (ITS) applications such as fleet management systems, in-vehicle navigation systems, collision avoidance systems, and adaptive cruise control.

Telematics represents the first major revolution since the radio for content delivered to the automobile. Combining personalization and telematics will allow companies to deliver real-time traffic alerts, specialized news programs, and targeted ads based on an individual's location and profile.

The future of telematics shows promise. As market penetration increases and the demand for enriched content grows, telematics becomes viable as a channel of information and entertainment. Eventually, telematics channels will permit us to communicate with the office and home, in ways well beyond simple voice conversations. Drivers will be able to turn on home lights, start and stop the sprinkler system, and set their office and home security systems all via their telematics systems. With a platform so flexible and robust, the potential scenarios are endless.

Peripheral Innovation

In the last five years, advances in mobile peripheral technology have been impressive. Mobile handhelds no longer are limited to simple voice or data functions; video and image capture, along with printing capabilities, are the new paradigm for these devices.

Web cameras. Web cams provide you with the ability to connect with co-workers and participate in meetings while you are on the road. With a Web camera, you can keep in touch and retain "face time" with your co-workers. Most Web cameras are easy to set up and use right from the box, so you don't need to spend time learning new software.

Camera PDA and smart phones. In October 2000, J-Phone launched its first camera-phone handset, the J-SH04, in Japan. A few years later, it is clear that camera phones are here to stay and that they are being integrated into everyday life. The innovation in the camera phone and PDA industry has been breathtaking. Each day brings new advances and better resolution. For instance, camera phones have created a whole new class of amusement called moblogging, for mobile Web logging; users post mundane and occasionally bizarre cell phone snapshots into online scrapbooks such as Mobog, Textamerica, and Yafro. What we have yet to understand is role of the still or video camera in transforming business processes. This should be an interesting trend to monitor.

Printers. Portable printers have long been prized by insurance agents, home inspectors, and real-estate brokers who wanted immediate approval or delivery of customized contracts. The big innovation was battery power, which eliminated the need to tote around the heavy AC bricks used with desktop printers. But it's only recently that portable printers have offered page-speed and photo-printing capabilities that rival desktop models. Now Bluetooth is allowing these devices to function without cables, enabling more convenience. Portable printers can access and print from PDAs, cell phones, or notebooks at a speed of one megabit a second at about 33 feet.

GPS, GIS, and LBS. New peripherals or extensions are coming to the market that provide the tools for building mobile and wireless applications that combine business-critical information with GPS, GIS, and LBS capabilities.

- A global positioning system (GPS) provides a set of coordinates for a mobile worker, a mobile device, or an asset.

- A geographic information system (GIS) supplies context within which GPS coordinates are meaningful.

- A location-based services (LBS) application uses context and location in order to simplify a task or an activity.

In field sales, field service, transportation, logistics management, law enforcement, homeland security, and other highly mobile situations, GPS, GIS, and LBS capabilities can improve productivity and responsiveness by an order of magnitude. The combination of real-time mobile data and geographic information provided in a location-based context is beginning to transform mobile applications in new and interesting ways.

Summary

> *"Learn from yesterday, live for today, hope for tomorrow.*
> *The important thing is to not stop questioning."*
>
> — Albert Einstein

Constantly questioning the current status quo is leading to more powerful technologies arriving at a dizzying pace. Yesterday's innovation becomes today's standard, then tomorrow's outdated concept. Steadily declining component costs and improvements in production economics are driving down the price of new technology. The price declines make mobile devices affordable to a broader set of consumers, greatly increasing the market penetration rate and creating user profiles more reflective of society.

In the face of this relentless change, the first task of executives is to understand the direction and velocity of technological innovation in their industries. Without such an understanding, the diligent efforts of thousands of employees are misdirected. Even worse, thousands of jobs and billions of dollars of market value are placed at unnecessary risk. Companies will invest scarce resources without producing any returns, and opportunities for more profitable growth will be lost.

Combining these broad hardware, software, and network trends to form sustainable mobile business models is truly a complex phenomenon that is bound by invisible fabrics of interrelated trends, which often take years to play out. Often, when we are in the middle of it all, it's hard to see the whole pattern of change. Instead, we tend to focus on snapshots of isolated problems and wonder why we were unable to see the whole picture. Innovation in the mobile economy is no different.

In the next chapter, we examine how SAP is developing a layer of functionality called Mobile Infrastructure that links the breakthrough technologies on the device side with the back-end applications.

Chapter Four

Mobile Application Infrastructure

Most business applications such as enterprise resource planning (ERP), customer relationship management (CRM), product lifecycle management (PLM), and supply chain management (SCM) are built for desktop interaction. Getting them to work on a 2 x 2 inch or 4 x 4 inch screen requires a piece of software called mobile middleware or mobile infrastructure. SAP Mobile Infrastructure is a core piece of mobilizing enterprise applications. It provides the foundation that businesses need to expand their mobile capabilities. Our goal in this chapter is to help you understand SAP Mobile Infrastructure (a component of SAP NetWeaver Mobile) from an architectural, feature, and integration perspective.

Introduction

Ask most people who invented the incandescent lightbulb, and they will say Thomas Edison. The truth is that Edison's version of the lightbulb trailed those of many other forgotten inventors.

What Edison did do brilliantly was work with his team of engineers at the famous Menlo Park, New Jersey, facility to develop a complete lighting infrastructure — sockets, switches, fuses, lamp holders, current generation and regulation, and wiring with distributing boxes, house connections, and meters.

Edison is remembered in history because he didn't just stop with a single innovative idea. He created an infrastructure to bring the idea to the mass market. SAP is doing something similar with its mobile infrastructure product. It is not interested in building the best lightbulb; it is intent on building the best lighting infrastructure.

Consider the typical business scenario to understand what kind of problems SAP is attempting to solve: The elevator division of a Fortune

500 company wanted to improve the productivity of its more than 1,000 mobile workers making repairs in the field. The division's managers set aggressive goals. They challenged the IT group to develop a solution that reduced the need for repeat visits, cut repair completion times, and simplified spare-parts inventory management. The division also sought to decrease its head count by 400 workers.

After studying the business processes involved in field service repairs, the IT group realized that significant productivity improvements could be achieved if mobile workers were given access to the SAP ERP and CRM applications. Analysis of the maintenance workflow revealed that workers needed remote access to work order dispatch, scheduling, equipment maintenance history, online reference manuals, job costing, order management, and call reporting functionality.

The IT group decided that a hybrid online-offline solution was the best option since adequate GPRS or 3G wireless coverage was lacking in the geographic areas the mobile technicians covered. The online-offline solution would allow the repair technicians to work in offline mode while performing repairs inside buildings or elevator shafts. Once they reached their truck, they could connect via wireless networks.

Another key decision for the IT group was determining the optimal handheld device for the technicians: Windows Mobile–based PDA or laptop PC. After studying the field workers, the IT group selected the rugged PDA over the laptop PC for several reasons: form factor, usability, PC start-up, and reboot issues. For future flexibility though, the group decided a Java-based, platform-independent runtime environment that could run on any operating system would work best.

The mobile infrastructure on the server side posed the biggest challenge for the IT group. The infrastructure had to integrate information from multiple data sources on multiple device types. Leverage was important too. The mobile infrastructure chosen had to be reusable for both "blue-collar" scenarios (field service or asset management), as well as "white-collar" scenarios (field sales and business intelligence alerts) planned for the following year.

In the following sections, we will look at the issues surrounding mobile middleware and infrastructure that businesses face when developing business-to-employee (B2E) mobile worker solutions. In particular, we will dissect different parts of the SAP NetWeaver Mobile component and specifically the SAP Mobile Infrastructure layer within it. Our goal is to lay the foundation for mobile application development and deployment.

Defining Mobile Middleware and Infrastructure

Enterprise applications are not necessarily synonymous with integration. Companies expend great effort to move information from a mobile device to a back-end application or between two systems. By installing mobile middleware (or infrastructure) they allow individuals to access and update any back-end application from one mobile device.

The term "middleware" describes a software product that serves as the glue between two applications. It acts as a connector, allowing applications to pass data between them.[1]

Thus, mobile middleware is defined as a software product that links the applications running on mobile devices with back-end SAP applications (ERP, CRM, SCM, PLM, human resources [HR], supplier relationship management [SRM], and various xApps).

Mobile middleware and infrastructure software consists of two pieces: a behind-the-firewall server and/or client software that combine to extend the reach of existing enterprise or collaborative groupware or messaging applications (including Microsoft Exchange, Lotus Domino, or POP3) or other applications.

Mobile middleware and infrastructure software also offers companies the opportunity to develop new applications for employees who use a variety of wireless devices including laptops, handhelds, smart phones, and other devices.

In terms of the business model, the software may be sold in a single offering (package of the platform, front-end client applications, and development tools) or as a hosted offering. For instance, SAP bundles mobile infrastructure into its SAP NetWeaver suite. On the other hand, mobile operators like Vodafone or Verizon try to provide the software (especially for messaging) as a hosted model.

To better understand the mobile middleware landscape, let's examine the three distinct generations that have shaped the application's industry.

Three Generations of Mobile Middleware

Mobile applications have been around long enough to have passed through three distinct phases: device-centric, application-centric, and user-centric.

Device-centric middleware implies that the organization has proprietary "point" middleware that can only support a specific manufacturer's device. Application-centric middleware suggests that the organization has more flexibility to support different devices but only for a specific scenario like mobile sales. User-centric middleware embraces a more flexible approach in which multiple devices and applications are supported by one middleware infrastructure.

Today, forward-thinking providers of software solutions are developing mobility applications with users in mind, but device-centric and application-centric solutions that fail to address the crucial issues of user experience and cross-application support are still being brought to market.

Enterprises that are planning for a mobile deployment must recognize that software based on the development paradigms of the earlier generations will likely be caught in a technological dead end, missing the ability to evolve. Moreover, since device- and application-centric technologies almost always create inflexible applications, even a short-term solution may be a complete failure from the end users' perspective.

The Device-Centric Middleware Approach

Device-centric middleware treats each individual device as the focal point for a distinct version of a mobile application, such as field service or asset management.

This proprietary, custom-developed method generally occurs when existing software solutions are not available or sufficient. In this approach, different middleware infrastructure is developed for distinct devices; that is, developers build separate software for desktop PCs, different PDAs, and specific smart phone products.

Device-centric solutions are tailored to meet the exact specifications of existing applications and devices and, therefore, may not be flexible enough to easily adapt to advances in technology. This development approach and the associated platforms are doomed because:

- They do not allow for rapid application deployment,

- They make application upgrades very expensive and difficult,

- They restrict the ability of application developers to respond quickly to new user requirements, and

- They are extremely costly.

Once adopted, custom-developed solutions may require duplication of application coding and content to support additional applications, new devices, and increased capacity. Each version of an application represents a different device, which means developers have to choose between adding features to all versions or writing new versions to support additional devices.

Application-Centric Middleware Approach

Developers that select the application-centric approach attempt to build "once size fits all" mobile applications for multiple devices. The applications are based on technologies such as transcoding, re-rendering, and Web screen scraping. They are often classified as custom solutions and involve inflexible programming languages like WAP (Wireless Application Protocol).[2]

Screen scraping gained popularity during 1999–2001. This method of rendering content on mobile devices basically excerpts Web-based content and applications by copying and converting the content of actual Web pages at a particular moment in time, rather than accessing the data and functionality of the template that is used to generate the Web pages.

These applications typically try to extend Web content to wireless devices. Unfortunately, changes to the source Web pages often cause the mobile applications to break down. The middleware in this approach features a server-side product that can dynamically translate and customize existing Web applications and content for viewing on any wireless Internet device.

The application-centric approach produces mobile applications that are inherently unstable and poorly integrated into the enterprise system architecture. From the perspective of the user, a single interface is defined that aims to satisfy the majority of user needs for a given context.

This "lowest common denominator" approach should be abandoned because it simply doesn't deliver a satisfactory experience on any device.

User-Centric Middleware Approach

The user-centric approach — the current, mature method for mobile application development — makes user experience the focus of development, regardless of the diversity of devices, communications standards, and applications. In this model, mobile middleware has to be flexible enough to support the goal of write once and deploy across different operating systems, networks, and platforms.

This approach allows application developers to refine the user experience for different contexts without having to write a separate application for every device.

For instance, in retail you find mobile workers on the sales floor and in the store-to-store delivery vehicles. In industrial markets, you see mobile workers in manufacturing and warehouses tracking work in process and managing inventory in shipping and receiving. In logistics markets, you find mobile workers on the road delivering and picking up products. In field service, you find mobile workers conducting inspections or creating work orders. In healthcare, you find mobile workers caring for patients and tracking medicines.

SAP is taking a user-centric approach. It is focused on building a mobile infrastructure that can support the needs of the mobile workforce in a host of different professions, industries, and applications. This is very much the same tactic that SAP adopted for SAP R/3 in the 1990s with great success in the PC client-server world. The same concept has been extended to the mobile world.

Mobile workers require more than just anytime, anywhere access. User-centric middleware aims to give mobile workers what they need where they need it in whatever context or on whatever device they prefer.

While each market for and application of mobility is unique, there are many common attributes and benefits for mobile workers. Providing that common foundation is the role of SAP NetWeaver Mobile.

Types of Mobile Connectivity

Now that you understand the different types of middleware approaches — device-, application-, and user-centric — let's investigate the specific type of connectivity that you will be targeting. Discerning the options for connectivity is a necessary part of choosing a middleware infrastructure.

As we wrote earlier, mobility refers to the action of performing your job away from your primary workplace regardless of connectivity. Connectivity could be offline, dial-up (using a standard landline), broadband (using a wired connection), or wireless.

Mobile infrastructure varies across several parameters including device types, enterprise needs, corporate policy, and user requirements. Typically, mobile infrastructure falls into three categories:

- **Connected:** the handheld device is connected continuously with the back-end SAP applications. In this scenario, access to the back end is available through the device's browser over a wireless (3G) or WiFi connection. Examples include RIM Blackberry for e-mail, CRM access (a thin client with always-on connectivity), or laptop-based CRM with GPRS card (a thick client with always-on connectivity).

- **Disconnected:** refers to local access on a PDA or rugged handheld computer where most of the interaction with the device is done offline in the field. The data is usually synchronized later, typically at the end of the day, using a cable to a PC or server. There is no wireless access in this scenario. Examples include laptop-based CRM (a thick client with sync-based connectivity) or handheld CRM (a thin client with sync-based connectivity).

- **Hybrid Online-Offline:** a more complex scenario that spans both connected and disconnected modes of operation. A user might go in and out of wireless coverage, resulting in periods of real-time connectivity and periods when he is completely offline. Making the application work seamlessly across these two modes requires an intricate infrastructure to ensure that the data is not corrupted and the task is done smoothly. Examples include laptop-based CRM (a thick or thin client with sync-based or always-on connectivity).

Figure 4.1 depicts the three categories of mobile middleware infrastructure. The figure shows that managers have four potential quadrants to choose from when they are looking at mobile investments. The quadrants can be further grouped into three categories: connected (quadrants 3 and 4), disconnected (quadrants 1 and 2); and hybrid online-offline infrastructure (quadrants 1, 2, 3, and 4).

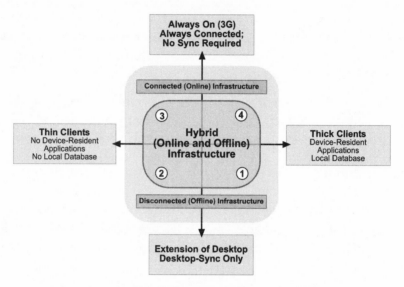

Figure 4.1: Three Types of Mobile Middleware Decisions

Ideally, you want a flexible mobile infrastructure (hybrid online-offline infrastructure) that can handle all these scenarios. If you are a global company, some areas of your business will have great wireless coverage, and some areas will have lousy wireless coverage. If your application does not work in both settings, you have to build multiple versions of the applications, which adds to the total cost of ownership (TCO).

Connected Application Infrastructure

A connected infrastructure works directly with your corporate back-end applications in real time. Companies with this type of infrastructure have users based in locations with adequate wireless data coverage that lets them be connected at all times. This category also covers companies that are extending their physical networks with WiFi-enabling access to corporate applications in an untethered fashion.

Connected mobile applications rely on back-end systems to perform complex transactions and business object validation, the results of which are transmitted to the connected device instantaneously.

The very popular RIM BlackBerry device offers a good example of a connected infrastructure. Users can log on in real time to multiple business or personal e-mail accounts from a single, push-based muiltfunctional device. For corporate customers, BlackBerry software tightly integrates with Microsoft Exchange or IBM Lotus Domino to enable secure, wireless access to e-mails and calendars.

With a connected infrastructure, mobile salesforces can link to SAP CRM applications via their BlackBerries. The application on the handheld synchronizes in real time with SAP CRM and encourages sales representatives in the field to update and access information they need for their sales calls anywhere, anytime. If they want to check the status of an open order when they are in front of a customer, they can do so immediately.

Other examples of connected infrastructure can be found in smart phone–based mobile consumer applications like gaming, Web browsing, and mobile commerce (banking, payments). They tend to be built on a connected infrastructure to provide the user with a real-time experience.

Disconnected Application Infrastructure

This is a typical mobile but not wireless (always connected) scenario. A disconnected application infrastructure entails downloading relevant data on the end-user mobile device, working with it remotely, and resyncing at the end of the day, the week, or whenever. This enables users to be productive even when disconnected or out of coverage.

The Palm devices from the late 1990s typified a disconnected application infrastructure. You could load all your contacts, mail, and Web site information onto the device while you were at home by syncing it with the desktop. Once you were on the road, however, the device was basically stand-alone.

Laptop-based mobile SAP CRM applications offer another example of this type of infrastructure. CRM users carry a full-blown PC application (thick client) on their laptops, including an application database. Laptop

CRM applications utilize the SAP Mobile Client framework to run business applications in a disconnected mode and later synchronize data with back-office systems.

Technically speaking, the disconnected model works using a store-and-forward messaging paradigm. The Mobile Client can make the complexities of wireless connections, including coverage gaps, connection management, and switching between multiple connections, transparent to the user. The Mobile Client uses message queues on both the client and the server. Messages sent from applications are stored in queues and are uploaded as soon as a connection is available. The client and server APIs enable the mobile application to submit and retrieve messages from the message queues.

Hybrid Online-Offline Application Infrastructure

A third interesting infrastructure possibility exists with the hybrid online-offline. With a hybrid, the device is "smart" enough to be online if there is wireless connectivity available and to revert to an offline mode when there is no wireless capability. Employees working remotely never have to wait for a network connection to complete mission-critical business transactions.

A hybrid infrastructure makes sense when real-time connectivity is often not possible, especially in areas where wireless coverage is sparse at best (remote regions, congested buildings, elevators, basements, and tunnels). In the case of multinational companies like Coca-Cola that operate in hundreds of countries, the assumption of ubiquitous wireless coverage in the design of applications may lead to problems in the field.

The lack of a high-bandwidth network means that data volumes that can be uploaded and downloaded must be kept to a minimum. To deal with this constraint, companies often deploy a hybrid infrastructure that places a significant amount of functionality on the device itself. Locating the functionality on the device minimizes the back-and-forth processing that normally occurs in the connected application infrastructure setting.

The big problem with disconnected processes is that with multiple people operating on the same data in parallel, it's very hard to maintain data integrity. An example of this could be a sales representative in the field updating the address of a customer while a call center agent updates the same customer's telephone number. Which version of the customer record is now correct? The answer is that some pieces of each new version are correct, and the data-syncing program has to be clever enough to sort this out.

During data synchronization, current data needs to be downloaded and obsolete (or old) data must be checked against it to avoid inconsistencies. Synchronization seems simple, but it becomes more difficult when back-end applications like ERP or CRM have numerous business objects that interact with each other to process business transactions.

Monitoring the connectivity and data integrity of mobile and enterprise applications is a serious undertaking and requires a sophisticated infrastructure like SAP NetWeaver Mobile Infrastructure.[3]

SAP NetWeaver Mobile Infrastructure

SAP NetWeaver Mobile is the technology foundation that powers SAP's solutions for mobile business. Its goal is to help insulate organizations from the complexities of user interfaces, device-level operating systems, and wireless networks.

SAP NetWeaver Mobile assists companies in designing, deploying, and executing end-to-end mobile business processes. It helps coordinate the flow of tasks, access to resources, and the exchange of information among various back-end systems. It also captures information about the execution of the process to enable continuous process improvement.

SAP NetWeaver Mobile is embedded within the broader framework SAP NetWeaver, which in turn establishes the technology foundation for the mySAP Business Suite. SAP NetWeaver and the different mobile clients interact primarily through the multi-channel access layer illustrated in Figure 4.2.[4] As Figure 4.2 illustrates:

SAP NetWeaver Mobile = SAP Mobile Infrastructure + Auto-ID + Web-based GUI + Voice Application Framework

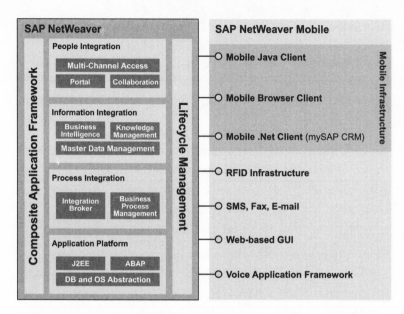

Figure 4.2: SAP NetWeaver's Multi-Channel Mobile Capabilities

SAP Mobile Infrastructure (SAP MI) is a subset of SAP NetWeaver Mobile. It includes Mobile Java Client (useful for disconnected infrastructure) + Mobile Browser Client (useful for connected infrastructure) + Mobile .Net Client (useful for disconnected laptop-based CRM).[5]

In the remaining sections of this chapter, we dive into the details behind SAP MI.

SAP Mobile Infrastructure (SAP MI)

According to SAP's Developer Network:

> Mobile Infrastructure (SAP MI) provides the foundation for extending enterprise class mobile applications to all Java-enabled devices regardless of connectivity mode. It provides an open standards-based universal platform for enterprise mobility enabling both standard ready-made applications from SAP as well as the ability for customers and partners to develop custom applications and extensions.[6]

The vision behind SAP MI is to give customers a platform-independent runtime environment for mobile solutions such as mobile sales or asset management that provides the flexibility to work in both connected and disconnected modes.

Constructing SAP MI was a complex undertaking. Unlike start-ups in the mobile application space that can get away with simple platforms, SAP had to develop a robust, scalable mobile platform on which a variety of mission-critical solutions could be built to meet a range of industry and cross-industry needs. SAP MI has evolved steadily since the early 2000s and is now widely used in the SAP community.

Key Capabilities of the SAP Mobile Infrastructure

Several of SAP MI's key capabilities follow:

- Support for mobile applications that can work in both connected and disconnected modes.

- Support for data synchronization that enables applications to store data offline on the mobile device and then synchronize the data on back-end systems as needed.

- Support for the development of industry-specific mobile solutions via a kit that helps developers build and customize applications.

- Support for central administration and deployment via a console that lets system administrators remotely manage mobile devices.

SAP NetWeaver Mobile also includes what is known as SAPConsole, which is widely used in the warehouse management and logistics area. Developed in the late 1990s to support text-based devices unable to take advantage of graphical user interfaces (GUIs), SAPConsole was helpful in translating SAP application interface information into text screens. These text-based devices were typically RF (radio frequency) devices, such as bar code scanners or character-based terminals.

As graphical interfaces became more prevalent, SAP's SCM customers started transitioning from character-based scanning devices to graphical devices running on Windows CE pocket PCs.

SAP developed an enhancement of SAPConsole called "WebSAPConsole," which allows companies to equip their graphical devices for mobile data entry. In principle, any device supporting a browser-based graphical display can be act as a data input device. In Chapter 9 we describe the architecture of SAPConsole and WebSAPConsole.

The Architecture of SAP Mobile Infrastructure

SAP Mobile Infrastructure serves as the foundation for extending mobile applications to all Java-enabled devices regardless of connectivity mode. The architecture has two primary components: client-side and server-side functionality.

The client side is called Mobile Infrastructure Client. The server side has two pieces: a synchronization and replication layer and a deployment console. Figure 4.3 illustrates the architecture.[7] Let's look at each layer in more detail.

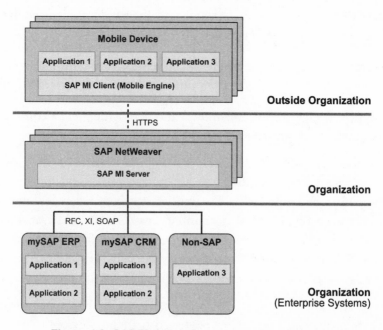

Figure 4.3: SAP Mobile Infrastructure Architecture

SAP Mobile Infrastructure Client

The mobile client includes its own Web server, database layer, and business logic — all part of a light-installation runtime environment that extends enterprise capabilities to employees and other users whether or not they are connected to the network. The different elements comprising the mobile client are depicted in Figure 4.4.[8]

The mobile client comes prepackaged with a Java Virtual Machine and an open programming model that allows developers to build applications with JavaServer Pages (JSP) or the Java 2 Platform, Micro Edition (J2ME). This open platform architecture delivers true device and network independence, while supporting mobile devices such as PDAs, laptop computers, and smart phones, as well as wireless LANs, Bluetooth, and GPRS.

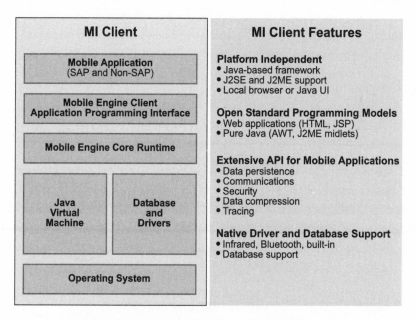

Figure 4.4: SAP Mobile Infrastructure Client Framework

In addition to wireless connectivity, the framework provides the following powerful application services:

- **Data synchronization.** Data synchronization ensures enterprise-wide data consistency in a mobile computing environment. Using the Simple Object Access Protocol (SOAP), modified data is transferred from the mobile device to back-end systems and vice versa. This minimizes data redundancy and inconsistencies, guaranteeing that both the mobile device and the back-end system have the most current data available. Other features include automatic recovery if a connection is broken, support for multiple back-end systems, and both synchronous and asynchronous processing of transferred data.

- **Secure and compressed data transfer.** The client uses the Hypertext Transfer Protocol (HTTP) for data transfer. The Secure Sockets Layer (HTTPS) can be also be activated for greater security. Compression enables efficient transmission of data from the mobile device to back-end systems.

- **Data persistence.** SAP MI allows users to access all required business data while working in a disconnected mode. The data resides locally on the file system or local database and can be retrieved and written through SAP MI.

- **Peripheral device support.** SAP MI provides native driver support for hardware controls (for example, battery life), device settings (for example, colors, back light), printers, scanners, serial and infrared ports, Bluetooth, magnetic strip readers, and radio frequency IDs.

The mobile client supports either a standard Web browser or a native Java-based user interface. Browsers offer maximum flexibility, and, with native applications support, developers can optimize solutions for screen size and user-interface controls. The advantage of native browsers is that this mode requires no installation and no client-side application maintenance or upgrades.

SAP Mobile Infrastructure Server Framework

The SAP Mobile Infrastructure server framework shown in Figure 4.5 resides within SAP NetWeaver and performs two important activities:[9]

- Synchronization and replication and

- Client deployment and administration.

Synchronization and Replication

Mobility is often associated with a continuous wireless connection to the network that provides real-time information access, retrieval, and update capabilities (known as connected applications). While this is ideal, wireless infrastructure is still relatively immature. Until wireless networks become more mature, a mobile infrastructure will have to span both connected and disconnected states.

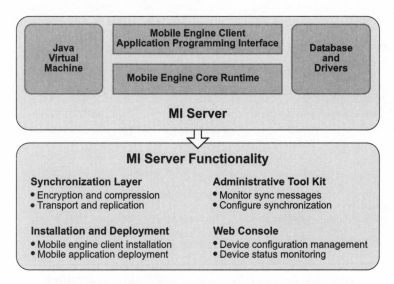

Figure 4.5: SAP Mobile Infrastructure Server Framework

For disconnected mobile business scenarios, SAP MI offers a synchronization and replication framework that resolves enterprise-level data redundancy by synchronizing mobile devices with back-end systems using a specially configured middleware server.

How does this work? In a disconnected scenario, mobile devices such as handheld computers, PDAs, and laptops can use a client-side version of SAP MI to run business applications locally without an active wireless connection.

Once a connection becomes available, the device synchronizes local business data with the SAP or non-SAP back-end application by linking up with the server-side version of SAP MI. Synchronization is accomplished via SAP MI middleware and can be executed in a wireless mode or by using a common cradle.

Synchronization components securely transfer encrypted and compressed data between mobile devices and any back-end server via the middleware server. Executed over a secure HTTP connection, synchronization uses standard wireless connection types such as GSM, GPRS, LAN, wireless LAN, and even cradles.

To monitor devices in the field, along with their data flow, usage, and error situations, the synchronization and replication processes are fully integrated into SAP's Computing Center Management System, so IT groups have all necessary information centralized to handle whatever situations arise in the field.

Synchronization and Replication Support	• Support of any network with TCP/IP protocol • Bidirectional and compressed data exchange based on XML • Delta-determination and conflict resolution • Data exchange based on business object level • Synchronization via floppy disc supported
Back-End Integration Support	• SAP and non-SAP back-end integration • Reuse of any existing SAP function module possible

Table 4.1: Technical Features of SAP MI Synchronization

Mobile Infrastructure Deployment Console

SAP Mobile Infrastructure also contains a centralized, role-based deployment console that simplifies deployment tasks in a global, multidevice IT environment.

This Web-based deployment component speeds up common administrative tasks such as installations, upgrades, and device configuration tasks. Integrated into mySAP Enterprise Portal, the deployment console provides:

- Central application installation and de-installation,

- Automatic download and deployment of new applications based on roles or device parameters,

- Central management capabilities by user, device, application, version, or role, and

- A central error log to locate and fix potential problems.

Central Software Distribution	Computing Center Management System (CCMS) Integration and Monitoring
■ Web-based user interface (Web Console) ■ Role-based application deployment integrated into SAP role concept ■ Registration, installation or uninstallation, and upgrade of remote devices ■ Status monitoring for installation processes of remote devices ■ Simplified software logistics for standard mobile application development (SAP and non-SAP) ■ Installation tool kit for mass devices	■ Central CCMS instance for all MI monitoring functions ■ Central alert infrastructure for MI components ■ Central tracing of remote devices

Table 4.2: Features of SAP MI Administration, Support, and Deployment

SAP Mobile Development Kit (MDK)

Developing applications (field sales, field service, asset management) on top of a mobile infrastructure calls for a development environment that can do three things:

- Create new mobile applications for different business scenarios, languages, and even target devices,

- Customize prebuilt SAP Mobile Client applications to a company's specific requirements, and

- Develop new extensions to integrate peripherals and other applications.

To meet these three needs, SAP is offering an object-oriented, visual development environment as part of its mobile infrastructure that provides everything companies require to start their efforts, including development guidelines, API documentation, sample applications, and technical support information.

Visual Development Environment

An essential part of the Mobile Development Kit is the visual modeling and development environment. The developer is given a prebuilt template environment in which business objects, the complete business logic and flow logic, or graphical screen elements can be configured with a single mouse click or by dragging and dropping them.

This prebuilt template environment helps improve speed of design, development, and testing since the developer does not have to change the lines of an application program or create program enhancements by coding objects and functions.

Development is streamlined because once a feature has been enhanced, a new one has been added, or a screen has been changed or created, the developer generates the application at the touch of a button. It is then fully functional without any additional work required.

Exactly how does this work? Let's say a service firm wants to reduce the cost of managing a repair work ticket from more than $10.00 to $0.75. The service firm completes more than 150,000 work orders each year. It wants to send work request data to its inspection team through BlackBerries to ensure that work is completed and the customer is billed accurately. Using prebuilt components, the developer combines work order, inspection, and time and attendance modules to automate the data collection and reporting process. Just like that, the service firm's solution is ready to be deployed.

Peripheral Support in Mobile Infrastructure

The peripheral support of mobile applications is a critical part of the mobile application studio. This support is enabled by the PIOS (peripheral input-output services) framework developed by Abaco Mobile for SAP. This layer also includes embedded support for peripheral access including generators and peripheral emulators.

According to Fernando Alvazez, CEO of Abaco Mobile, "PIOS provides an abstraction layer and a common architecture across multiple peripheral types that isolates the mobile applications from specific peripheral model implementation details. PIOS is model, platform, processor, virtual machine, and connection agnostic."[10]

The business value of PIOS is that mobile applications no longer need to target a specific peripheral model; instead, they define the expected peripheral functionality — a bonus for developers who are building applications on SAP MI. They can select from supported mobile peripherals (printers, bar code scanners, RFID readers, and so on) based on features, cost, support, and regional availability considerations rather than vendor-specific technical implementation details.

PIOS allows the mobile application developer to focus on improving the application feature set rather than devoting time to developing the plumbing required to connect to each peripheral. PIOS simplifies developers' lives by offering wizards and emulators that help them define the application peripheral requirements and features, select models that satisfy those requirements, and emulate their behavior.

PIOS results in a lower overall cost of development and greater flexibility as new peripheral models become available. The concept of hardware and operating system abstraction is a key differentiator of SAP Mobile Infrastructure.

Making a Business Case for a Mobile Infrastructure

The stakes are enormous. The right mobile infrastructure decision can either make you wildly successful or land you years behind your competition.

A comprehensive assessment of the business value of any mobile infrastructure acquisition and implementation requires the consideration of three items: cost savings, risk reduction, and business process improvement. To make a solid business case for the acquisition and deployment of SAP Mobile Infrastructure, IT managers need to demonstrate the value to their companies in as many of these categories as possible.

In many corporations, SAP Mobile Infrastructure replaces existing mobile middleware implementations built and managed as a collection of custom or point products. When using a variety of products — synchronization engines, integration adaptors, device drivers, device management — from numerous vendors to deliver mobile infrastructure services, IT organizations face a host of potential problems, such as:

- High acquisition costs — Time is wasted evaluating and acquiring mobile point products from multiple vendors because each component is evaluated, acquired, and delivered independently.

- Deployment delays — Mobile application projects cannot get off the ground until all point products have been evaluated, tested, and deployed. Integration and quality assurance (QA) of middleware can delay the start of mobile solution design and deployment.

- Cost of managing complex licensing agreements — With different types of middleware components priced independently, managing license agreements can be painful.

- Overhead costs due to version control and release schedules — Release schedules for disparate products are not aligned, making upgrading of the mobile infrastructure difficult, risky, costly, and time-consuming. This puts the burden on IT staff to track and control versions of point products that are deployed throughout the organization, adding to overhead costs.

Assess your organization to see if it faces any of these problems. As a next step, quantify the cost of these problems. If you are an SAP customer, you can avoid this cost by migrating to SAP Mobile Infrastructure (which is provided as a part of the SAP NetWeaver stack).

Lastly, as part of your business case make sure that you identify and meet the critical application infrastructure demands stipulated by your end users. We end this chapter by summarizing these requirements in Table 4.3.

Multiple Wireless Devices	Can the mobile infrastructure support all major wireless devices - smart phones, BlackBerries, PDAs, and Pocket PCs - from one platform and an architecture that allows support for future devices and wireless protocols?
Multiple Data Sources	Can the mobile infrastructure supply a single platform that meets an organization's entire set of wireless needs?
Security	Can the mobile infrastructure encrypt data and authenticate users to ensure secure transactions? For added protection, can it eliminate the risk of denial-of-service attacks or attacks on sensitive corporate data?
Scalable and Available	Can the mobile infrastructure scale to support thousands of users and hundreds of concurrent sessions? Would it be available 24x7?
Easy Integration	Does the mobile infrastructure provide developer tool kits and a customizable application program interface for connectivity to business systems and enterprise data sources?
Device Personalization	Can the mobile infrastructure support customizable settings and preferences that allow each device's look and feel to match user needs, optimizing each device's interface for maximum effectiveness?
Disconnected Scenarios	Can the mobile infrastructure support intermittent wireless connectivity? Can it support thin client and thick client architecture, thus providing a functional solution even in areas without wireless coverage?

Table 4.3: Summarizing Key Mobile Infrastructure Considerations

Summary

"If you build a better mousetrap, you will catch better mice."

— George Goble, 1996 Ig Nobel Prize Winner for Chemistry

As enterprises seek to support their growing mobile requirements and expand their mobile computing deployments, the need for a comprehensive and flexible mobile infrastructure becomes evident. The ideal mobile infrastructure must 1) enable your mobile strategy, 2) support your target devices, application platforms, and network choices, and 3) leverage existing IT investments.

Unfortunately, mobile infrastructure decisions are complicated and not well understood. The marketplace is awash with mythology that keeps most companies from investing in viable, long-term strategies. Our goal in this chapter was to explain the critical issues of mobile application infrastructure and supply a framework for selecting appropriate products and development strategies.

Choosing an infrastructure for your corporate mobile strategy is not trivial. As we wrote in Chapter 3, mobile business is a knot of multiple standards, devices, and protocols. Large enterprises are typically full of applications software such as ERP and CRM that must be integrated with mobile devices in order for field employees to do their jobs effectively.

The dual demands for flexibility and a low total cost of ownership (TCO) place a premium on picking a long-term infrastructure that addresses multiple needs, rather than a point solution for a very specific device or limited application.

Throughout the chapter, we focused on clarifying the different elements of SAP NetWeaver Mobile, SAP Mobile Infrastructure, and SAP Mobile Developer Kit.

The value of SAP NetWeaver Mobile is clear: It automates and streamlines the many processes that are the lifeblood of a field organization. From processing work orders to notifying managers, SAP MI provides a process management layer that controls how people and technology interact to get things done. Now that you have a good grounding in the mobile infrastructure technology, it's time to look at the specific applications that you can build on top of it.

Chapter Five

Mobilizing Field Service

There is one constant in business: Products break, and when they break, they need to be repaired. As a result, for some industries, break-fix field service workers may represent a sizable chunk of their workforce. However, while enterprise applications seem to be everywhere in business, field service workers traditionally remained beyond their reach. Now, with an increasing push to keep every facet of business in sync with each other, the challenge is to bring field service employees into the real-time business loop.

Introduction

Field service, workforce management, fleet management, post-sales support, enterprise service management and service dispatch management — a diverse lot. What do these areas have in common? They are the next targets for productivity enhancement, cost savings, and revenue generation in service chain automation.

A logical question to ask is why mobilize field service. The answer becomes apparent when you look at companies that support consumer services or complex finished goods and machines: They rely on their field service organizations (several hundred to several thousand workers) to maintain customer satisfaction and loyalty. Failing to equip these armies of field technicians with the right handheld tools kills productivity. Simply slapping a handheld on an existing process isn't the answer. You have to rethink field service processes.

When it comes to service, customers have high expectations. Look at Sears Product Repair Services, a business unit of the $41 billion giant Sears, Roebuck and Co., which claims 12,500 technicians in 180 U.S. cities. For companies like Sears, managing and coordinating a vast, dispersed group of mobile technicians using paper and clipboard is no longer tenable. Instead, Sears' field service workers use a ruggedized device to receive, capture, and transmit critical information from the remote location to Sears' back-office system.[1]

The Sears example is not an isolated one. Numerous best-practice companies are racing to optimize field service by coordinating and synchronizing four critical elements:

- People (call center reps, control desk employees, and field workers),

- Parts (service parts inventory management),

- Process (operational hand-offs, client interactions, logging/reporting, aftermarket up-sell and cross-sell), and

- Data (service level agreements such as contracts or warranties).

Firms that achieve this level of coordination and synchronization are not only squeezing latency and costs out of their field service operations but also edging out competitors by retaining more customers. Efficiently managing field service workforces has grown to be part of corporate strategy in certain vertical markets.

The responsibilities of mobile field technicians have expanded beyond traditional break, fix, or support duties to include more intricate, revenue-generating activities aligned with the broader enterprise.

Mobile Field Service Innovators: Telecom and Utility Firms

The telecom and utility industries have led the early adoption of mobile field service applications. Their speedy adoption stems from one constant factor in the telecom and utility businesses: Things break often due to natural and unnatural events. When they break, they need to be repaired.

In addition to unavoidable break and fix requirements, these two markets are undergoing rapid changes that are driving demand for mobile field service products.

Some of the most important drivers include the following:

- **Deregulation.** The telecom, cable TV, electrical, and other utility markets are being deregulated worldwide, with the incumbents forced to shift from a monopolistic, uncompetitive marketplace to a world filled with new competitive start-ups where productivity, customer service, and speed are crucial to survival. Mobile workforce management products aim to meet the needs of this new competitive environment by allowing field service workers to offer a higher level of customer service and operate more efficiently.

- **Revenue generation opportunities.** The field service worker is typically the only face-to-face contact between the utility and the customer. Mobile field service products can help turn a field service call into a revenue generating opportunity by using mobile computers to present marketing promotions or product information to educate or influence a purchase decision.

- **Advancement of wireless and mobile computing technology.** The quality of field interactions is increasingly dictated by the quality of the wireless capabilities. As a result, the price, performance, and size of mobile computing devices and wireless systems are key issues. In addition to the business need to provide the required functionality at affordable levels, the ability to integrate with core back-office SAP applications is a must-have for productivity reasons.

The solutions deployed by early adopters have typically covered a business process that spanned the customer call center (order taking, scheduling), the dispatch center (workload distribution, vehicle location, map-based dispatching), the mobile worker (call-ahead, dispatch, wireless connectivity), and management (reporting, analysis).

First-generation proprietary solutions provided this functionality through constant real-time two-way communications with all mobile workers over a variety of mobile data networks. These solutions provided a significant improvement in efficiency over previous paper-and-clipboard-based or batch (dial-up) systems where field workers could not receive dynamic updates to their work plans.

Industry Sectors	Suitable Work for Mobile Solutions
Telecommunications and cable industries	▪ Installation of residential services such as phone, cable, and DSL ▪ Repair of business services such as virtual private networks (VPNs), frame relay, and private branch exchange (PBX) ▪ Maintenance of wireless base stations and other field equipment ▪ Inside diagnostics and repair and maintenance of service disconnects ▪ Preventive maintenance by contractors
Utility industries: electric, gas, and water	▪ Customer service requests such as connects or disconnects ▪ Trouble shooting special needs such as energy audits ▪ Installation and meter repair ▪ Meter reading and collections

Table 5.1: Mobile Field Service Activities in Telecom and Utilities

The Next Generation: Mobile Field Service for the Mainstream

Historically, only large organizations within a few industry verticals (utilities, cable, and telecom) attempted to implement software with the goal of improving their mobile field workforces. Mobile functionality was limited in terms of market adoption due to unclear ROI, expensive proprietary devices, slow networks, and workforce resistance. This is no longer the case. Technology such as mobile cameras has progressed to the point where it has the potential to transform field service.

Consider this likely scenario: A customer was having issues with her computer. Upon arriving at the site, the field technician was baffled by the problem. Instead of describing the problem, he took a few digital photos of the computer screen and e-mailed them to the engineering team in India. Engineering was able to diagnose and troubleshoot the problem quickly by looking at the screen shots. Collaboratively, they were able to solve the customer's problem within minutes.

In parallel to technology changes like the integrated cameras described above, the demand situation is changing. The drive to mobilize field service workforces is extending to new sectors such as oil and gas, real estate, financial services, and high-tech manufacturing. The global demand for mobile field service solutions is also heating up among service providers specializing in home repair (painters, electricians, and plumbers), landscaping, and office and medical equipment repair.

Taking these trends into account, E-Business Strategies recently forecast that U.S. sales of mobile field service solutions will rise to more than $800 million in 2006, from around $140 million in 2003. The field service market is growing for several reasons:

- Companies want to increase their ROI on existing ERP or CRM applications, which automate basic dispatch, work order, and scheduling functions. The effectiveness of these applications, however, plummets when workers leave the premises. New mobile applications let workers input and retrieve work orders, parts, time, labor, mileage, customer comments, and other information directly to or from ERP or CRM systems, eliminating a key bottleneck.

- Increasing productivity by re-engineering onsite field service processes — root-cause analysis, reporting, and recommendations — is a goal many businesses have set. The focus on productivity means that companies are determined to maximize billable field time, minimize idle time, improve service reliability, and reduce call errors.

- A keen desire to leverage technology innovations exists. Mobile devices, including PDAs, notebook PCs, and mobile phones, are increasing in functionality and decreasing in price. (Device costs form the highest portion of the initial purchase of a mobile field workforce automation system). Specialized mobile software and devices, some ruggedized, boast better functionality and reliability.

- Off-the-shelf solutions are available. Most large companies have traditionally developed mobile information systems in-house. This situation is now reversing, with companies purchasing systems from third-party vendors. The rapid pace of innovation means that utilities can no longer keep their own systems current, and off-the-shelf systems have advanced to the point where internal development is no longer a viable alternative. The bottom line: Mobile field service is moving from the realm of proprietary homegrown solutions to that of standards-based solutions.

The focus on field service is accelerating as the economy has slowed, competition has mounted, and customers have become more demanding. Table 5.2 illustrates the typical problems that management is attempting to tackle with field service automation investments.

- Missed appointments
- Unnecessary overtime
- Repeat customer visits to get the job done right
- Jobs that take too long to complete
- Delayed status reports
- Inadequate information collected from or supplied to the field
- Redundant data entry work
- Excessive driving time

Table 5.2: Typical Problems with a Disconnected Field Force

Mobile Field Service Business Scenarios

Several industries could stand to improve their efficiency and productivity through mobile solutions:

- Home repair and installation services,

- Transportation and logistics, and

- Insurance: property, home, and auto.

What do these industries have in common? In all of them, field workers are unique in their pattern of mobility and data use. They typically move from location to location, many spending 90% of their time on the road on a response or route basis, and they use data tied to the field service business process, which involves dispatch and scheduling, asset management, field technical support, mapping and workforce scheduling, inventory access, contract management, and shipping and procurement.

Home Repair and Installation Services

Home repair and installation services are mobilizing in a hurry. Over the past two decades, companies in the home repair and installation business — Home Depot, Lowe's, GE, and Sears — have worked to perfect installation and repair process productivity and enhance workforce automation, while maintaining a knowledge-driven employee base.

The first mobile solutions for these industries revolved around the pager and the cell phone and were backed by call centers with dispatchers. The idea was to improve dispatch and communication with workers, but the process was alarmingly paper-intensive.

In a typical service situation, the technician arrived at a customer's location, performed service as needed, and filled out paperwork. The billing department received paperwork for the entire route only after the driver returned. In addition, frequent errors led to customer questions and billing disputes, requiring technicians to spend hours helping to resolve these issues. Ultimately, these first-generation solutions created fluctuating demands on resources, making workforce planning difficult.

More recently, home repair and installation companies have prioritized transactions between the back-end enterprise systems and their thousands of field service technicians in order to increase productivity. The goal of these process improvements is to ensure the following:

- Repairs are performed with the right resources and tools to ensure that 90%-plus of repairs are completed successfully on the first attempt.

- Dispatch centers have real-time information concerning the availability of service technicians.

- Managers are able to view the status and type of all jobs assigned to technicians, view travel time between jobs, and manually override assignments if there are conflicts.

- In-vehicle mapping provides technicians with the best routes to the next service call, decreasing drive time.

- Better wireless links to the back-end parts database make remote inquiries and order entries more seamless. Superior schematics reduce return trips and improved parts management.

The outcome of these improvements is more flexibility for customers when choosing appointment windows. With better coordination and control, technicians can visit customers the same day they call for service.

The evolution of field solutions through new technologies, namely laptops and rugged handhelds, has allowed home repair companies to improve customer service and productivity. Keep in mind that best-practice field service solutions are designed to be as transparent as possible, to require little field training, and to offer the technicians support tools to enhance and improve customer service.

Figure 5.1 illustrates the end-to-end process flow for mobile service that is tightly integrated with back-end CRM applications.

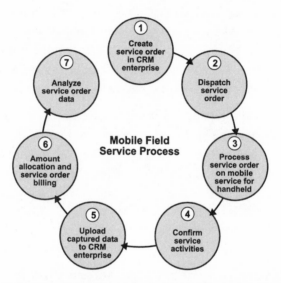

Figure 5.1: Service Order Management Integrated with mySAP CRM

Transportation and Logistics

For transportation and logistics providers that handle millions of shipments daily, managing and tracking the volume of these packages has proved to be a daunting task.

In the past, many companies built customized solutions that let delivery drivers use bar code scanners to download shipment data to keep track of packages. These solutions lacked the near-real-time benefits of a wireless environment.

Today, best-practice companies are using packaged solutions to provide real-time track and trace capabilities, visibility into customer shipment status, and more efficient dispatch services. New mobile field service solutions for the transportation and logistics industry mean that

- Drivers don't have to remain in their vehicles to communicate with dispatch, thanks to text messaging.

- Timely pickup and delivery information can be transmitted to back-end mainframe systems, allowing for near real-time visibility of shipments for customers.

- Paper can be eliminated from the equation since signature capture is a standard feature and devices can quickly retrieve signature information.

- Pickup dispatching is improved since drivers can now view and process their pickup stops easily from the scanner screen on their new device.

Logistics and transportation firms are changing the way they do business to satisfy the needs of customers — all within a paperless system.

Insurance: Property, Home, and Auto

For the insurance industry, a mobile workforce is a way of life. Storms, tornados, and automobile accidents result in claims that take only an instant to create. Processing those claims is another matter. It is well known in the industry that next to the amount of the settlement, claim-processing speed determines customer satisfaction.

Insurance companies were among the first to use notebook computers as a productivity tool for appraisers. Though certain efficiencies were attained, the lack of real-time connectivity between the appraisers and the servers still created challenges.

First-generation solutions for the insurance industry had the following related shortcomings: inefficient methods to receive new assignments on a timely basis, a lack of precision in scheduling appraiser appointments, a minimum of one business day between an assessment and settlement offer, and the need for appraisers to phone or fax requests for total-loss assessments.

Today, insurance companies are rolling out second-generation mobile solutions that tightly integrate with back-office processes (see Figure

5.1). These deployments have caused a steep drop in appraiser drive time; some companies are reporting an average of an hour a day in time savings.

In the case of automobile insurance claims, customer satisfaction has bounced back thanks to a much quicker settlement process. Many times when appraisers determine vehicles are an obvious total loss after an accident, they will upload that information to the mainframe quickly and come back with a fair market value. The appraiser can make the settlement offer on the spot, get the papers signed, and have the car towed away.

Elements of Mobile Field Service Solutions

If you could document the wish lists of home repair, logistics, and insurance companies in the business of delivering field service daily, many would go something like this: We need to improve customer service, boost service revenues, reduce our operating and warranty expenses, and increase the reliability and performance of the products we service.

How do businesses realize such results? Leading companies are showing that the single biggest opportunity for improvement on all of these fronts is through a new way of thinking about the business of delivering service on the front lines — mobile field service management.

Mobile field service management spans software applications and mobile devices and services that wirelessly mobilize and automate processes related to your customers, assets, and workforce. Its foundation, as Table 5.3 shows, is built on three disciplines:

- Customer relationship management,

- Enterprise asset management, and

- Workforce management.

Unlike any one of these individual disciplines, which concern themselves solely with customers, assets, or workforces, respectively, mobile field service management concentrates on processes.

Mobile field service is a business process management (BPM) layer that takes the islands of knowledge, data, and business rules in CRM, PLM, and ERP systems, which represent the core of enterprise activities, and unites them into a business system that is accessible to field workers.

Field service management focuses on the business flows within and across each of these disciplines and the integration required to achieve new levels of performance.

	Customer Relationship Management	Enterprise Asset Management	Workforce Management
Entity Focus	Customers and work orders	Assets, inventory, and work orders	Field technicians
Scope	All customer interactions from point of contact to point of service	All assets and work necessary for the delivery of service	All resources for the execution of work
Critical Capabilities Required	Ability to manage the entire customer relationship and revenue cycle	Ability to manage the complete asset lifecycle and all work types (installation, scheduled, and emergency work)	Ability to schedule, dispatch, and optimize resources for short duration tasks as well as multi-day projects and crews

Table 5.3: The Different Applications Touched by Mobile Field Service

The Functionality of Mobile Field Service Solutions

Specifically, mobile field service solutions provide schedule management, workload forecasting and leveling, and rule-driven service monitoring and control (drives the flow of orders through the system according to client rules).

Modules, some of which may not be part of the mobile field service applications but are covered by other enterprise applications, include:

- **Customer service** — transaction management (receipt and processing of requests for service from enterprise and call center applications), billing (passing service order data to billing applications), contracts (track client contracts and related activity), and entitlement management (client entitlements based on contracts, warranties, and service policies).

- **Workforce management (WFM)** — workload management (work scheduling, forecasting, dynamic workload leveling) and service order monitoring and control.

- **Logistics** — parts planning (handling and disposition of parts) and reverse logistics (supporting and tracking return material authorizations).

- **Communication** — wireless support (wireless data presented to and gathered by the field workers on different devices and networks, including store-and-forward mode where connectivity may not be continuous).

- **Business intelligence** — analytics, reporting, and data mining (displaying and analyzing real-time and historical data).

Scheduling	Appointment booking to manage customer commitments, automated assignment to allocate work to technicians, and reassignment to adjust workloads as conditions change.
Staff scheduling	Management of technician attributes, crews, shifts, and rosters.
Order management	Order entry, modification, and cancellation, and work order precedence management for each type of work performed by the organization.
Work progress	Real-time tracking of technicians, vehicles, orders, and work results.
Dispatch management	Tools to monitor technician and work order status and alerts to notify dispatchers of jeopardy situations.
Wireless enablement	Real-time wireless communications across private and public networks, and wireless awareness (for example, technician is out of wireless coverage) to deal with the unique problems of operating remotely and communicating across a wireless network.
Technician workflow	Providing technicians with the information they need to do their jobs when they need it; enforcing an efficient technician workflow from the start to the end of the day; enabling access to work order information; collecting and validating work results; and managing inquiries to enterprise applications.
Decision support	Key performance measures and reports to help managers assess the effectiveness of the workforce in meeting work commitments and planning for the future.

Table 5.4: Mobile Field Service Features and Functionality

To be useful, mobile field service solutions have to integrate with existing enterprise and external systems. In the case of utilities the system that supports customer service activity usually also creates service orders. In the cable industry, it is common for a third-party billing system to provide customer information, billing, and creation of service orders for both provisioning and trouble calls. If a CRM system is in place, it will typically provide complete call center support (which varies by vendor).

Table 5.4 illustrates the detailed functionality that comprises SAP's mobile field service solution. In the next section, we show how Messer Griesheim GmbH deployed it.

Case Study: Messer Griesheim GmbH

Messer Griesheim GmbH has been associated with industrial gases for more than 100 years. The company supplies gases, specialty gases, and gas mixtures to many industries in Europe and around the world.[2]

The distribution of millions of gas cylinders to thousands of customers occupies a large part of Messer's business. A centralized system, with the ability to track the status of every one of these containers, is essential to maximizing asset utilization and keeping customers happy.

Until recently, Messer did not have such a system in place. Instead, it relied on a decentralized process composed of piecemeal solutions that did not adequately integrate back-end operations and information with Messer's operators, partners, or customers.

SAP enabled Messer to replace its heterogeneous system with an integrated, centralized system capable of tracing each gas cylinder and determining its status at any point during the cylinder's lifecycle. With the centralized system in place, asset utilization has gone up by more than half and cylinder losses have fallen sharply.

Messer's customized service solution consisted of arming truck drivers with rugged, bar code–scanning PDA devices, so they can scan each container of gas, thereby keeping better track of the containers that have been delivered to or returned by customers.

The company's mobile solution eliminates stacks of paperwork and results in customers receiving their gas orders more quickly. The delivery and the billing departments have more accurate records, can better anticipate customer needs, and complete the billing cycle faster.

The Business

Messer Griesheim manufactures and supplies oxygen, nitrogen, argon, carbon dioxide, hydrogen, helium, inert welding gases, specialty gases, gases for medicinal use, and a range of gas mixtures to a broad array of global organizations. Global customers include companies in the steel and metal, pulp and paper, chemicals, food, pharmaceuticals, automotive, and electronics industries, as well as those in the medical, research, and environmental technology fields.

To service these organizations, Messer maintains operations in more than 50 countries with 400 facilities, including production plants, distribution and filling stations, and research centers. Employing more than 8,000 people and generating sales of approximately €1.5 billion (more than $1.9 billion), Messer remains one of the largest industrial gas producers in the world, with leading market share in Germany and other countries in Europe. More than a quarter of a million customers worldwide choose Messer to supply their diverse gas needs.

Messer organizes its business according to how it delivers industrial gases to its customers:

- Delivery of large volumes from onsite production facilities or by pipeline;

- Delivery in bulk tanks by truck or rail; or

- Delivery in gas cylinders for medical, scientific, and construction applications.

More than one-third of the company's overall gas sales are represented by gas in cylinders. In fact, Messer owns approximately 4 million gas cylinders serving 250,000 customers worldwide.

Needless to say, Messer urgently needs to trace and track cylinders on its premises, as well as cylinders at customer premises and with other business partners, like agents and suppliers. With its investment in so many cylinders, the need for a reliable solution to trace and track cylinders is paramount to Messer. It is essential to maximizing cylinder usage, reducing cylinder losses, improving rental invoicing processes, and complying with government regulations regarding products, product packaging, and tracing ability.

The Business Dilemma

The process Messer was using to achieve these goals was not integrated, centralized, or free of errors; consequently, Messer could not effectively trace individual assets or track cylinder status, which led to inefficient asset utilization and customer dissatisfaction.

Previously, some Messer subsidiaries had tried to develop their own applications to trace and track the lifecycle of their cylinders and wound up with nonscalable legacy systems, which were minimally, if at all, integrated with back-end systems. These legacy systems resisted being upgraded to support modern tracking functions or processes, such as bar coding, scanning, and radio frequency identification (RFID) tagging.

Furthermore, Messer's heterogeneous applications resulted in a shortage of integrated information during different process phases and made individual asset tracing and cylinder-status tracking, even at the regional level, practically impossible. The outmoded process also became prone to error, which resulted in increased error-handling costs, due to physical counting of gas cylinders at the customer site, and decreased service quality, due to errors in rental invoicing, for example.

Messer went in search of a mobile solution to resolve these problems.

The New Tracing and Tracking Process

Messer's requirements for a mobile-based solution make more sense when you follow a cylinder through its lifecycle of being filled, commissioned, loaded, delivered, unloaded, sorted, and refilled again.

Messer's mobile solution addresses all the steps in the cylinder lifecycle and traces each one individually. They are identified via bar code labels. The steps of the cylinder lifecycle follow:

1. Once the gas cylinders have been purchased or returned by customers, they are filled with the corresponding gases in a Messer filling station.

2. After filling, they are stored and commissioned in pallets for the next delivery to the customer.

3. As soon as the truck driver is available for the next delivery, the driver picks up the commissioned pallets and the delivery tour starts.

4. The driver delivers the filled gas cylinders to the customer site.

5. The customer returns empty cylinders and the truck driver prints the delivery note for the customer.

6. Once the truck driver arrives at the central storage, Messer operators sort the empty gas cylinders and store them until the next filling.

7. Finally, customer history data, cylinder status, filling, delivery, and other details are stored for reporting purposes.

The filling process: The filled cylinder is scanned by bar code scanners attached to PDAs. Relevant data is gathered and stored in SAP Web Application Server (SAP Web AS), a component in SAP NetWeaver, to improve cylinder management. In the filling process, the mobile solution helps answer questions like these: Which cylinders? When and where were they filled? With which gas and gas tank? Who filled it?

The picking and commissioning process: The tour (or route) planning occurs in SAP R/3. The warehouse operators, who are responsible for commissioning the cylinders, access the tour information through the mobile solution. The information is grouped according to product type and tour. The operator processes the electronic commissioning lists through the integrated bar code scanner in real time, the cylinder's status is changed to "commissioned," and the database is updated. The mobile solution enables answers to questions like these: Is the product necessary for the tour? Is the cylinder size correct? Is the cylinder status right?

The truck loading process: The truck driver arrives at a Messer warehouse, where the commissioned cylinders are platted and now ready for delivery. Through the wireless local area network (WLAN) connection, the driver downloads the tour information, the transport order, and the corresponding delivery orders to the mobile solution. The driver scans each loaded cylinder, and the information is automatically stored in the mobile solution. In parallel, the database is updated with the new cylinder status. In addition, the driver can download information from SAP Web AS regarding which cylinders the customer already has since some will be returned.

The delivery process: When the delivery tour starts, the mobile solution runs in disconnected (offline) status; however, all of the entered data in the delivery process is stored locally. At the customer site, the cylinders (corresponding to the delivery order) are unloaded. The driver scans each delivered cylinder. If the wrong cylinder is scanned, the system alerts the driver. Once all the delivered cylinders are unloaded and scanned, the system automatically confirms the delivery order. The driver then loads and registers all returned empty cylinders. The driver prints out the delivery note for the customer. The driver can also register special services performed at the customer site, as well as any customer complaints.

The truck unloading process: The driver arrives back at the Messer warehouse after completing the delivery order. The mobile solution can now work online through the WLAN connection. The driver synchronizes the offline data with the database. The cylinder movements and status (full or empty) are updated, as well as delivery orders with returned cylinder-withdrawals information and special services items. The billing process can now start. Because this process involves no manual tasks, Messer can reduce the risk of error during information processing.

The sorting process: After the gas cylinders are unloaded and stored in the warehouse, the sorting process begins. Each returned gas cylinder is scanned and sorted for such actions as filling, a compliance check, or repair. The database is updated again with the cylinder status.

The reporting process: All of the cylinder movements registered in the database during the process are passed to SAP Business Information Warehouse (SAP BW), and this information is available at any time and can be used to generate reports.

Messer employees can access the following information online whenever they like:

- List of cylinders at each customer site,

- Customer history (deliveries and returns),

- Cylinder history (filling, delivery, and storage history),

- Status (commissioned, empty, filled, or delivered) and the location of a cylinder,

- Filling information for a cylinder (date, operator, filling station, and gas tank),

- Delivery information (delivery date and truck driver), and

- Batch information (which cylinder is filled with which gas).

Results and Business Benefits

Process improvements: Messer replaced its paper-based processes with a computer-based tracing and tracking process that integrates information between subsidiaries, delivery partners, and customers. The solution centralizes the information storage in the same database, as well as the administration of mobile devices and their users.

By introducing a unified mobile technology and a standard mobile platform capable of supporting country-specific processes and enhancements, Messer offers its partners, customers, and subsidiaries a solution that can be customized for each target group and country.

Return on investment: Messer estimates a 26-month payback period. In determining ROI, the company considers two key parameters: the number of assets in circulation and the cost per asset. In a company that owns approximately 4 million gas cylinders (with some of the larger customers invoicing between 500 and 4,000 cylinders on a monthly basis), the improvement in the cylinder lifecycle process generates substantial benefits.

Tangible benefits: The tangible benefits include reduced cylinder losses and better asset utilization. The benefits span increases in cylinder filling speeds and cylinder rotation (less storage time), which also helps boost sales and margins. With an average price of €100 for a new cylinder and over 4 million cylinders in circulation, a small improvement in the recuperation of lost cylinders can dramatically affect the bottom line.

Messer has also cut costs through a country-specific legacy system and information integration, as well as the integration of quality management and logistics to eliminate process errors. A unified cylinder tracing solution reduces the maintenance costs of additional tools and legacy systems. Lastly, manual entry of information ceases to be an issue. This means back-office employees can focus on improving processes and not on data processing.

Intangible benefits: Messer's mobile solution is also producing numerous intangible benefits, such as the ability to comply more efficiently with government and legal regulations, as well as complete documentation to meet ISO standards for cylinder identification.

The mobile solution is live, and Messer Griesheim is in the midst of rolling it out to its many operators, more than 1,000 delivery partners, and hundreds of customers.

Making a Business Case for Mobilizing Field Service

There is a new reality in field service: Workers in the field are beginning to shoulder the responsibilities of customer relationship managers. They communicate with customers face-to-face; frequently, they are the only representative of the company the customers ever see. Field service workers can sell to existing customers by understanding their needs. They represent the brand in what they do and say, and they have to service the customers.

Given the importance of field service, companies are carefully evaluating the purchase of a mobile workforce management solution. In this section, we guide you through creating a business case for investing in mobile field service solutions.

The Business Need

Long considered a tactical cost center, field service is fast becoming a strategic focus among enterprises. Why has field service climbed to the top? Demanding customers and the unflagging quest to improve employee productivity.

Enterprises ranked demanding customers as the strongest pressure behind their decisions to optimize field service operations. A majority of firms classified this pressure as a top priority. Others chose shrinking profit margins and competitive pressures. (see Table 5.5).

External and Business Pressures	Organizational Imperative	Tactical Imperative	Technology Imperative
Demanding customers	Build a customer service-centric organization	Increase worker productivity	Customer relationship management
Shrinking profit margins	Integrate business processes	Connect field personnel with back office	Work order scheduling and tracking
Pressure from competing firms	Establish performance management procedures	Focus on cross- and up-sell opportunities	Service inventory and logistics management
Contract or warranty compliance	Train field workers	Track warranties and service level agreements (SLAs)	Accessing contracts in CRM and ERP systems
Mandates for service parts inventory cost reductions	Provide visibility into inventory levels and locations	Plan field service inventory positions	Homegrown custom solutions
Government regulations	Improve data collection associated with compliance	Outsource some or all of field service operations	Real-time data collection using mobile software and hardware devices

Table 5.5: The Business Drivers Behind Mobilizing Field Service

In response to these external forces, companies are setting strategies and taking actions primarily around maximizing field service worker productivity. The reason: It is the proverbial "low-hanging fruit." Deficiencies in overall field service quality and customer satisfaction can frequently be pinned on inefficient management of technician skills, availability, and locale.

It is not surprising that many firms cite increasing worker productivity as their primary strategy for optimizing their field service operations and connecting field personnel to the back office as a means to this end. However, it is not enough to show the need. Field service projects are approved when decision makers are convinced that they will deliver tangible business benefits.

Focus on the Specific Business Benefits

Mobilized field service operations must help enterprises improve operational efficiency, data integrity, and utilization of corporate assets.

Applications must enable mobile professionals to send and receive work orders, document service calls onsite, and order parts, all at the point of work. By being able to access critical data from the service site, the technician can complete the job correctly the first time, reducing callbacks and improving customer service.

Sample target benefits include:

- Improved first-time fix rate,

- More efficient parts selection and availability,

- Increased customer satisfaction through more rapid response,

- Better regulatory compliance, and

- More accurate assignment planning based on availability and competency.

Mobile technology empowers companies to view, monitor, and measure every step of the offsite service-management process. Mobile technology also lets businesses plan and assign service requests to the right service representative based on worker availability and competency. Representatives can note complaints about goods or services when visiting a customer and record orders at the customer site. They can also access master data and maintain records about service activities. Empowerment of mobile employees is a key side effect of mobile field service.

Understand the Operational Requirements

Using a mobile device, the field service technician logs everything that occurs during the service call. The technician can view a list of all visits and for each visit either perform the necessary activities — diagnosis, repair, invoice issuing, and cash collection — or update the customer's status with a reason code indicating why the service could not be performed, such as the customer wasn't home. Customers benefit from this real-time exchange of information as evidenced by the decreasing call-to-resolution time.

These types of field workers, as identified previously, are usually traveling by foot, car, or van. In order to carry out their work, they often need parts and materials, maps, plans and design instructions, specific test and repair equipment, and specialized knowledge. They also need to capture and maintain data necessary to support back-office systems.

Since they operate independently of the headquarters' management and administrative structure and systems, they also are not fully aware of the changing characteristics and parameters of their workloads, customer requirements and needs, travel times and costs, availability of parts and supplies, or new priorities. In essence, they constantly have to make decisions based on uncertain knowledge and yet are directed to optimize their working time to achieve the most cost-effective response to meet changing customer needs and requirements.

Examining the duties, skill sets, and operational conditions found in these types of mobile field service operations and the types of current assignments, travel times and distances, and parts availability shows that productivity and efficiency of service employees can be improved by 20%–30% or more if they are provided with a workable, reliable infrastructure and supporting process application.

Align Operational Requirements with the Infrastructure

Achieving this level of improvement becomes plausible when you combine two new technological developments:

- The rise of technology and related communications software to allow real-time communications and applications support to and from the central core management systems for dispatch and assignment and logistics support operations to service personnel in the field.

- The advances in software application and optimizing algorithms for workforce management, assignment and scheduling, field diagnostics and repair, logistics coordination, and administrative support.

The development and deployment of these technologies, plus the addition of expanding capabilities for precise geographic positioning and real-time reporting for field personnel, is leading many organizations to seriously consider implementing advanced field service communications and automation systems and technology for centralized and mobile (field personnel) support.

Quantifying the Expected ROI

In a tough economy and a restricted IT spending environment, mobile field service implementation must have a strong, measurable ROI, based on improving efficiency — sending the right person and equipment to the right place at the right time — via cost and head count reductions or improved productivity and customer service.

Some of the metrics that are useful for monitoring the effectiveness of field service investments follow.

Calls Serviced per Technician

If the mobile solution can help the technician work faster and more effectively, you can expect an increase in the number of calls that each technician can service.

First-Time Fix Rate

When the technician cannot fix the equipment on the first visit, he or she must then schedule a follow-up visit. This affects customer satisfaction and increases the cost of service.

Delays often occur for several reasons: 1) the right information is not communicated to the engineer at the time of dispatch or 2) the information communicated was wrong. In either case, the engineer might show up with the wrong documentation and spare parts.

Another reason technicians cannot fix equipment on the first visit is that they need help from colleagues or they need more information. If they cannot collaborate effectively from the customer's premises, they have to schedule another visit.

A mobile solution helps in many of these cases by allowing technicians to retrieve parts information as needed. The first-time fix rate is directly measurable before and after the mobile implementation.

Time to Repair

The quicker the appliance or equipment is inspected, diagnosed, repaired, or serviced, the more satisfied the customer is going to be. If the equipment sold is down for a long time, the customer is not likely to be happy. Because there is a potential to reduce dispatch and repair time, measuring the average time to repair can help measure the value of the mobile solution.

Reduction in Paperwork

Mobile field service solutions should reduce the amount of paperwork — invoicing, billing, and proof of service — required to start and finish onsite transactions. Reducing paperwork translates into more time for technicians to visit customers.

Dispatch Time

Mobile solutions can cut the dispatch time by keeping track of technicians through GPS or location tracking technology. With this knowledge, a dispatch system is able to select an engineer for a job based on proximity, availability, and skill set. The benefit of reducing average dispatch time is measurable.

Winning new customers, never an easy task, is tougher than ever. Keeping them satisfied is even more important. How do you build customer loyalty? With great service each time you encounter a customer. Great service at all touch points means that businesses have to measure, monitor, and control processes. The different metrics that we presented in this section will help you to calculate the value of mobile field service investments.

Summary

"A sale is not something you pursue; it's what happens to you while you are immersed in serving your customer."

— Anonymous

Historically, manufacturers have serviced their products — directly or through a third-party provider — reactively, responding to customer repair requests often after an outage or breakage has occurred. Enterprises have treated their field service organizations as a necessary cost of doing business.

Companies that provide repair, maintenance, and other field-based services can no longer afford to treat post-sales service as an afterthought. E-Business Strategies research indicates that after-sales service accounts for 10%–40% of revenues for many industrial and service companies and up to 50% of inventory investment. Still many firms servicing equipment, facilities, and other high-tech and industrial assets rely on outdated, inefficient processes for call logging and tracking, work scheduling, contract and warranty management, and service parts management.

In summary, there are several reasons driving companies to mobilize field service:

- In response to intense customer demand for quality service, enterprises are focusing their strategies on maximizing field service worker productivity via better processes and tools.

- Strategic focus of field service is on the rise, as more than three-quarters of firms currently run or plan to run field service as a strategic operation with revenue and profit goals in place. As a result, there is a sea change under way in the field service arena, from a tactical cost center to a strategic profit center.

- Hampered by insufficient tools to measure and improve field service performance, companies are tackling the challenge by mobilizing processes that are tied to overall customer experience. Delivering an optimal experience involves the coordination and synchronization of four key components: people, parts, process, and data.

- To remain competitive, enterprises must intimately understand and document criteria for customer satisfaction and reverse engineer their field service organizations to meet or exceed these criteria. A key goal is worker empowerment — doing more for the company with less effort.

The bottom line: Best-practice service organizations are proactively supporting their products via field service automation technologies and collaborating with their mobile workforces to improve operational efficiencies, profitability, and satisfaction levels.

Chapter Six

Mobilizing Asset Management

Dow Chemical, ChevronTexaco, and other large companies usually own many pipeline and manufacturing assets scattered across different locations. When this internal plant machinery or equipment breaks down, the asset management process is set in motion. Mobile asset management, or MAM, allows the plant maintenance technicians, auditors, and warehouse personnel at these companies to access relevant business processes anywhere, anytime. In this chapter, we describe the different trends, features, and functionality shaping MAM. We illustrate the real-world application of MAM via three case studies: Fraport, Infraserv, and Wesertal.

Introduction

In the last five years, BASF, the world's largest chemical company, spent $4 billion on new plants and equipment for its U.S. operations. Like many companies, it wants to optimize the usage of its machines to increase production before it turns to hiring new workers. According to Klaus Peter Löbbe, who runs BASF's North American operations, "Now comes the time to make the assets sweat."[1]

Asset management is a core business activity for several industries as the following examples explain:

- Manufacturing companies depend on equipment uptime and performance to meet production goals; for them, monitoring, calibrating, and maintaining plant machinery is mission-critical.

- For electrical utility companies, ongoing asset maintenance is a prerequisite for trouble-free, 24x7 service. When catastrophic events such as hurricanes occur, repairing assets becomes even more critical.

- Hospitals, hotels, and airports require glitch-free facilities to deliver the high-quality service their customers expect.

- Public transit and logistics companies depend on the reliability of their fleets to move people and goods.

- Banks rely heavily on their computer servers and networks to keep online and offline financial processes working seamlessly.

It's no secret that physical or capital-intensive companies in the utilities, telecommunications, transportation, mining, and oil and gas industries want to improve the efficiency of their asset management operations by increasing the effectiveness of predictive and preventive maintenance and emergency repairs, by meeting compliance regulations, and by capturing more accurate real-time data.[2]

In the past, field technicians who serviced equipment either on the factory floor or in a remote location were beyond the reach of tethered networks. Technicians could not download or upload information electronically or provide real-time feedback. As a result, their processes were mostly paper-driven and prone to errors, which made plant maintenance and equipment management a time-consuming exercise.

Emerging MAM applications change that. They empower internal field technicians and engineers that provide preventive maintenance and repair functions to access the information — essential equipment data, work orders, documentation and inspection forms — they need and perform required functions when and where they need to, regardless of connection state (from a utility pole, factory floor, loading dock, or even inside an mine shaft).

MAM applications can be deployed on laptops or handhelds. Field technicians can work in a disconnected mode, complete their tasks, and later update back-end systems through synchronization. In this way, all parties involved in the process, from the asset operators to the field technicians and engineers, via the maintenance planner, can access the real-time data that is relevant for them.

Business Objectives Driving Mobile Asset Management

Have you ever visited Disneyland or Disney World? Did you stop to think about the army of maintenance workers quietly laboring behind the scenes to ensure you a safe ride? Whether it's a natural gas pipeline, an electric substation, a manufacturing plant, a hospital, an office complex, or a trucking fleet, maintenance organizations share the same mission: to keep their critical assets and operations running as reliably and efficiently as possible.

The business objectives driving investments in mobile asset management include:

- Improving overall field productivity,

- Providing management with more accurate and timely data,

- Ensuring regulatory compliance,

- Promoting accountability and control, and

- Outsourcing asset management.

Improve Field Productivity

Transforming maintenance operations from paper-based systems to digital ones can lead to a wealth of productivity gains that benefit users and the organization as a whole.

Eliminating unproductive activities such as time-consuming paperwork, data entry, and travel and incorporating measures such as "record as you work" models for technicians keeps companies' critical assets in peak working condition, that is, no unscheduled downtime and more efficient operations.

Delivering critical information to the point of performance is a surefire way to improve field productivity. Technicians, engineers, and other mobile workers can do their jobs faster when they can retrieve data at point of need. Lacking proper information at the point of performance reduces first-time fix rates and contributes to asset downtime.

More organizations are realizing that technicians could benefit from immediate access to job plans, safety plans, and work histories while performing equipment maintenance. Rounds inspectors need to view acceptable operating ranges while taking asset readings, enabling them to spot problem trends and request repairs before breakdowns occur.

Provide Management with Better Data

Managers want more visibility into activities in the field. They face pressure to capture timely, accurate field data such as:

- **Labor and resources information.** With up-to-the-minute tracking of technicians' time and attendance, management gets the necessary data to deploy its workforce more optimally. Work-completion data is available almost immediately to management, providing them with the knowledge for better planning, scheduling, billing, and tracking.

- **Asset condition and history information.** Collecting accurate equipment measurement points, maintenance histories (such as mean time to repair, or MTTR, and asset downtime), product warranties, and condition assessments helps businesses to isolate problem assets and assign technicians most effectively.

By digitizing the asset maintenance workflow, companies and workers spend less time completing forms, transferring data, and reconciling actual with reported work and actually gain time for more planned and preventive maintenance activities.

Ensure Compliance

External regulations and internal quality assurance have led some overwhelmed companies to adopt electronic auditing and verification capabilities in hopes they will have an easier time with compliance. For instance, in the pharmaceuticals industry, the FDA's 21 CFR Part 11 regulation stipulates that all work and user data have to be recorded and validated during equipment maintenance to ensure the highest levels of quality and safety. The call for new point-of-performance compliance capabilities to meet strict FDA, OSHA, and other reporting requirements has helped spur mobile investments.

Internally, maintenance organizations worried about document security are electronically tracking the change history of a work order and requiring electronic signatures and labor certification. This requirement means that only authorized personnel can complete or modify work-order steps. In addition, controls are necessary to certify that only the proper tools are used to complete equipment maintenance tasks.

Industries such as aviation, transportation, utilities, food processors, pharmaceuticals, and others will benefit from accurate, thorough maintenance data that is easily available for regulatory compliance and internal quality monitoring.

Promote Accountability and Control

Many organizations are searching for ways to improve tracking and auditing to maintain updated counts on assets and materials, from tools and spare parts, to high-cost, far-flung equipment and machinery.

Promoting accountability and control means conducting accurate cycle counts without paperwork and keeping track of materials when they travel between the technician and the storeroom. It also involves inventorying assets and collecting critical information on those assets wherever they are.

Lastly, promoting greater accountability and control entails managing the complete lifecycle of strategic assets through planning, procurement, deployment, tracking, maintenance, and retirement, especially if they are expensive or life-sensitive (like an aircraft engine). Inadequate accountability and control can expose companies to significant liability in the event of problems.

Outsource Asset Management

Outsourcing is another trend that is changing the nature of asset management. Asset owners responsible for management of the four key asset groups — production, facilities, transportation, and IT assets — are considering outsourcing instead of overseeing it themselves.

Since outsourcing entered the debate, internal asset management organizations are shouldering intense pressure to provide superior services at lower costs. We expect this pressure will continue as companies focus on core competencies and contemplate outsourcing noncore business processes to third-party service providers. The goal is to drive down their costs and improve bottom-line performance.

Ultimately, the outsourcing trend will build more momentum for mobile solutions. Managers will need greater real-time control and visibility into business metrics — what their contractors are doing and how service is being delivered.

Summarizing the Business Objectives

Recent business trends have underscored the need for integrated asset management and greater asset visibility. The pressure to manage assets strategically and for bottom-line impact grows.

Next-generation asset management solutions are helping companies to improve production reliability, labor efficiency, material optimization, software license compliance, lease management, warranty and service management, and provisioning across the asset base.

Until recently, enterprises had a hard time managing assets. Different assets have distinct management needs, resulting in a patchwork of systems that make a corporation's assets nearly invisible at the field worker level. MAM solutions address some of these problems.

Elements of Mobile Asset Management

SAP's MAM solutions empower workers to perform their daily activities related to plant maintenance and customer service in the field — at customer sites and within plants — while disconnected from the back-end SAP system.

As Figure 6.1 shows, these solutions tend to have certain core functionalities: order management, notification management, measurement and counter reading capability, technical object management, inventory management, business partner management, and contract management.

Order Management

This functionality allows businesses to manage work order tasks for maintenance and service orders. By setting parameters at the back end, companies can guarantee that their field employees receive only the downloaded data relevant to them, such as their assigned tasks.

Figure 6.1: Overview of SAP's Mobile Asset Management Solution

In addition, field employees can view operations for work orders, check the terms of a service contract or warranty, create new work orders, and track details of services provided. The order management function also allows field employees to see historical orders related to technical objects, giving them complete information about the jobs at hand.

Notification Management

Equipped with this functionality, field employees can handle the entire notification process: creating new notifications (related or not related to orders); displaying and modifying existing notifications; and adding tasks, items, reasons, and text to existing notifications. This functionality improves notification quality and increases the amount malfunction information that field employees and enterprises exchange. A good notification management system helps companies troubleshoot equipment, thus decreasing equipment downtime and increasing customer satisfaction.

Measurement and Counter Readings

This part of an MAM solution allows field employees to perform measurements and counter readings on handheld devices. They can insert a new reading or check a previous reading to verify that appropriate parameters have been observed. They can also use the measurement and reading function to:

- Measure points and counters linked to the equipment and functional locations, and

- Create a measurement document.

Technical Object Management

For field employees, the benefit of this functionality is gaining access to important information about technical objects that can help them better manage their workloads. For example, technical object management lets employees monitor equipment that needs servicing. They can also:

- Display equipment,

- Connect to the business partner record from the equipment object,

- Retrieve equipment warranty information,

- Show the equipment or functional location lists to the work center,

- Install or uninstall equipment at a functional location, and

- Link to service contracts from an equipment object.

Inventory Management

This application lets field employees track and manage inventory quickly and cost-effectively. When they create material consumptions, inventory count is updated automatically, which allows the accurate tracking of mobile inventory. Mobile inventory can be either local stock or customer consignment stock.

The inventory management capability also supports:

- Validating part numbers during an inventory check,

- Checking local availability of storage location or consignment stock,

- Supporting customer consignment stock, and

- Updating stock records when an order transaction is saved.

Business Partner Management

With this functionality, field employees can review customer records (beyond basic details such as address and location) that correspond to orders. It also enables them to

- Display the business partner master record and

- Survey the business partner list.

Contract Management

Contract management contributes to excellent customer service by giving field employees access to the latest contract information related to a technical object. They can also view contract information in synopsis or detailed form, depending on their needs in the field, and they can display contract header information related to an order.

For a quick review of the functionalities associated with SAP's mobile asset management solution, see Table 6.1.

Case Study: Fraport

On April 11, 1996, a tragic incident took place at Düsseldorf Airport. A fire in an occupied passenger terminal killed 17 passengers, seriously injured 72, and inflicted minor injuries on several hundred people. The cost of the damage is still not completely known, as some areas of the airport have not been restored to full operation.[3]

Fire safety is a core concern and business process. In this case study, we follow a leading airport operator to see how mobile asset management helps the company with the complex compliance process of maintaining and repairing fire shutters in the air conditioning systems.

Company Overview

With 2003 revenues of €1.8 billion (about $2.3 billion) and an average of 23,544 employees as of mid-2004, owner and operator of Frankfurt Airport, Fraport AG, is one of the leading airport operators in the world.

The company, which has subsidiaries in Europe, Hong Kong, and Peru, is split into four business divisions: traffic and retail, aviation ground services and logistics, information and telecommunication, and real estate and facility management.

Function	Description
Order Management	▪ Display and review orders for a day or a week ▪ Confirm the tasks and activities to be performed ▪ Create new work orders ▪ View the operations for a work order ▪ Create time and material confirmations ▪ Display the technical object involved and access its maintenance and repair history
Inventory Management	▪ Manage and track inventory in a mobile storage location or a customer consignment ▪ Perform a local availability check on materials ▪ Get an inventory list and the count of materials in the storage location
Notification Management	▪ Process customer service or plant maintenance notifications or create new ones ▪ Display detailed lists of notifications ▪ Modify or release notifications
Measurements and Counter Readings	▪ Perform measurements and counter readings using a handheld device in offline mode ▪ Create new measurement documents for the measurement points of a technical object ▪ View the last measurement document history
Business Partner Management	▪ Access the details of a customer record, such as address, contact person, or telephone number
Technical Object Management	▪ Download relevant information about the installed base ▪ Manage and monitor all technical objects that need maintenance or servicing ▪ Enter details of items you have installed or removed

Table 6.1: Elements of SAP's Mobile Asset Management Solution

Fraport's business strategy centers on growth and consolidation in Frankfurt, as well as external growth. The air transportation market is booming. In Germany alone, passenger volume is expected to double by 2015, and Fraport intends to embrace this increase by expanding its runway system and passenger terminal at Frankfurt, as well as by optimizing its technical systems. Ongoing quality measures at Frankfurt secure continuous improvement of efficiency and productivity.

In its real estate and facility management division, Fraport is responsible for around 420 buildings and facilities at Frankfurt Airport. An important activity of the planning and management partner is safeguarding fire protection measures in all the buildings that have been selected for use in a pilot project of the SAP MAM solution.

This pilot project involves the maintenance of 22,000 fire shutters that can seal vents in seconds, trapping heat and smoke in a local ventilation unit. Increased safety was the top priority, and Germany's strict safety requirements demand that fire systems be reliable and stable.[4]

What Is the Business Problem?

Maintenance of the ventilation units is an essential element of Frankfurt Airport's fire protection measures dictated by legislators and the related trade association. The manufacturer of the units also stipulates stringent conditions of use. In case of fire, the fire shutters close automatically, isolating the blaze. This prevents or slows the spread of the fire.[5]

Fraport coordinates the maintenance work for the ventilation units, although third-party companies are responsible for the work itself. The costs incurred depend on the number of fire shutters and the difficulty of the maintenance work. By law, the maintenance work must be documented and stored for at least ten years. Responsibility for compliance with the fire protection measures lies with Fraport. Full maintenance is now ensured by sample surveys and checks by Fraport employees.

The pilot project is Fraport's first step toward implementing a mobile solution that increases safety in the maintenance of fire protection devices. The pilot was seen as the forerunner to the implementation of mobile solutions in different areas. The strategic goals of the pilot were:

- Increase safety by preventing defects, create transparency, and ensure maintenance work is carried out,

- Perform maintenance work efficiently to safeguard fire protection measures (shutters) in the buildings,

- Integrate with the SAP Plant Maintenance (PM) system for quick access to safety information,

- Implement an integrated mobile scenario as the platform for additional mobile applications, and

- Archive maintenance documentation efficiently in the central system.

Mobilizing the Process

The new processes for performing maintenance work were geared first toward raising safety levels. In contrast to the previous procedure, paper-based orders no longer form the basis for employee activities. The employees now rely on PDAs and transponders for all relevant information and instructions. The mobile devices contain all the order information and are used to identify fire shutters, to perform maintenance work, and to document the results of maintenance.

To ensure the maintenance was completed and to raise the level of safety and efficiency, the airline operator introduced a new procedure. Fraport loads the maintenance orders on the mobile devices centrally, so its employees can start on the work as soon as they receive their devices. The employees are equipped with a bar code ID, which is scanned to identify an employee before he or she begins each maintenance order. This procedure is not used to monitor performance (neither quantity nor quality), but instead is used for activity reporting and guarantees that the work is done by the employee responsible for it.

When the employee's ID is scanned, the maintenance order is activated on the mobile device. The next step involves checking the feasibility of the maintenance. This means assessing whether the fire shutter is in place and a readable transponder is visible. If the work cannot be carried out, a message is generated with three possible types of defect in the form of a code (shutter not available, transponder not available, or transponder not readable). The employee then assigns the appropriate defect and saves it.

By now, employees have recorded electronically a great deal of information, and suitable measures are triggered directly after evaluation of the maintenance work (when the devices are read). This may entail correcting the ground plans if a transponder does not exist or requesting a repair to insert a missing transponder or replace a damaged one. With the old, manual, paper-based procedure, there were no guarantees that defects of this type would be found.

To activate the order, the employee scans the transponder with the mobile reader, holding them a maximum of 3 centimeters apart. This shows that the fire shutter was accessible and that the employee was physically present to carry out the maintenance work. The individual steps of the maintenance are documented on the handheld and the instructions are confirmed with a checkbox.

At this point, a request that the individual maintenance task be carried out and confirmed is created, thereby ruling out the possibility of any steps in the procedure being omitted. When documenting defects, the employee selects from a list of standardized error codes. This prevents the types of misunderstandings that occur with handwritten documents. The wording of an error description or illegible handwriting leaves room for interpretation by the reader, which can lead to confusion.

After the maintenance tasks are completed, the transponder is scanned a second time, and the order is deactivated. At this stage, no more activities can be performed on this work order. When all the orders are finished, the employee returns the mobile device to Fraport. Using a docking station, the company retrieves the information from the mobile device, uploads it to the SAP R/3 system, and evaluates it in predefined time intervals. Getting rid of manual entry means the data is available to Fraport as soon as it is transferred from the device.

Fraport's method for mobilizing asset management included the following:

- Define an efficient process for the performance and administration of maintenance orders and implement this process using an integrated mobile solution.

- Base the approach on SAP MAM in tandem with SAP R/3 Plant Maintenance, mobile devices (RFID readers), and transponders.

- Electronically recognize and record facilities that require maintenance. Generate maintenance orders with relevant data.

- Implement menu-based maintenance, procedure registration, and recording of defects.

- Read and archive the maintenance order information in the main SAP PM system.

Details of the Implementation

December 2002 saw the start of the pilot project. Two employees each from Fraport and SAP tackled project organization. After they produced the business blueprint in February 2003, the task list was implemented. Five months later, a test run was carried out.

How did it work? All the fire shutters were assigned RFID labels in the same maintenance period. The RFID transponders, or tags, had to be protected with an integrated ferrite layer. It must last for at least ten years because by law the data must be stored for this long. The memory of the transponder contains important information: the bar code for identification, an equipment number issued by the SAP system, and the time of the inspection. Any defects are stored on the PDA, the Psion Teklogix netpad model, which is well suited for engineers. MicroSensys contributed the reader for the RFID chip.

Results and ROI

Fraport's pilot project illustrated the value of mobilizing the asset management process. The benefits from this project include:

- **Increased safety.** A new mobile process guarantees that necessary maintenance is actually carried out on site by engineers, the main objective — compliance monitoring — of the project.

- **Close-knit process integration.** The solution is fully integrated into the administrative processes of plant maintenance and prevents errors.

- **Traceability and transparency.** Documentation of the entire maintenance process and the results increases transparency.

- **Savings.** By cutting the cost of order archiving and administration (handling and assets), Fraport saves €100,000 in processing costs yearly. Additional savings came from the gradual dismantling of the old archives, with no need for archiving in the future.

- **Streamlining of the maintenance process**, administration of maintenance orders by Fraport, and increased transparency (documentation of maintenance steps for reporting) create greater scope for a new pricing structure with the service provider.

Based on the experience gained, Fraport is considering additional scenarios such as maintenance of fire doors, smoke detectors, security doors, and baggage transporters. Fraport's next step is to map the entire maintenance system (fire shutters, fire doors) and leverage SAP MAM to handle its service assurance activities.

Case Study: Infraserv

Infraserv GmbH & Höchst KG, headquartered in Frankfurt am Main, Germany, was founded in 1998 by its former parent company Hoechst AG. Today Infraserv is an integrated site operator and service provider for chemical and life-science production sites. Infraserv Höchst employs 3,700 people and recorded 2002 sales of more than €873 million (nearly $1.1 billion).[6]

Infraserv operates the Frankfurt-Höchst Industrial Park, which has had an international reputation as an innovative and efficient location for chemicals and pharmaceuticals for more than 140 years. More than 80 companies call the industrial park home. As a system provider, Infraserv pools the services necessary for integrated site operation.

The company encompasses all the competency areas expected of a professional site operator, from providing a complex infrastructure platform, through supplying utilities, goods, and raw materials, to environmentally friendly waste disposal. Technical and logistics services, plus comprehensive support in the areas of environment, health, and safety, complete Infraserv's offerings. Infraserv's main objective is to make it easier for companies in the chemical processes industry to concentrate on their core business.

The Mobile Maintenance Project

The motivation for Infraserv's mobile maintenance project was clear: to optimize the value chain, thereby ensuring that customer satisfaction and service quality remained consistently high.

According to Jochen Schmidt, Infraserv's manager of new business development, "We see ourselves as a quality-oriented operator of sites, buildings, and systems, and we align our processes to optimize customer benefit using value-oriented management."

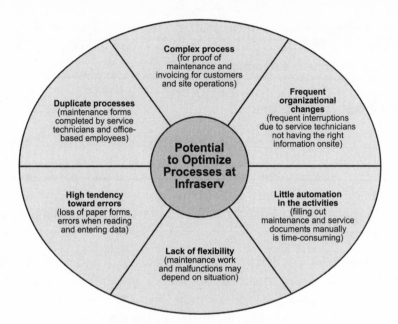

Figure 6.2: Challenges at Infraserv Höchst

Infraserv's project focused on the processes for the maintenance of technical objects (elevators, heating systems, and air conditioning and ventilation systems) and the repair of malfunctions in its sites and facilities division. Ultimately, Infraserv hoped the project would lead to more efficient processes and better customer service. After some initial analysis, it became clear that more automation in the processes was the way to achieve this goal.

Business Case Development

As a first step, Infraserv's sites and facilities division investigated the possible uses of mobile solutions, searching for ways to optimize existing processes and to define more efficient ones for the future, including increased automation through mobile technology. The division also undertook to examine the quantitative and qualitative advantages and disadvantages of using the software. An additional goal was to construct a decision making basis for the project sponsors and to convince the service technicians that the right action had been taken.

The research for the business case, the definition of the target processes, and the alignment of the detailed requirements with SAP MAM took place between March 2003 and July 2003.

Business Process Target Selection

For the business case, Infraserv selected processes that could significantly benefit from the use of a mobile application. The focus was, therefore, on performing maintenance and repairing malfunctions that were previously recorded predominantly on paper.

Infraserv focused on the most important processes service technicians use everyday. This enabled the company to narrow its scope and make the processes more efficient — quickly and pragmatically — and to measure this efficiency. According to Joachim Litzinger, mobile maintenance project manager, "Employees will only support process optimization when they see it for themselves."

To map the entire process, the project team analyzed the processes and functions used by the service technicians, as well as the process interfaces to the MRP planners and to internal plant maintenance coordination. The team assessed the processes by calculating their average duration and frequency. In line with the project goal to extend and improve service for customers, the team examined weaknesses in the old processes and looked at customer requests and complaints to identify potential candidates for optimization.

The process analysis revealed that the main processes, which were manual, should be automated more. Sometimes, excessive paperwork was leading to some processes being carried out twice — an information bottleneck that could be prevented by automation. Also, the service technicians onsite needed better information that they could use to handle malfunctions immediately, in accordance with the local conditions, or to notify colleagues.

Infraserv's analysis revealed that process automation would add value in three ways:

- Prevent processes from being delayed due to frequent organizational changes, such as different contact persons at the customer site.

- Greatly reduce the error rate resulting from coordinating the service technicians' work on paper.

- Provide proof of maintenance evidence to chemical and pharmaceutical customers that Infraserv carried out maintenance checks.

Implementation

After evaluating the seven other providers of mobile solutions, Infraserv opted for SAP because implementation and operating costs were low and because the mobile devices could be integrated with its existing SAP back end. In fact, due to existing SAP knowledge and skills, Infraserv was able to deal with many integration tasks itself.

After the project team analyzed the potential for optimization, the team drafted the new processes that SAP MAM would support going forward. Here too, the duration of newly defined main processes for maintenance and repairing malfunctions was estimated and then multiplied by the frequency per year.

During the weeklong design phase, Infraserv employees implemented the Web Application Server (SAP Web AS), Mobile Infrastructure, and MAM application. The mobile device selected was the handheld Panasonic Toughbook CF-P1 with bar code scanner.

In August 2003, Infraserv implemented the requirements of the service technicians in its sites and facilities division and followed up with a five-day test phase. Later in August, the division signed off on the software, and the pilot operation began. Within three months, Infraserv had a solution.

Benefits and Results of the Business Case

As part of the business case, the project team was able to verify the cost efficiency of using SAP MAM for maintenance and for repairing malfunctions. The initials calculations estimated that ROI for automating just these two processes was 108%, with break-even after 1.9 years. The annual discounted free cash flow is positive after just two years. The ROI analysis helped support the decision to move forward.

In addition to the savings from cost efficiency, SAP MAM generated other qualitative improvements for Infraserv. They included an increase in service quality and the expandability of the existing range of services in the sites and facilities division because of the implementation.

Mobile computing enables the service technicians to call up the information they need onsite, then to process it and add new data. In particular, electronic data exchange for maintenance plan orders, maintenance processing, time recording, verification recording, and activity confirmation have been improved and speeded up. Automation means that the technicians can now react more flexibly to exceptional occurrences and detected malfunctions.

Rollout for the 120 Infraserv service technicians began in early 2004. In the pilot phase, the project team checked the efficiency of the new processes by measuring them. The results showed that the times for the processes examined were better than what the team was expecting.

Next Steps

In the second phase, Infraserv is planning to implement more mobile SAP applications in subsidiaries and divisions. Other projects for mobile maintenance and malfunction repair are also in the pipeline.

The bottom line: MAM helps Infraserv pursue its competitive strategy of using innovative processes to provide its customers with continuously improved services and additional high-quality offerings.

Case Study: Wesertal GmbH

Wesertal GmbH is a regional power supply company headquartered in Hameln, Germany. The €250 million company, a fully owned subsidiary of the German E.ON Group, employs 500 people. Of these, 100 are mobile service technicians who cover a 2,800-square-kilometer grid to service the equipment that supplies electricity, gas, solar power, drinking water, and heat to the company's customers.[7]

An innovator among German power suppliers, Wesertal was the first company to offer Internet services. The company is similarly innovative in its response to the business driver in the European utilities marketplace today: the elimination of electricity and gas supply monopolies and the resulting tough competition, lower profit margins, and the need for cost efficiency.

Looking for Asset Management Process Improvement

Wesertal was generating 15,000 service and maintenance work orders annually for its service technicians using the SAP Plant Maintenance (SAP PM) component.[8] Wesertal was looking for a technology solution to add value and decrease operating costs.

The goal was to streamline the current paper-based business processes. Let's see how this worked. The service technicians had to drive to service centers before and after work to pick up orders and drop off reports. The work orders SAP PM generated were printed out and carried around in the technicians' briefcases. The technicians had to record working hours, kilometers driven, wage-paid hours, work performed, and inspection results. Their handwritten reports were then entered manually into a data acquisition system.

"For a long time now, it was a nuisance that our field service employees managed their work papers by hand and their entries were transferred to the goods management system manually," says Burkhard Menzel, CIO at Wesertal. "We urgently had to get a hold of a mobile solution. Our idea of what it was to look like was very clear: as far as possible, it had to integrate perfectly into our SAP systems and constitute a professional solution based on standards that offered a secure future."

Improving Maintenance and Service Operations

The first step to automating and mobilizing the asset management process was to establish the enabling infrastructure. Wesertal wanted a mobile infrastructure that could work both online and offline because the region had many hills and mountains, and it was hard to maintain a constant online connection.

Wesertal selected SAP Mobile Infrastructure to leverage its existing systems and provide its technicians with a mobile business solution to support their maintenance and service work. Once the infrastructure was in place, the company was able to implement a mobile service application in only three months.[9]

The service technicians at Wesertal use PDA devices from Symbol Technologies that allow them to connect any time they wish. Each morning they link wirelessly from their homes to the SAP systems via the SAP Internet transaction server to receive the day's assignments. At the service sites, they navigate a simple checklist to enter information into the mobile device, including hours worked, distance driven, equipment serviced, and inspection results.

Using the capabilities of SAP Mobile Infrastructure, the mobile application automatically saves and buffers this information. Technicians synchronize with the main SAP system in real time or at a later point to transfer their information and receive new instructions.

Two-Year Return on Investment

After conducting a detailed ROI assessment, Wesertal expects a fast payback in around two years. The ROI comes from three areas:

- The technicians no longer have to drive to one of the seven service centers to pick up work orders and return paperwork when they are finished.

- No one at the service centers has to type in the technicians' handwritten notes.

- The quality and comprehensiveness of information is improved because technicians enter it electronically at the service call site.

Wesertal's next step is to allow technicians to enter information on materials consumed during the service visit. The company will also bar code–enable the system, which will allow technicians to scan equipment bar codes onsite then enter associated information about the service requirements.

Making a Business Case for Mobile Asset Management

Managing assets is an integral part of a larger business process: product lifecycle management (PLM). Asset lifecycle management consists of two functional areas: plant maintenance (internal use) and customer service (external use). As the case studies illustrated, MAM addresses both areas.

Now that you understand how companies are implementing MAM, it is time to turn the attention to your organization. Are you a candidate for implementing MAM in your organization?

Answering the following questions can you help you determine if a MAM solution has a place within your organization.

- In nonwireless mode, are you constantly shifting resources and demands, making it difficult to optimize work routes, deploy available workers and equipment against tasks, and manage other resources in real time, while continuously balancing cost (including minimizing overtime) with customer responsiveness?

- Are your technicians and engineers using paper in the field and wasting time on petty administrative tasks (sorting, recording, talking to dispatch) that could be otherwise automated? Are they traveling to the office for orders and to drop off completed data, which affects billable field time and increases "idle time?"

- Are nonwireless processes limiting two-way information flows between field and dispatch, hampering service quality, customer satisfaction, and revenue (up-sell) opportunities? Do they inhibit workforce and workload balancing?

- Is inefficient data entry (or re-entry from field to office) introducing errors, omissions, and redundancies in work and data, affecting service reliability and customer satisfaction? Does data entry duplication add to your costs?

- Without wireless connections, do your maintenance operators have low visibility into active order and technician status, problem situations, and resolution status?

- Without real-time data from the field, are managers able to monitor KPIs to optimize asset performance? Are they able to analyze field engineer performance and track mean time between equipment failures and performance improvement without having to run reports?

- To better understand your situation map the current AS-IS business processes and mobile TO-BE processes to gauge the impact of implementing a mobile asset management solution. Figure 6.3 illustrates an example of an AS-IS and TO-BE process model.

As you map your AS-IS and TO-BE processes, analyze your organization by asking the following questions: Are your mobile field engineers unique in their pattern of mobility and data use? Do they typically move from location to location, spending 70%–80% of their time on the road? Do they rely on processes such as dispatch and scheduling, asset management, field technical support, mapping and workforce scheduling, inventory access, contract management, and shipping and procurement? If you answered yes to these questions, then you are a candidate for an MAM solution.

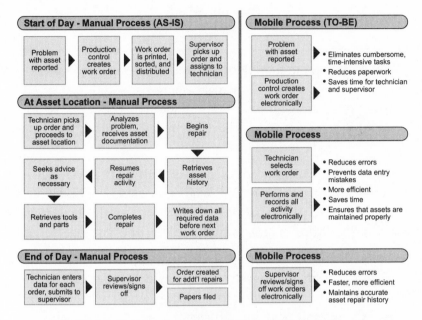

Figure 6.3: Reengineering Asset Management Processes

Just look at SBC Communications. In June 2000, SBC launched its multimillion-dollar "Technician of the Future," initiative, which equipped 27,000 network technicians with intelligent field devices (IFDs) — wireless laptops that contain diagnostics/line testing, detailed cable wiring maps, and access to service call and product information. With the IFDs, technicians have access to manuals, reference materials, and simplified administrative work procedures. IFD ease-of-use features allow technicians to complete routine tasks using touch screen functionality. The IFDs also let technicians run multiple diagnostic tests (15 in 15 seconds), replacing at least six pieces of equipment that were needed to do the same work.[10]

SBC is just the tip of the iceberg, an example of a mega-trend. In closing, it's pertinent to point out that MAM applications is one area in the enterprise software economy that is receiving multimillion-dollar investments.

Summary

"Normal people… believe that if it ain't broke, don't fix it. Engineers believe that if it ain't broke, it doesn't have enough features yet."

— Scott Adams

Technicians, engineers, and maintenance operators perform work on critical assets out on the shop floor, in the field, and in many other places far, far away. Employees who manage spare parts and inspect critical assets travel to wherever those assets are located. These people are not performing work at their desks. They are out at the point of performance taking care of assets and materials.

These mobile employees need to interact with SAP to do their jobs. They require information from SAP when they are in the field. Similarly, they provide the SAP back end with information from the field — crucial information that helps managers plan, analyze, and make decisions.

Armed with mobile asset management solutions, technicians are finally able to capture field data quickly and accurately, giving management a thorough view of the organization to enhance planning, scheduling, billing, customer service, and operating efficiency.

Connecting mobile employees with back-end SAP applications can benefit companies in unexpected ways. For example, some organizations are leveraging SAP to implement advanced asset management concepts like reliability centered maintenance (RCM), total productive maintenance (TPM), and overall equipment effectiveness (OEE). These concepts revolve around reducing the amount of reactive work, eliminating preventive maintenance backlogs, and ensuring the reliability of critical assets.

The bottom line: To achieve higher corporate performance — whether measured in terms of shareholder value, revenue growth, profitability, or customer satisfaction — companies have to become more sophisticated in their approach to asset management.

Chapter Seven

Mobilizing Direct Store Delivery and Route Accounting

This chapter provides an understanding of the direct store delivery (DSD) process and the value of mobilizing it. Mobile DSD and route accounting solutions are increasing the productivity and efficiency of account sales managers and delivery drivers in the consumer products and retail industry. Mobile DSD solutions are improving productivity as employees spend less time correcting mistakes and more time working with customers. The information velocity from the field has improved, which leads to real-time insight into orders, delivery, invoicing, and pricing. Mobile DSD solutions help companies to rationalize head count as the technology enables employees to switch between the roles of sales and distribution. We present two case studies, Frito-Lay and Earthgrains, to help illustrate the nuances of DSD.

Introduction

When you walk into your supermarket, do you expect your favorite snack to be waiting on the shelf? As you walk to the refrigerated section to pick up some ice cream, do you ever stop to think about how it landed there? Technology, particularly wireless handheld computers coupled with direct store delivery (DSD), plays a large role in guaranteeing that your snack, beverage, or ice cream of choice is always in stock.[1]

DSD is shorthand for delivering high-turnover and perishable products from suppliers (manufacturers, brand owners, or distributors) directly to retail stores, vending machines, restaurants, or convenience stores. The key word is direct: DSD bypasses intermediaries and additional warehouses. Manufacturers or distributors that choose DSD assume responsibility for shelf inventory, while product check-in is handled by the manufacturer, distributor, or retailer.[2]

The DSD model of store replenishment prevails in the consumer goods and grocery industries. DSD is especially suited for products that are restocked often and that respond to in-store promotion and merchandising. Greeting cards, magazines, beverages, generic drugs, baked goods, snacks, dairy products, and coffee can all be delivered directly to stores and are classified as either perishable or nonperishable.

DSD operates on the theory that no one understands a product better than the manufacturer that created it. Retail stores that favor DSD allot space in their establishments to individual manufacturers and ask them to create in-store displays that highlight their products.

Market Overview of Direct Store Delivery

DSD is an outgrowth of the pressures that grocery distribution and supply chains face. Miniscule margins, competition from the likes of Wal-Mart, industry consolidation, smaller and more frequent deliveries, and a proliferation of product categories and stock-keeping units (SKUs) are some of the challenges looming in the trillion-dollar industry.

DSD is a major reason why products move faster and more efficiently to retail store shelves today. Managing shelf space is a big issue in retail, and DSD enables companies to merchandise with maximum visibility and appeal.

The market adoption of DSD has grown over the past decade. Currently, DSD accounts for as much as 25% of U.S. supermarket sales volume and a higher percentage of convenience store sales volume.[3] In fact, many DSD categories, such as beverages, snacks, cookies, crackers, and baked goods, are among the best performers in stores.

To better grasp the scale and scope of DSD, consider the fact that an average convenience store stocks 1,500 SKU items delivered directly to each store. Each store is supported by an average of 20 separate manufacturers or distributors that make more than ten deliveries in a typical day. Within the beverage category alone, stores deal with 18 separate beer wholesalers and 10 carbonated soft drink bottlers.[4] All these transactions can create friction if the component steps — sales, delivery, invoicing, and returns — are not operating smoothly.

The Business Value of Direct Store Delivery

Before we go any further, we should outline the business value of DSD for both retailers and the combined category of manufacturers, brand owners, and distributors.

Retailers with high-turnover products can benefit from DSD through labor savings — eliminating labor overhead from the warehouse to retailer delivery, from shelf replenishment to inventory control. In fact, with most DSD products, the first time retail employees touch the products is when they scan them at checkout.

In a retail environment that experiences high employee turnover, DSD process automation and standardization can result in savings due to lower errors and training costs.

Manufacturers, brand owners, and distributors can profit from DSD if it is implemented properly. They can better manage the space containing their company product(s). From a marketing standpoint, they can monitor and execute in-store merchandising. They can also manage and control store-level category management to benefit from products with high-velocity returns and large profit margins. From an operational standpoint, they can leverage their control of store-level inventory to ensure maximum sell-through from shelves and displays and minimum out-of-stocks.

DSD's multiple benefits have led many businesses on both sides of the retail equation to adopt the model. The Grocery Manufacturers of America estimates that half of the top ten packaged foods in retail are delivered directly. These categories are merchandised frequently; some even daily. They experience extremely high turns (beverages and breads) and are very susceptible to impulse buying (snacks, crackers).

Why Mobilize Direct Store Delivery?

DSD is becoming critical to maximizing shelf turns in the retail industry — a trend that is expected to continue as consumer demand for "freshness" and "the right product at the right time" speeds up the movement of products from manufacturers to retail shelves.

DSD's prominent role in food and consumer packaged goods sales means that improving the daily operational practices of DSD through mobile technology is an industry imperative.

The three drivers for mobilizing DSD include:

- **Operational complexity** stemming from an ever-expanding array of brand groups and product lines, new product varieties, slimmer margins, increased globalization, and more promotions.

- **Razor-thin margins and continuous profit pressure** due to the retail industry's high-turn, high-velocity processes, complete with administrative overhead. With such processes, investments in better execution and process automation become a must.

- **The movement from conventional sales methods to sophisticated pre-sell environments.** Many existing systems are paper- or DOS-based, presenting a barrier to adapting quickly to ongoing industry concerns.

Mobile DSD solutions help firms overcome these obstacles. They aid in capturing, moving, and managing information to and from the point of activity. With rugged, wireless enterprise mobility systems deployed at every point of activity — in the field, production facility, distribution center, warehouse, depot, or retail location — companies are regarding mobile solutions as key weapons in the battle for shelf space.

Table 7.1 summarizes the benefits of mobilizing DSD processes.

Benefit	Associated Tasks
Productivity Improvements	- Errors and resolution issues - Data entry costs - Merchandizing productivity - Eliminate product delivery errors
Supply Chain Process Improvements	- Control of cash and inventory - Access to timely data - Consolidation of routes - Just-in-time (JIT) delivery of finished products - Real-time updates
Competitive and Positioning Improvements	- Competitive shelf-space advantage - Shelf-space analysis - Elaborate pricing schemes - Multimedia promotions

Table 7.1: The Benefits of Mobilizing DSD Processes

Mobile Solutions for Direct Store Delivery Processes

We, like many others, believe DSD and the newer mobile technologies — handheld computers, application software, mobile printers, wireless communications, and scanners — are an excellent match.

At the front end, the heart of a mobile DSD operation is located on the mobile device and on its application software. Dramatic improvements have taken place in this area. DSD software has evolved from very basic, two-line, and text-based handhelds (running proprietary operating systems or MS-DOS) to very sophisticated, full-screen, graphical user interface (GUI) applications.

Manufacturers and others that practice DSD typically implement small screen, GUI handhelds running a Pocket PC-based operating system. With technology improvements, it is conceivable that screens sizes will expand, allowing mobile workers to interact with applications using fewer keystrokes and even voice commands.

The Symbol MC9000 exemplifies a DSD handheld computer. This handheld includes a high-resolution color screen for easy reading indoors and outdoors; WiFi networking; up to 64 megabytes of memory; Microsoft Windows Mobile operating system; and rechargeable, extended-use lithium-ion batteries. The MC9000 incorporates a bar code reader capable of reading both one-dimensional and two-dimensional bar code symbols from multiple angles.[5]

While mobile devices have been involved in the DSD process for a while, it is only recently that the application software has advanced to the point where mobile applications can be integrated smoothly into back-end customer relationship management (CRM) and supply chain management (SCM) business processes to produce a more efficient, more profitable supply chain.

Several benefits arise when companies integrate mobile applications with core business processes: the ability to speed up back-door check-in, reduce distribution of unapproved items, and eliminate invoice discrepancies (and therefore invoice deductions). Integration also allows supply chain partners to spend less time discussing data, errors, and discrepancies and more time discussing business-building activities.

The bottom line is that linking mobile solutions and enterprise back-end systems (enterprise resource planning, or ERP, CRM, and SCM) will give companies more visibility at the store and the account levels, a big help for those in low-margin industries that want to manage their operations on the street more effectively.

Direct Store Delivery Process Models

In order to identify and develop the potential that mobile solutions hold for DSD, it is critical that we outline the DSD business processes. Within DSD, the individual processes can vary by category due to product type or legal requirements, but the basic processes fit into one of two models: two-tier or three-tier (see Figure 7.1).[6]

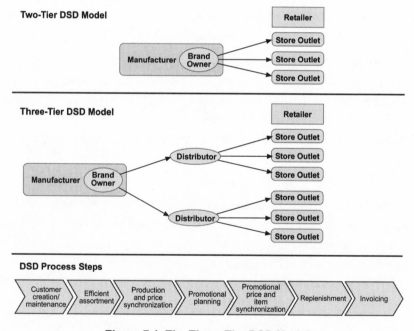

Figure 7.1: The Three-Tier DSD Model

The Two-Tier DSD Model

A two-tier model means manufacturers (or brand owners who contract out manufacturing) and retailers conduct business with each other directly. In this model, the manufacturer distributes products to the store without any intermediaries. The relationship between P&G and Wal-Mart offers an example of the two-tier DSD model.

The manufacturer uses its salesforce to help determine the right items for the store and control product pricing on the shelf. The manufacturer in some cases may use a third-party distributor, but that distributor acts only as an agent, almost in an outsourced sales function.

The Three-Tier DSD Model

In the three-tier model, the brand owner hires distributors to manage its products. For example, Coca-Cola uses a soft drink bottler (Coca-Cola Enterprises) or wholesaler to get its product to the store. Exclusive territories are owned by or assigned to the distributor by the brand owner. In most cases, no other distributor may sell the same branded product within that specific area.

The distributor delivers the product to the retailer on behalf of the manufacturer. The distributor determines which items will be sold at what price to the retailer and makes the service policy decisions. The distributor also handles many of the interactions with the retailer and, in some cases, may manage products for multiple brand owners.

Each distributor has its own separate back-end system that is independent from the brand owner, creating an information integration and consistency problem. The challenge is to make the information flow between all the partners more efficiently.

Some elements of the business process that need to be synchronized include: distribution (movement of product to store), merchandising (building displays, permanent and temporary point-of-sale, or POS, placement), monitoring dispensing or vending equipment if required, and collecting information related to marketing agreements (programs related to image and product distribution within the exclusive territory).

Elements of Direct Store Delivery

Consider this: Coca-Cola Enterprises is going mobile. The world's largest producer, bottler, and distributor of nonalcoholic beverages purchased 28,000 handheld computers as part of a enterprise mobility solution for its North American and European mobile workforces. Many of these handhelds will be deployed in a DSD process improvement initiative.[7]

PepsiCo is not standing still either. PepsiCo's three biggest bottlers — Pepsi Bottling Group, PepsiAmericas, and Pepsi Bottling Ventures — are rolling out their own lightweight handhelds and sales software. They sought a technology solution that could streamline sales and delivery processes, increase efficiencies, decrease errors, and grow with the company into the future.[8]

How exactly will Coca-Cola, PepsiCo, and the others sure to follow use the handhelds? To answer this question, we need to examine the DSD process in detail. The typical DSD process begins with start-of-day activities. Orders for each route, the six-to-eight week sales history for each customer, and any notes or special instructions for route drivers are downloaded to handhelds before drivers arrive in the morning.

During the day, DSD involves checking materials out of the warehouse and visiting customers. At the end of the day, drivers come back to the warehouse, check in returned materials (unsold products, returned products, and redeemable containers), submit collected payments, and balance and settle materials and payments accordingly.

Figure 7.2 illustrates the complete DSD process when it is paired with mobile technology. Mobile DSD aids delivery personnel with three key tasks: 1) loading the truck, 2) making the deliveries, and 3) settling up at the end of the day.

Load the Truck

In the morning, the handheld devices are loaded with data from the back-end server. The start-of-day data downloaded (customer master file, sales orders, deliveries) depends on the driver ID, vehicle ID, route, and other assignment criteria. In the best-case scenario, downloading occurs before the drivers report for work. Some data may be uploaded back into the server such as beginning odometer reading.

Once the truck is loaded, the driver begins checking out for the day. Checkout covers validating the loaded outgoing material and cash quantities. After the driver is done, an employee checker can perform the verification count and sign for the checkout load. Supervisors can verify discrepancies.

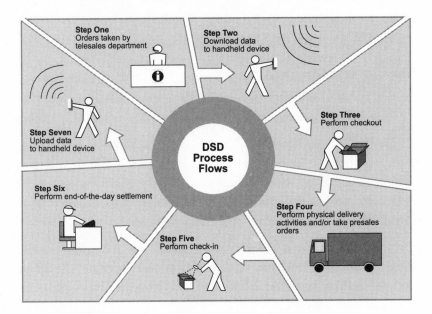

Figure 7.2: The Mobile Direct Store Delivery Process

Make the Deliveries

Now on the road, the driver follows the route plan and delivers the presold goods to the customers on his route who had ordered them. In addition to deliveries, the driver can also visit customers on the route and try to sell them products, advise them of new promotions, or complete customer information surveys.

The following handheld capabilities support the driver during his travels:

- Easy access to lists detailing associated activities for each visit. Variability is easily managed by updating visit status with reason codes indicating why activities are not performed (customer closed, lack of time, and so on).

- Full delivery activity management that spans support for presold and direct-from-truck deliveries (van deliveries made without presold orders), invoice issuing, customer data (customer master file, sales orders, deliveries) and truck inventory updates, payment collection, and future delivery order taking (new sales orders).

• Visit management functionality, a feature that allows drivers to rearrange the order of visits and create unplanned visits on the fly.

Settlement and Check-In

Back at the distribution center at the day's end, the driver checks in, which consists of counting and verifying the inventory on the truck and the cash on hand.

Along with check-in, handhelds help drivers at the end of the day by maintaining a list of customers not serviced (with reason code); recording messages for the sales department and miscellaneous driver expenses, and printing settlement reports and any tour reports.

Other end-of-day reconciliation capabilities include recording odometer readings, submitting customer payments, and reconciling checked-out materials against returns. This step also may include supervisor verification functionality.

Once the driver finishes the final settlement process, the system posts the appropriate sales, financial, and materials management transactions in the back-end system.

Three Roles in the Mobile DSD Process

The value proposition of mobile DSD is simple: enable salespeople and drivers to capture critical inventory and sales data at the retailer and transmit it back electronically, eliminating the need for redundant data entry by back-office staff and speeding up the overall business process.

The mechanics of mobile DSD tends to vary by geography and role. There are three critical roles in the mobile DSD process: the delivery driver, the van seller, and the preseller (see Table 7.2).

• The delivery driver primarily is a 100% focused role. He only delivers exactly what was predetermined in the warehouse, in the order taking area, or in the sales area of the back-end business.

• In the van sales model, the driver acts as both an order taker and a delivery person. In this model, the customers don't specify what they want beforehand; they decide based on what the van seller has in stock.

- Presellers don't even have any goods on their trucks, should they be lucky enough to have one. If presellers happen to be in large cities, then they might only walk around to nearby restaurants. They just take the orders, which are delivered later.

Functionality	Related Tasks
Presales (take orders to be delivered later)	▪ Download route or tour information at the day's start ▪ Check out ▪ Process route or tour with visits ▪ Sales order processing ▪ Create new order for future delivery ▪ Pricing; collect payment; inventory cash ▪ Issue order confirmation ▪ Process return orders ▪ Record expenses ▪ Reports; check in; end-of-day settlement (back-end)
Delivery (deliver presold orders)	▪ Download route or tour information at the day's start ▪ Check out ▪ Process route or tour with visits ▪ Delivery of presold orders including quantity changes and cancellation ▪ Returns (full goods and empties) ▪ Pricing; issue invoice or delivery note ▪ Collect payment; inventory cash ▪ Inventory adjustment ▪ Record expenses ▪ Reports; check in; end-of-day settlement (back-end)
Van sales (combine the delivery driver and the sales role)	▪ Start-of-day tour information ▪ Check out ▪ Process tour with visits ▪ Process sales orders (create new orders for immediate and future deliveries) ▪ Deliver presold orders including quantity changes and cancellations ▪ Returns (full goods and empties) ▪ Pricing ▪ Issue invoice or delivery note ▪ Collect payment; inventory cash ▪ Inventory adjustment ▪ Issue order confirmation ▪ Process return orders ▪ Record expenses ▪ Reports; check in; end-of-day settlement (back-end)

Table 7.2: Role-Based Functionality Requirements

For each of these different roles, the DSD solution must be both full-featured and easy to use. It must have:

- A driver-friendly user interface with touch screen buttons, function keys, and simple screen layouts,

- Task-driven screen flows in which completing a task automatically takes the user to the next logical task, and

- A nongraphical "heads down" user interface.

In addition to enhancing productivity, mobility in the delivery process can also augment accuracy. Moving from a paper to a mobile solution can reduce mistakes and re-work, but the most important result is more accurate information.

The two case studies on Frito-Lay and Earthgrains that follow will help you understand the dynamics of DSD better.

Case Study: Frito-Lay — The DSD Pioneer

Catering to the demands of a country that munches and crunches $15.1 billion worth of snack foods each year, U.S. snack makers scramble to maintain lucrative shelf space for their products. One of the tools of their trade is DSD, and Frito-Lay was the first to try it.[9]

Frito-Lay showed that mobile technology could foster better retailer relationships and enhanced customer service. The company established that when workers have information at their fingertips and can address customers' questions and concerns quickly and confidently, they form a stronger customer bond. This operational improvement proved to be a significant long-term competitive advantage for Frito-Lay.

Company Overview

The snack food industry got its start in September 1932 when two separate events took place. The first event occurred in Texas when Elmer Doolin bought the recipe for a corn chip that resulted in a new salty foods category. The product was Fritos brand corn chips, and his firm became the Frito Company.[10]

That same year in Nashville, Tennessee, Herman Lay started his own business distributing potato chips. Mr. Lay later bought the company that supplied him with his product and changed its name to H.W. Lay Company. Nearly thirty years later in 1961, the two companies merged to become Frito-Lay, Inc.

In 1965, Pepsi-Cola and Frito-Lay merged to create PepsiCo. Frito-Lay's snack foods contributed 34% of PepsiCo's net revenues and generated sales of $9.1 billion in 2003. The multinational company calls Plano, Texas, home and employs 30,000 people nationwide.

Frito-Lay brands account for more than half of the U.S. snack chip industry. Some of Frito-Lay's banner product lines include brand names such as Lay's, Ruffles, Doritos, Tostitos, Fritos, Rold Gold, and Sunchips. Eight of the company's brands rank among the ten best-selling snack brands in major U.S. supermarkets.

Today, Frito-Lay North America claims 50 food manufacturing and processing plants and approximately 1,900 warehouses, distribution centers, and offices. On the sales side, Frito-Lay is split into four geographic business divisions (north, central, south, and west) to be more responsive and closer to other marketplaces. With more than 14,000 salespeople, Frito-Lay has the largest direct store salesforce in the world.

A Pioneer of Direct Sales and Distribution

Frito-Lay owes some of its success to its direct sales and distribution strategy. In Frito-Lay's DSD model, merchandisers go into every store, stock and service the shelves, and generate new product sales nearly every time they are in the store. This is what has made Frito-Lay famous. They deliver fresh product with a 30-day shelf life and a guarantee to accept unsold product from customers. The salespeople keep a good mix in the stores, they know what sells, and they keep their shelves looking clean and fresh.

These salespeople use handheld computers to generate sales data daily. Frito-Lay first introduced mobile data communications to its route drivers in 1986. Its automated route sales system is based on handheld input devices linked to back-end systems in distribution centers nationwide.

The initial units were dinosaurs by today's standards — 10 inches long with one-line screens — but they were effective. Frito-Lay revenues jumped 14% per year to $5 billion from $3 billion between 1986 and 1990. Operating profits grew at an even faster rate of 30% to $934 million in 1990 from $348 million in 1986.

Competition was another reason why Frito-Lay improved the distribution process. In the mid-1980s as regional players proved themselves worthy opponents in the snack food industry, Frito-Lay began to price its products regionally. Whenever the company changed prices, it had to print and distribute new forms. It became unmanageable, and Frito-Lay became inefficient at doing what it had done so well for so long.

Automating the Sales Process

The first-generation handheld device that Frito-Lay used for sales processing was a lightweight, portable computer that could be used for order entry, route sales accounting, and sales ticket generation. It also kept track of inventory for the route salesperson.

How does this work? When reporting to one of the company's distribution centers, a Frito-Lay salesperson inserts the handheld unit into a cradle, which then sends data to the mainframe at headquarters. Information on customers, products, promotions, and sales routes are downloaded from the server, and new orders, sales tickets, and daily reports are uploaded. An uploading-downloading session usually takes two to three minutes.

Direct EXchange Commerce System

A typical DSD system produces thousands of invoices daily, with numerous line items and totals ranging anywhere from a few dollars to thousands of dollars. The volume of transactions poses data accuracy problems if not properly automated.

To solve this problem, Frito-Lay has tried to improve information exchange with retailers through Direct Exchange (DEX). DEX is defined as the electronic exchange of information between a vendor's handheld computer and a store's DSD system.[11]

DEX offers a way to automate check-in and synchronize data. Many retailers use the document that is generated by their receiving system as proof of delivery; however, with DEX, invoice details are immediately entered into the retailer's receiving system. The receiving system sends the invoice details to its accounts payable system for payment. Statements or invoices become unnecessary.

Since DEX eliminates a significant amount of paper for retailers, they tend to offer suppliers incentives for DEX participation. Some of the common incentives include honor check-in or case check-in and priority check-in over non-DEX vendors.

The ROI of DEX is considerable. Saving an hour or even a half-hour in verifying delivery-related transactions can result in sizable dollar savings. Solutions such as DEX are critical innovations that help streamline the DSD process. Otherwise, simply automating the front-end interactions with handheld computers will result in minimal efficiency gains.

Entitiy	Benefits of DEX for the Partners
Retailer	▪ Closes the loop for inventory management ▪ Provides opportunities for administrative cost savings
Joint (retailer and supplier)	▪ Shortens check-in time ▪ Enables electronic billing and remittance ▪ Reduces chargebacks for unauthorized items
Supplier	▪ Decreases sales ticket errors ▪ Avoids manual data entry into DSD system

Table 7.3: Benefits of Direct Exchange in DSD

Case Study: Earthgrains and DSD

Earthgrains is one of the leading manufacturers and marketers of fresh packaged bread and baked goods in the United States and Europe. Earthgrains, an SAP customer, has proven itself quite adept at using DSD to optimize sales and distribute products with low shelf lives.

The following Earthgrains case study illustrates the concept of scan-based trading (SBT), which in many retail circles is seen as the next generation of the DSD concept.[12]

Company Overview

The Earthgrains Company of St. Louis, Missouri, was established in 1925 as Campbell Taggart. In 1982, Anheuser-Busch acquired the publicly traded company and made it a company division. In February 1996, a month before Anheuser-Busch spun off the company once known as Campbell Taggart, it changed its name to Earthgrains.

After 1996, Earthgrains was busy transforming itself into one of the most profitable and fastest-growing wholesale baking companies in the industry. It expanded by making acquisitions and developing its product portfolio in the premium and superpremium bread segments to augment its lineup of popular breads and other bakery products sold under leading brand names such as Earth Grains and IronKids.

In July 2001, Sara Lee acquired Earthgrains for $2.8 billion.[13] With the acquisition, Sara Lee more than quadrupled its annual bakery sales to become the nation's second-largest packaged bread company, and gained a strong distribution system to extend its Sara Lee brand franchise. The new division is called Sara Lee Bakery.[14]

Earthgrains and SAP

The bakery products business is highly competitive, particularly in the areas of price, product, and service. Companies in this industry strive to separate themselves from their peers through product quality, price, brand loyalty, effective promotional activities, and the ability to identify and satisfy emerging consumer preferences. Customer service, including frequency of deliveries and maintenance of fully stocked shelves, is an important differentiator and a crucial factor in how much retail shelf space fresh-baked goods manufacturers are granted.

The competitive nature of the business means that the industry is often an early adopter in terms of information technology innovation. Market leader Earthgrains has built an industry-leading DSD model through the development and use of state-of-the-art information technology.

Earthgrains successfully implemented SAP with the rollout of the first modules in 1996. Earthgrains installed SAP because it could help the company better manage the business from both a control and an administrative standpoint. Over the years, Earthgrains used SAP and other IT links with retailers to help it manage the bakery category and to take costs out of the system. Specifically, Earthgrains became a leader in category management through proprietary ordering and assorting software that ensures unique customer needs are met.

Category Management and Mobile Direct Store Delivery

On the sales and distribution side, Earthgrains uses handheld computers to get the right product to the right location at the right time. Distributing fresh packaged bakery products involves determining appropriate order levels, transporting the product from the production facility to the customer using DSD, stocking the product on the shelves, visiting the customer daily to ensure that inventory levels remain adequate, and removing stale goods.

Through mobile handhelds, the company is able to track and monitor sales and shelf inventories more actively. The fresh packaged bakery industry relies on mobile handhelds to provide information that allows companies to make and distribute products capably and resourcefully.

The handheld computers accompany Earthgrain's employees on over 5,000 company-owned routes. The routes span a range of customers in multiple distribution channels where bakery products are sold, including traditional supermarkets and their in-store delis or bakeries, foodservice distributors, convenience stores, mass merchandisers, club stores, wholesalers, restaurants, fast food outlets, schools, hospitals, and vending machines.

In summary, mobile handhelds have helped Earthgrain's sales representatives take orders at customer locations, automatically update their route books, and access product and account information, thereby improving customer service. Prior to automation, sales representatives would have to phone and transmit orders to the office via other one-way communication devices. Now information updates are performed at the beginning of each workday.

Scan-Based Trading — The Next Generation of DSD

At Earthgrains, the mobile DSD projects constituted part of two major ongoing initiatives — vendor-managed inventory and scan-based trading. These two initiatives have sought to allow Earthgrains to exchange information with customers, eliminate administrative costs, and obtain current information to manage the shelf and the fresh product that consumers want.

An innovative use of technology, scan-based trading facilitates trade between DSD grocery suppliers and retailers. Typically, retailers pay for the DSD supplier's products after they are scanned through the store's front register, rather than when they are delivered to the retailer's back door. The supplier retains ownership of the product up until the point of sale, and the back-door receiving process is eliminated.[15]

Scan-based trading has lowered costs for retailers and suppliers and increased supply chain efficiencies. Retailers can shift their time from promotions and cost changes to category planning systems and better customer service. Suppliers can deliver their product whenever the store is open. Figure 7.3 illustrates the differences between DSD and scan-based trading.

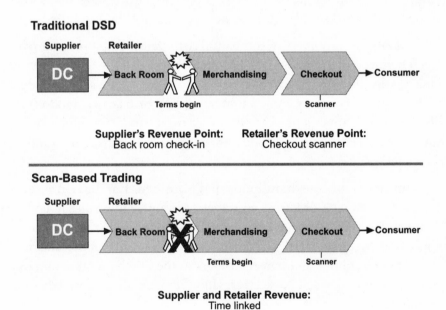

Figure 7.3: Differences Between DSD and Scan-Based Trading

With scan-based trading, the supplier counts the stock in the store, and the retailer reports product sales. The key to successful scan-based trading in theory is that trading partners jointly share all the product movement and inventory data on a routine (sometimes daily) basis. Retailers and DSD suppliers synchronize pricing, promotions, sales, inventories, invoices, and other data via the Internet. This sharing of data also keeps both parties aware of the shrinkage. Since the price of the product is predetermined, the invoice for the goods is the number of units sold times the price, added to the agreed upon shrinkage cost.

The industry's current approach to scan-based trading is the work of the Grocery Manufacturers of America's DSD committee, which was formed to improve upon the route accounting process. After much review, the GMA's committee suggested a new approach: supply stores with product and pay the suppliers when the consumers purchase the goods. It was an idea that they called scan-based trading. To determine the viability of scan-based trading, the committee has conducted studies that tested the possibility of:

- Eliminating back-room receiving so vendors could deliver products whenever a store is open,

- Establishing a paperless flow of scan-based information in order to get rid of invoice discrepancies, bill backs, and large amounts of paperwork, and

- Utilizing a perpetual inventory system so each store could replenish products based on sales of that product.

According to the GMA, the findings of the first study (1996) were positive. Sales rose 2.9% compared to control stores, and shrink averaged 0.5%. Moreover, eliminating back-door check-in saved the retailer 20 minutes and suppliers 30 minutes per delivery.

However, because price data was not synchronized between the retailer and its suppliers, invoice discrepancies persisted, and the number of unauthorized products delivered rose (because of the elimination of back-room check-in), underlining the importance of tighter synchronization of products, price lists, and promotional calendars.

Incorporating mobile devices into DSD should decrease invoice discrepancies and reduce back-door check-in time.

Creating Your DSD Strategy

Now that you seen what best-practice firms Frito-Lay and Earthgrains (Sara Lee) have done with mobile DSD, let's look at how to create a DSD strategy for your organization.

A robust business case is your best weapon for overcoming internal reluctance and the naysayers who say things like "We know it is good for us but..." or "Yeah, it might be a good thing for the other firms, but we are different."

To develop a DSD strategy, you have to start by asking yourself the following questions:

- What is my current process?

- What do I want my next-state DSD process to be?

- How do I get from the current state to the next state?

- What mobile investments should I be making?

- What is the expected ROI of making these investments?

Many DSD projects owe their success to the IT and business project teams who conduct extensive analyses of route operations and determine exactly what is needed from their hardware and software.

Assess Your Current DSD Process

The first step in developing any strategy, DSD included, is to study the current processes in place, which helps to establish a baseline for any improvement efforts.

Most companies execute DSD in the following fashion: Each morning, often well before dawn, drivers arrive at a local distribution center or warehouse. They pick up a rugged handheld computer and log in with a PIN code. The drivers place the device into a cradle to download that day's route, inventory, and pricing information — a process that may take 2–10 minutes per person (longer if there are 50 or more drivers sharing a small number of cradles at each warehouse). While waiting for their turn or for the information to download into the device, drivers remain idle and unproductive. Next, they head to the truck, where they count their load to be sure the proper inventory is aboard for that day's deliveries. Then they hit the road to make their rounds.

While making the rounds, route drivers arrive at retail locations and review orders with customers. Customers preview invoices before approving them. To accept, the customer may even sign on the handheld's screen using a pen stylus. At each store, drivers count by hand and unload the prescribed number of units ordered and accept any returns. The driver keys this information into the handheld device, confirming the delivery. An immediate invoice may be printed out as well.

In large retail operations, the handheld device may be physically cabled to a special data exchange computer in the back of the store in order to electronically invoice the store. If another company's delivery person is already there, the driver needs to wait his turn.

In smaller operations, like a local delicatessen or convenience store, which may be a single-store, cash-and-carry account, the driver must collect cash or credit card payments. Again, all information about each stop needs to be manually entered into the handheld device to ensure proper accounting of billing and payments.

At the close of the day, the handheld device is returned to its cradle, where the accumulated, or batched, route data is uploaded to the consumer packaged goods company's inventory and ordering systems. At this point, the master distribution control software can begin the process of figuring out the final order or route adjustments to make for the next day. The next morning, the daily ritual of drivers queuing up at the syncing cradles repeats itself again.

Improving Direct Store Delivery with Wireless

Once you understand the current DSD process, it's time to analyze it for areas of improvement, such as streamlining the flow of information and minimizing the number of hand-offs or repetitive data entry.

Wireless Connectivity Driven Improvements

One common bottleneck in the process described above is the driver queue at the start and end of the day. It turns out that wireless local area networks (WLANs) can easily eliminate this problem. In the new scenario, the handheld computers can either be left in the vehicle cradle in the truck each night or they can be brought into the depot for storage and recharging. Drivers simply get into their truck or pick up a recharging handheld and key in their PIN numbers as usual, but now the day's information is transmitted wirelessly to the handheld, whether it's inside the warehouse or in the driver's hand while he is inspecting his daily load. The morning lineup becomes a thing of the past.

One properly positioned WLAN access point can support the upload and download of information to 100 or more handheld devices. If companies opt to still use the centralized cradles inside the warehouse, they can be less expensive "recharge-only" cradles, since they no longer need to provide for data communications. The WLAN technology quickly pays for itself in terms of time and equipment savings.

With the lineup problem erased from the shift, the total time savings can easily add up to an extra delivery stop per day per driver. Since many drivers are compensated for sales, they can use the extra minutes to cross-sell and up-sell. A few extra minutes a day can be converted into larger orders for existing products as well.

Wireless has the potential to eliminate the time-consuming electronic invoicing, or DEX, process. Instead of lining up to plug in a DEX cable for invoicing at each store, wireless can streamline the information transfer. Since the majority of large retailers have WLANs in place for their own inventory tracking and other productivity-enhancing applications, it is possible to transmit these invoices directly to store applications from the handheld. Access agreements are being developed to support this capability in major chains.

Cash collection and credit authentication are two other parts of the route accounting process that wireless connectivity simplifies — this time via GPRS and 3G networks. The available connectivity makes it possible for route drivers to obtain credit authentication from their handheld devices after swiping customer credit cards through readers mounted directly on the handhelds or in the trucks. This process speeds up cash collection and minimizes billing issues, should there be a problem with the payment.

Handheld and Mobile Infrastructure Improvements

The new handhelds deliver tremendous computing power, while conserving battery power; therefore, far better software solutions with greater ease of use and improved navigation can now be delivered. For instance, with a few clicks, the driver views a list of all visits, and for each one either performs the necessary activities — sale, delivery, invoice issuing, cash collection — or updates the customer's status with a reason code indicating why the visit could not be performed, such as the customer store is closed. The driver also can rearrange the order of the visits and create new unplanned visits.

In the past, DSD devices had small, black and white screens and ran closed, proprietary operating systems and single-vendor software. This was great for the handheld vendor because consumer packaged goods companies were tightly tied to that single vendor once they made their initial selection.

There was little incentive for hardware and software prices to decline over time in this scenario, and some vendors took advantage of the situation. All this has changed recently. CIOs are demanding a switch to more open industry-standard platforms to allow for greater flexibility in choosing hardware and software vendors.

Handheld designs with options such as high-resolution color screens and integrated bar code scanners can also improve the overall process. Bar code scanning capabilities eliminate hand counting entirely and ensure far greater accuracy. Some new handheld devices even incorporate image capture capabilities. Imagine snapping images of the competition's new package or display designs to send back for analysis.

Reliability Improvements and Better End-to-End Integration

Cutting-edge technology is not enough. Every element of the infrastructure needs to function in an integrated fashion. For instance, using the DSD capability for high-rate order taking, sales and delivery professionals can enter orders into handhelds and then seamlessly upload the orders into a main order log in the ERP back end. The orders are then routed to the warehouse management system for picking, packing, and loading and dispatched onto the trucks in order to be delivered according to customer-specified periodic delivery cycles.

Another critical improvement related to mobile DSD is reliability. Distributors and manufacturers are not going to deploy handhelds until the technology is mature and stable enough to be supported by a small IT staff.

Since the DSD system is replacing paper, it has to be fault-tolerant, as fault-tolerant as paper. Paper is never going to fail, unless pencils or pens are broken or unavailable. Paper doesn't run out of batteries or stop working because a system goes down, and it's great for disaster recovery.

The ROI

The tangible ROI for DSD investments comes from the following:

- Cutting down on the use of paper,

- Minimizing staff, and

- Eliminating data transfer errors.

The intangible ROI, which is harder to measure, comes from the typical results of eliminating the process inefficiencies. For example, sales revenues could grow since salespeople would spend less time on administrative work and more time with their customers.

The strategic ROI comes from the ability to use the data for decision making. Imagine a complex distribution chain for a typical Fortune 1000 company with a direct salesforce and several hundred distributors that sell to tens of thousands of stores. That's a lot of detailed data.

Today, with DSD applications, it is possible to know what was actually sold to a store by stock-keeping unit (SKU). Companies can monitor and track promotion and service activity at any level. This level of insight enables companies to better plan and forecast demand.

Summary

"During my eighty-seven years I have witnessed a whole succession of technological revolutions. But none of them has done away with the need for character in the individual or the ability to think."

— Bernard Mannes Baruch, American stockbroker, public official, and political advisor

One of the most ubiquitous business processes benefiting from mobile technology is route accounting or DSD — that is, the regular delivery of a vast array of fast-moving consumer packaged goods (CPG) to global retail stores.

DSD has gained prominence in recent years for streamlining shelf assortment and replenishment of high-turnover and perishable products in the retail industry. Soft drinks, beer, bottled water, potato chips, bread, cigarettes, magazines, and newspapers all have to be sold, delivered, and accounted for, often on a daily basis. Today, a sizable percentage of CPG companies depend on handheld computers to keep track of their global operations.

As outlined in this chapter, DSD simply refers to the processes required for a delivery representative to service multiple customers within a day's route (or tour). The delivery personnel represent a vital, customer-facing extension of the modern manufacturing and distribution enterprise.

Increasingly, the delivery personnel are being asked to do three things in the context of the DSD business process to keep customers satisfied:

- Ensure that deliveries arrive on time. While the typical route or tour often consists of deliveries to a set of customers, significant variability can occur. Eliminating this variability is critical.

- Solve customer order problems as they arise. Customers might adjust delivery quantities unexpectedly, resulting in incongruities between ordered amounts and delivered amounts.

- Perform sales, merchandizing, and field audits in addition to delivery.

These requirements call for on-demand, remote access to customer data, account information, and enterprise application functionality. As we outlined in this chapter, mobile DSD can help meet these information and functionality needs.

Clearly, we at the beginning of a huge business process upgrade cycle. Companies are poised to leverage powerful mobile applications capable of tracking everything that happens in the course of a day's delivery tour. With the dramatic advancement of today's wireless handhelds, a new batch of sophisticated systems is ready to be unleashed.

Chapter Eight

Mobilizing Sales and Marketing

Name a single industrial products, consumer goods, pharmaceutical, or medical products manufacturer that doesn't have a field sales operation. For many industries, field sales is the critical revenue engine that keeps business running, so supporting and enhancing the processes surrounding field sales is mission-critical. In this chapter, we examine the different facets of mobilizing field sales solutions and address the question of what it takes for a mobile sales initiative to be successful. We will illustrate the key ideas behind mobilizing sales via two case studies: a global pharmaceutical company we call PharmaCo and TÜV Nord Group.

Introduction

In 2003, Michelin, the international tire company, snapped up more than 500 Palm Tungsten handhelds for its commercial fleet salesforce. When they perform tire inspections at customer locations, sales consultants now have a device that can store the collected data. Information such as tire wear, age, and mileage is recorded, analyzed, and sent to commercial customers in order to provide them with current, reliable knowledge on Michelin tire performance.

The business value for Michelin is found in the now paperless tire-inspection processes and in a product development team that is better informed on tire performance. The data gathered by the roving salesforce is centrally stored and shared within the Michelin extended enterprise (commercial tire dealers and the Michelin and fleet service departments).[1]

Fast-moving salespeople depend on access to relevant information and using that time-sensitive information to their advantage. Top-performing field salespeople are always eager to learn about sales leads, account details, contracts, quotes, product pricing, and inventory figures as soon as new information becomes available. They constantly ask themselves the following questions: What do I need to do today to close the sale? What does my pipeline look like? Where am I against my quota? What information does this long-standing customer need to buy more? What issues do my customers have, and what are we doing about them?

As sales, marketing, and service processes become more enmeshed, sales and marketing professionals in the field are assuming a front-line role in customer relationship management. They require anytime, anywhere access to critical customer account and product information to keep customers happy, close more deals, and grow revenues faster and more profitably. They seek less paperwork and speedier transactions.

In order to understand the future of field sales, it is important to assess the current state. Today, with the widespread adoption of CRM, sales personnel at many companies have access to a sophisticated customer management system running on their desktop PCs. Once they leave their desk, however, they still have to keep track of their sales contacts using pen and paper. This is inefficient. It means that information has to be entered twice: first by hand in the field and then into the back-end system on the desktop when they get back to the office.

Best-practice firms are solving the problem of keeping the field sales and marketing staff fully connected by establishing handheld systems and processes for recording, tracking, and sharing information about sales opportunities, leads, and forecasts, as well as the sales process and closed business. They are deploying mobile solutions that can do the following:

- Automate manual tasks and provide access to current and prospective customer knowledge at the point of customer contact, thereby improving the effectiveness of the sales pitch.

- Replace paper-based systems with interactive forms, which results in faster information exchange and a more efficient operation.

- Supply the information necessary to respond to customer queries about products, quotes, pricing, and order status. Salespeople who can instantly answer customer questions stand a good chance of boosting customer satisfaction.

- Streamline and automate repetitive tasks, a functionality that allows employees to focus on generating revenues rather than on procedures and can lead to more satisfied employees.

These mobile sales solutions work on a wide variety of mobile devices, including the RIM BlackBerry, Pocket PC, mobile Linux, and Palm PDA devices and smart phones.

The connectivity infrastructure between the mobile device and the back-office applications situated behind the corporate firewall greatly influences the capabilities of the mobile sales application.

Why Field Sales Investments? Why Now?

Despite all the investments in enterprise applications, many sales interactions in the field occur with the help of pen and paper. The sphere of influence of CRM is mostly limited to the four walls of the enterprise. The minute the salespeople walk out the door to visit customers, they rely on low-tech pen and paper or spreadsheets.

The problems with the manual ways of doing things are several: 1) they're slow; 2) they impede productivity; and 3) they are prone to errors. Every customer interaction with a paper-based model is a point where you can see process variation and the potential for errors to propagate.

The possibility of leveraging existing CRM and salesforce automation (SFA) investments is motivating companies to allot money for high-tech and high-touch mobile field sales. The best CRM system in the world does no good if few salespeople are in the office to use it.

The ROI of any enterprise software directly correlates to the number of users. Low salesforce adoption hinders many organizations that hope to realize a return on their CRM and SFA investments. In many organizations, access to valuable CRM tools is restricted to the desktop, thus limiting their value for the highly mobile salesforces that exist today.

One indication of a successful CRM initiative is real usage to drive revenue growth. By giving field sales professionals customized access to time-critical information through handheld devices, leading companies are seeing CRM adoption rise.

As a result, every company is trying to achieve the same objective: give the salesforce access to vital information in the CRM application anytime, anywhere. The competitive environment is also forcing companies to provide the right sales tools and pipeline visibility to make the field salesforce more efficient and effective.

It does not take a genius to realize that a high-touch mobile salesforce needs access to multiple applications — SFA, CRM, ERP, and SCM. These apps contain data that can be invaluable to closing sales and maintaining customer relationships. For instance, to quote a price, it is common for a salesperson to extract data from multiple systems and integrate the responses before sending the quote to the customer.

The bottom line: Consistent, reliable data is the backbone of mobile sales. It does not matter what CRM application you have; it is how you use it in the field that counts. A mobile sales solution offers an excellent way to lift the ROI of existing enterprise software.

Typical Field Sales Scenarios

Examining field sales scenarios in the consumer packaged goods, industrial products, and life sciences industries sheds light on the needs of the mobile salesforce.

Field Sales in the Consumer Packaged Goods Industry

The consumer packaged goods (CPG) industry is mobile by nature, but even in this fast-paced industry, sales representatives were kept informed through printed product data sheets and inventory lists until recently. Since the distribution business constantly changes, printed materials became outdated as soon as they were delivered.

A large beverage distributor with an extensive salesforce that frequently visited its outlets and sales channels, keeping a close eye on existing business and looking for new revenue sources, typified the state of the industry before mobile sales. While on the road, the sales representatives could not transmit customer orders immediately, which led to delays in order entry and fulfillment.

The distributor realized that it desperately needed a more modern technology infrastructure to enable the nationwide sales team to complete an array of customer transactions onsite. These transactions included order taking, offering discounts and promotions, managing contracts, compiling customer profile information, and producing and dispatching invoices in a mobile environment.

Automating onsite transactions also yielded back-end benefits. The mobile sales solution helped optimize manufacturing planning and supply chain processes based on actual customer demand. In the distribution industry, mobile sales solutions have created a ripple effect for optimizing the entire manufacturing and fulfillment chain.

Field Sales in the Industrial and Heavy Equipment Industries

The industrial products industry is quite competitive. With salesforces generally away from the office, keeping them informed of hot sales and inventory levels is a constant challenge.

To address this issue, many industrial manufacturing companies are dismissing the days of manual order entry and tracking in favor of providing salespeople with interactive access to back-end systems using handheld devices.

With the new system, sales reps can input and retrieve key information through their PDAs while in the field on sales calls, regardless of connectivity. Key functionality that industrial manufacturing companies look for includes:

- Sales tools to track and manage opportunities, accounts, contacts, sales leads, calendars, and action items;

- A quote capability that allows sales reps to map solutions to customer needs by presenting what-if scenarios to achieve the optimal terms and conditions of the sale;

- Personalized and fully integrated pipeline management to build and manage sales opportunities by leveraging tools like real-time customer lifetime value analysis and customer scoring; [2]

- Up-to-the-minute intelligence about customers, prospects, and competitors. This flow can be bidirectional where salespeople collect survey data using Adobe interactive forms, for example; and

- An expense reporting tool that automatically prepares reports with the click of a single button.

The expected ROI from mobile solutions for industrial product sales includes improved employee productivity, shortened sales cycles, and increased visibility into the sales process.

Field Sales in the Healthcare and Life Sciences Industries

The healthcare and life sciences industries are made up of pharmaceutical, medical products, and biotech companies that survive by selling products to the healthcare sector.

In the pharmaceutical industry, the primary sales channel for prescription drugs is the physician, so companies strive to educate the physician about their latest products in order to become the prescription of choice. They do this by sending sales and marketing representatives to meet physicians to talk about the drugs and leave behind samples and brochures — a process known as detailing in the industry.[3]

So what is the business problem? Since detailing is a mechanism by which companies gain market share, the doctor's office is a battleground in the pharmaceutical industry. A sizable percentage of pharmaceutical marketing budgets are spent on salesforce effectiveness.

The detailing process is reaching a point of diminishing returns as mushrooming armies of salespeople compete over dwindling access to physicians — sending the cost of sales through the roof. Each day, pharmaceutical companies find it more difficult to differentiate themselves, build relationships with physicians, and influence them to drive adoption and sales. The goal of mobile sales solutions is to drive market share while improving productivity and lowering sales costs.

What is the solution? Since the sales reps get only a few moments with physicians, they have to be extremely organized throughout the entire call to have maximum impact. A new breed of mobile sales solutions customized to the needs of pharmaceutical sales reps offers an improved foundation for building better relationships with physicians.

Figure 8.1 illustrates the range of tasks that mobile detailing solutions must cover. The solution requirements are clear: convenient, easy to use, and efficient. The successful solutions must make better use of sales reps' time by offering them a comprehensive view of the company-physician relationship, easier access to the information they need to be prepared for their sales calls, and other productivity tools.

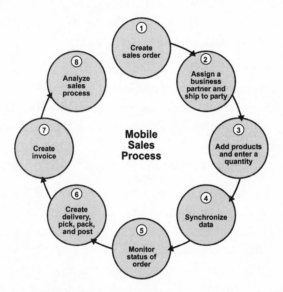

Figure 8.1: Mobile Detailing in the Pharmaceutical Industry

From an ROI standpoint, mobile detailing solutions can also boost CRM system adoption by more quickly and accurately capturing and updating critical call reporting information, giving management the power to see what is actually happening in the field.

A Typical Mobile Sales Scenario

Marcia is an account executive for a multinational industrial systems manufacturer. On average, she visits 14 customers per week, generating around $3 million in annual revenues for her company.

The Sales Scenario Before Mobile

Marcia starts her day with a sales call to an existing customer that she just acquired through a merger. Having reviewed yesterday's printout of the account profile, pending orders, and support history, she feels sufficiently knowledgeable about the new customer and dials.

Once on the phone, Marcia is totally unprepared for the customer's anger over an order that was supposed to have arrived two days ago. The delay has put the company behind schedule, and the customer wants to know when he will receive his order. Marcia is not aware of the missed shipment date, nor is she able to provide an immediate answer as to a new delivery date. She places a call to the factory, leaves a message, and tells the customer she will get back to him as soon as she gets a response.

Marcia's next meeting is with a customer that she hopes will place an order today, the last day of the third quarter. The customer surprises her by doubling the order size. He asks for a revised quote so that he can enter the purchase order into his company's SAP financial system. Marcia has no way to create a quote onsite. She takes all the changes down and rushes back to the office to create the quote and update her sales forecast.

While Marcia is creating the new quote, she receives an urgent e-mail from a customer whose equipment has failed and needs a field engineer dispatched immediately. Marcia is unable to reach any of the engineers supporting her region and leaves messages for all. Several hours will elapse between now and the time an engineer who understands the application is able to ascertain what exactly went wrong. Then the engineer will need to download the technical history on the equipment in question and perhaps the technical manuals as well. This amounts to almost a day's turnaround to get an engineer to the site.

Marcia calls the customer back to tell him that it will be Monday before there will be a field engineer available who can visit the site. The incensed customer threatens to cancel a pending order. Marcia placates him by offering a large discount on his next order for the inconvenience caused.

The Scenario After Mobile Sales

After hearing about the problems salespeople routinely faced, Marcia's IT department decided after due diligence to roll out a mobile sales solution. The IT staff wanted to make sure that salespeople had at their fingertips up-to-date customer information, order status, price query and quote generation, and dispatching and technical information.

Marcia and the field engineers now are equipped with handhelds running applications enabled for mobility, and Marcia's much improved day goes something like this:

- Much better prepared when she arrives at customer sites, Marcia has eliminated most unpleasant surprises, like missed ship dates, from her day. She updates sales forecasts and customer contact information on the fly and synchronizes whenever she is connected to the Internet.

- Her customers are happy when she retrieves order status and shipping information and creates price quotes onsite. Phrases like "I'll have to get back to you on that" are gone from her vocabulary. Buy decisions can now be made at the point of customer contact.

- Engineer status and availability are at her fingertips. Their updated schedules are available in real time.

This is an example of a sales scenario where a cumbersome set of sales tasks were transformed by the implementation of a mobile sales solution.

Elements of a Mobile Field Sales Solution

As the sales representative starts his day, either from home, the office, or on the road, he can review his business and personal activities at a glance and receive alerts and reminders throughout the day.

While on the move, he can prepare for customer calls and stay on top of things with access to e-mails, customer histories, and contacts. As he meets with customers, he notes new information such as contacts, orders, and follow-up activities. Throughout the sales process, the mobile field sales application supports the sales methodology and best practices, and makes it easy to enforce them.

The functionality that is available on mobile devices, like that of the hypothetical sales rep we just discussed, varies considerably depending on the industry and situation. The following key mobile sales capabilities may be included on a device:

- **Order management** — manages all the data collected from the first customer contact to the most recent order. Sales staff can access data from quotations, contracts, orders, availability, open purchase orders, and sales history at their desktops or on laptops. Orders entered offline at the customer site are uploaded to the main system for additional processing, guaranteeing that sales reps always have the latest status information concerning orders.

- **Sales planning and forecasting** — supports analysis and reporting of all planning and forecasting information. These critical capabilities paint a complete picture of estimated revenues and product quantities over time, ensuring accurate plans and forecasts.

- **Account and contact management** — enables companies to capture, monitor, store, and track all critical information on customers, prospects, and partners. This information includes detailed profiles, sales activities, and overviews of critical relationships. It allows users to quickly retrieve account information such as complete customer interaction histories.

- **Activity management** — lets sales professionals schedule and manage tasks, reducing sales times and increasing productivity. Activity management is responsible for capturing and accessing every customer activity, including all communication transactions, such as appointments, dates, telephone calls, e-mails, letters, and meetings.

- **Campaign management** — gives field sales professionals the ability to track, measure, and execute the results of marketing or sales campaigns. Mobile users can also define, plan, and execute their own unique campaign offerings or product launches across multiple communication channels, including direct sales, call centers, mail, e-mail, Internet, and mobile devices.

- **Opportunity management** — gives professionals complete visibility into each prospective sale. The goal is to make it easy to capture, manage, and monitor the business contact and account information of potential opportunities including identifying the main decision makers, sales histories, milestones, progress, outbound activities, and internal tasks.

- **Quotations** — handles the data required to generate quotes so field sales reps know that quotes are always consistent and complete. They can even configure quotations to meet specific needs.

- **Pricing** — enables all sales staff to provide accurate, offline pricing information. With the sales pricing engine, reps have pricing tools at the point of sale and at their fingertips.

- **Configuration** — supplies comprehensive, easy-to-use functions for both single and multilevel sales configurations. It delivers the powerful variant configuration to the laptop, so there's no need for an online connection to the system. It requires no additional maintenance of master data or of interdependencies.

- **Time and travel management** — ensures that field sales personnel adhere to company travel policies. Mobile users can record, review, and update travel information, enter the corresponding receipts, and maintain time sheets.

- **Sales analytics** — helps managers quickly determine the financial status and overall effectiveness of the sales organization. It provides all the data needed to monitor trends proactively and measure customer retention and revenue shortfalls.

The subset of functionality that is implemented in a mobile sales scenario depends on the specific requirements of the organization.

Solution	User Requirements	Characteristics
mySAP CRM Mobile Sales for Handheld (handheld sales)	• Easy-to-handle, lightweight mobile device • Limited function set • Quick access to a limited amount of customer and product data • Simple and not extensive text input • Able to handle small and medium data volume	• Up-to-date, but not always real-time • Network coverage not always available (disconnected scenario) • Integration with back-office applications required

Table 8.1: mySAP CRM Mobile Sales for Handheld

Case Study: TÜV Nord Group

TÜV Nord Group, known throughout Germany for the "TÜV" seal of approval, provides technical, scientific, and safety certification services through its 2,500 mobile technicians. TÜV Nord maintains dual headquarters in Hamburg and Hanover in northern Germany. The company, which was founded in 1869, employs more than 4,000 people and provides services to 250,000 customers.[4]

TÜV Nord serves more than 200 areas through its state-of-the-art measuring and testing equipment and technical experts. TÜV Nord implemented mySAP CRM Mobile Sales and Mobile Service to make its technicians more efficient *and* to transform them into entrepreneurs, in anticipation of the upcoming liberalization of its marketplace.

TÜV Nord's activities are regulated by the state but it is expected that the European Community will open up the marketplace. In anticipation, TÜV Nord implemented mySAP CRM Mobile Sales and Mobile Service to change business processes from those of a monopoly organization to a customer-oriented one.

TÜV Nord's technicians have a reputation for trustworthiness with their customers. The company equipped them with TÜV Mobile Stations — mySAP CRM mobile tools loaded onto laptops and linked to mySAP CRM in the central office — to capitalize on that trust and expand business relationships.

By capturing valuable customer information at the source, the TÜV Mobile Station transforms service engineers and technicians into marketing intelligence gatherers. Transmitted directly from the front end to the back end, this information translates into useful insights.

mySAP CRM Mobile Sales and Mobile Service are linked tightly with TÜV Nord's enterprise SAP solution to enable that cross-sharing of data. That was a key reason for selecting the solution.

According to Gunnar Thaden, TÜV Nord's CIO, "The main reason why salesforce automation and mobile technician projects have not been successful in the past is because of the lack of integration between the back-office system and the mobile application. mySAP CRM offers this close integration. It also provides the CRM functionality we need and straightforward interfaces to other specialized applications our service people use. And it gives us the capability to tailor a mobile CRM solution for multiple tasks and business processes, in areas as diverse as checking cars, inspecting elevators, and qualifying nuclear plants."

TÜV Nord Mobile Stations incorporate tightly integrated mySAP CRM mobile sales and service functionality for customer and prospect management, contact persons, material masters, and calendar tools. Service engineers obtain a comprehensive view of customers, current and historical orders, service contracts, and other relevant information. They also gain the ability to collect crucial customer information about the account, which can be accessed at all touch points. The mobile solution ensures that a reliable, high-quality customer data stream serves as an input to applications like mySAP Business Intelligence.

Solution	User Profile and Requirements	Characteristics
mySAP CRM Mobile Sales (laptop sales)	▪ Professional users who need many features and functions ▪ Solution must work well with large data volumes ▪ Require easy text input	▪ Disconnected for long periods ▪ Information up-to-date, but not real-time ▪ Network coverage not always available ▪ Integration with back office required

Table 8.2: mySAP CRM Mobile Sales

Case Study: PharmaCo

The case of PharmaCo, a major pharmaceutical company, illustrates how the industry is eagerly adopting mobile field sales.

PharmaCo sells its products to wholesaler and distributors, as well as directly to physicians; therefore, the company has several sales channels (field force, specialty field forces, call center, and e-business).[5] In the past, PharmaCo's salesforces worked on separate systems, which required employees to share information and coordinate work for the large client base in an ad hoc, paper-based manner.

Updating client and prospects information with all its complexity and linkages was a nebulous process. For instance, how could a PharmaCo employee know if a physician office belonged to one or several buying groups or was in a relationship with a broader network?

In this context, PharmaCo sought a solution that would consolidate the disparate systems its salesforce was operating on to a common platform that provided an integrated, single view of each customer and contact. In addition to improving overall customer satisfaction, other project goals and objectives included:

- Maximizing the effectiveness of the salesforce by improving teamwork and productivity. The challenge was to eliminate downtime costs due to long stays in waiting rooms as they made their visits to various administrators' and physicians' offices.

- Integrating all users with a common platform and providing "everyone touching a customer with an integrated view of the customer."

- Leveraging existing architecture and technology where possible and integrating the new solution seamlessly with the current environment.

PharmaCo's New Solution

After months of planning, it was decided that the first phase of the project would focus on the following SAP components:

- Customer Interaction Center (CIC),

- Mobile Sales, and

- CRM Enterprise (Marketing [limited functionality in phase one]).

To implement the solution, Capgemini was selected, along with SAP and Biltmore, to implement the SAP CRM solution that would meet PharmaCo's business, data, and technical needs.

Customer Interaction Center

The CIC was selected to replace the existing call center application to provide the "integrated view of the customer" that PharmaCo desired. All inbound and outbound customer interaction, from sales orders to product inquiries, was recorded using Activities within SAP CRM. This ensured that anyone viewing a customer record would have a complete history of PharmaCo's interaction with that customer. The call center screen was then designed to display a customer's complete interaction history, providing the call center representative with the information necessary to provide prompt, accurate service to each customer. Capturing customer interactions with Activities allowed PharmaCo to improve call tracking. Salesforce managers could also access calls by status, helping them with their management and coaching function to optimize the performance of their field sales and call center reps.

Recording all customer interaction with Activities also ensured that all interactions by field sales reps would be captured in a similar manner to those of call center reps. This continuity not only guaranteed that all customer interactions would be visible to both field sales and call center reps, it also improved communication and helped facilitate accurate data capture throughout the salesforce.

Mobile Sales

Mobile sales functionality was deployed on field sales reps' laptops in an initial pilot. Using the activity and calendar functionality within the mobile environment, field sales reps were able to schedule activities for their customers at the beginning of each trimester (every four months).

When detailing customers, representatives would record the visit within the Activity Journal, and update any account changes. The bidirectional replication of this data allowed both salesforce managers and call center reps to see notes and scheduled visits for each account, increasing the collaboration within the salesforce and allowing PharmaCo to present a consistent face to the customer.

Marketing

Marketing functionality was limited to capturing key information on the physician's practice. This information, in addition to geographic and product details, was used to dynamically segment business partners and create target lists for both field sales and call center reps.

With this functionality, salesforce managers could create target lists specific to a customer's product base, a physician's specialty or geographic region, for example, and assign them to specific field sales or call center reps. Managers also used this functionality to collaborate with their salesforce; the common platform allowed field sales and call center reps to create their own target lists and make recommendations to the salesforce managers.

PharmaCo's Technology Architecture

Before pursuing this project, PharmaCo had looked at several options for a field sales tool. The decision to use SAP CRM was based not only on functionality and robustness, but also on the tight integration SAP CRM would have with its existing R/3 instance.

PharmaCo's new infrastructure included the CRM components required for both the Interaction Center and Mobile Sales, and leveraged an already existing investment in Business Warehouse. It should be noted that PharmaCo also committed both time and energy to cleansing the data warehouse prior to the launch of SAP CRM as it recognized that redundant data would reduce the long-term benefits.

ROI and Business Benefits

The system implementation improved the selling team's capabilities, especially in the areas of customer knowledge and collaboration:

- Collaboration between field forces and sales managers with increased quality and relevancy of data shared; and

- Collaboration between salesforces (field, phone, and specialty).

After the implementation, PharmaCo gained the ability to refine targeting and its implications for territory coverage in an efficient manner. The new system also provides the company with a better understanding of key customers' preferred touch points (face to face, phone, and e-business) and can serve as a basis to better serve them and increase their satisfaction.

The successful deployment of SAP CRM 4.0 supplied PharmaCo with the common platform they needed to provide "everyone touching a customer with an integrated view of that customer," meeting both business and technical project goals.

The outcome: PharmaCo's salesforce is more connected and organized. Salesforce managers are now able to communicate and collaborate more effectively and accurately with both the field salesforce and the call center reps. Salesforce managers have a greater insight into the daily tasks and productivity of their reps and can closely monitor their success and provide support when needed.

By consolidating the number of applications needed to perform daily responsibilities, business processes were refined to be more efficient and time-saving. Call center reps and field salesforces have, within a single solution, access to all key information required to effectively do their jobs. They also can be assured that the information they view is the same across sales groups.

In addition to business process efficiencies, the implementation of SAP CRM has benefited PharmaCo's in-house technical staff, who now have fewer applications to maintain. The common SAP platform also allows PharmaCo to cross-train its existing technical resources to manage both front- and back-office applications, providing additional cost savings.

Developing a Strategy for Mobilizing Field Sales

Mobile sales applications executed by workers in the field are business process subsets of larger CRM enterprise applications. A good example is the pharmaceutical sales person who calls on doctors and is responsible for the distribution of samples, the collection of feedback, and efficacy information regarding the effectiveness of a particular drug.

Like pharmaceutical companies, many other organizations in a variety of industries — aerospace and defense, consumer products, and utilities — regard mobilizing their salesforces as a priority. Their objectives are clear. They want to attack four problems that plague field sales operations:

- Limited insight into critical prospect, customer, and product information, as well as contracts and sales documents,

- Failure to capture and save accurate interaction information on customers, prospects, and partners,

- Inability to recognize or effectively address competitive threats or cross-sell and up-sell opportunities, and

- Wasted productivity as reps spend time researching basic contact, contract, and account information instead of selling products.

Addressing these problems requires solutions that can do the following:

- Provide field sales representatives with mobile access to up-to-date customer and account information,

- Establish an easier, more efficient way to manage customer accounts, including activity and opportunity management, and

- Allow managers to view sales orders and perform CRM analytics reporting, giving the business a 360-degree view of its sales pipeline.

Looking at the above list, you could conclude that mobilizing the sales process should be relatively easy. Unfortunately, the reality is that mobilizing sales is anything but easy. Why is there a discrepancy between expectations and actual execution?

The answer is simple. Most organizations don't analyze the sales process carefully enough before they embark on creating and coding a mobile solution. They deploy solutions that are difficult to use, time-consuming to access, and of limited value in the field.

Another reason for the low success rate is misjudging the complexity of sales interactions. Sales is a complex web of activity interrelated with numerous other processes such as quotes, inventory, production, and post-sale support. Streamlining the sales process requires careful analysis of the different tasks that constitute the overall process.

Understanding the current field sales processes is the first step of any mobile sales or CRM strategy.

Mapping the Current Field Sales Process

The initial goal of sales process modeling is to depict what is currently happening in an organization.

- What tasks or activities are involved in accomplishing sales objectives? How do they happen? How frequently do they occur?

- What sales activities are involved in interactions with other applications inside the organization?

- What factors control these activities? What information is needed, and what information is produced?

When you create a sales process model, you can also analyze the difficulty of the activity and whether mobilizing the activity would reduce the time it takes. In short, develop "what if" scenarios. This can help identify tasks that you might be able to mobilize or eliminate in order to streamline the sales processes.

Once you have identified what is currently happening in your organization, you have a baseline that can enable you to optimize and mobilize your current sales practices, respond to changes in the marketplace, and define requirements for new mobile applications.

Now you are ready to map these business process flows and the resulting functional requirements onto the mobile infrastructure technology.

Which Mobile Solution? Connected or Disconnected?

The next step is to decide whether you want to roll out a connected or a disconnected model based on the requirements. As we noted earlier, mobile sales solutions are of two types: connected (always-on or online) and disconnected (sync-based or offline). Which one is right for you?

The connected model is straightforward. It links the salesperson with the enterprise applications as long as the wireless coverage is there. The always-on capability avoids the need to wait for a laptop to start up and connect. The handheld mimics the desktop and serves as a mini-portal into the back-end applications. For a busy salesperson, the connected model has the potential to save many hours per week.

The disconnected model is more involved. Consider the scenario: A sales manager working on a desktop will access a list of leads from an intranet site and assign certain contacts to a salesperson. The next time that salesperson synchronizes the handheld with the desktop, the new contacts are transferred to the mobile sales application running on the handheld. When the reps make sales calls, they capture information about the customer and location using the mobile application. The next time they synchronize, the new data is integrated with the central server, eliminating the need for duplicate keying.

Both the connected and disconnected mobile applications help keep the salesforce apprised of the latest information about customers and prospects. Rather than relying on pen and paper, reps now have current databases full of customers on their handhelds. In addition, the data captured in the field allows managers to develop more effective sales programs because they now have a more up-to-date view of the market.

Most companies in the early 2000s implemented a disconnected model since high-speed coverage was spotty. As 3G spreads, more businesses are turning to the connected sales model.

Expected ROI from Mobile Field Sales

As you prepare to invest in field sales applications, take a moment to contemplate the different sales processes. Analyze the link between the different sales and marketing process metrics listed below with strategic and tactical goals of the organization.

Number of Calls and "Best Value" Calls

If your field sales solution is making your salesforce work more quickly and efficiently, you can expect an increase in the number of sales calls that can be made per salesperson. This is a measurable metric. In addition, a strategic metric exists that is more difficult to measure: the number of "best value" calls. The mobile solutions equip the salesforce with a richer understanding of customer revenue and behavioral patterns that can help them concentrate their sales efforts on the most profitable customers.

Number of Products

If your field sales solution is designed properly, it can increase the ability of the salespeople to cross product lines, business units, and geographies to meet customer needs. The number of quotes given to prospects or products sold per visit is a measurable metric.

Number of Orders

If your salespeople are bogged down by manual order entry, your field sales solution can keep the process humming smoothly by guiding the sales person through the workflow. The average number of orders per month can be measured to demonstrate the mobile solution's value.

Average Size of Order

If a salesperson has access to more information to sell higher-value items, you might expect an increase in the average order size. For example, with a mobile solution a salesperson might be able to explore complex product configurations with the customer. As part of this process, the salesperson can work out the price and the margins of such unusual configurations while in front of the customer.

Number of Up-Sells and Cross-Sells

If your mobile solution includes functionality that enables the salesperson to cross-sell and up-sell across product families, you should consider measuring the number of times a cross-sell or up-sell occurs. This is a complex functionality that depends on the capabilities of the back-end CRM applications to make the correlations between products.

Close Rate

The mobile solution can act as a virtual sales advisor and recommendation assistant that provides context-specific advice through interactive questions and choices to engage customers. This feature can help a salesperson move toward a close. You should measure the rate at which a salesperson is able to close deals. You can expect a bigger change in this metric for low-value products than for high-value items.

Revenue per Salesperson

The goal of every company is to take in more revenues per salesperson, definitely something you should measure. In the short term, it might be difficult to see a difference, but you should see improvement in revenues per salesperson over the long term (six months to a year).

Reduction in Paperwork and Better Data Quality

Mobile field sales solutions should reduce the amount of paperwork required to start, rework, and finish transactions. The benefit of reducing the paperwork is seen in the time the salesperson has for actually selling.

Summary

"There are two ways of being creative. One can sing and dance. Or one can create an environment in which singers and dancers flourish."

— Warren G. Bennis, University of Southern California sociologist

After wireless e-mail and field service, sales is the primary target area for mobile applications. Most sales professionals have to be on the road in front of customers, and extending enterprise applications to these road warriors makes sense.

In this chapter, we discussed how mobile sales solutions for managing time-sensitive and mission-critical tasks are being deployed in different industries. We also illustrated with two case studies the nuances of deploying mobile sales in the pharmaceutical industry versus laptop-based sales applications in TÜV Nord.

Before a mobile sales project can be successful, companies have to determine if they are committed to making the necessary changes in their processes, culture, and technology to achieve a different business result than they realize today.

When it comes to using mobile sales applications effectively, the following tips gleaned from best-practice companies should prove useful:

- **Tip number one:** proactively manage the salesperson's experience by creating tailored role-based experiences that consistently deliver information at the point of need.

- **Tip number two:** transform sales from an art to a science by using advanced mobile tools and techniques to constantly improve the effectiveness of specific interactions and to home in on what works in cross-selling, up-selling, and keeping customers loyal.

- **Tip number three:** be prepared to continuously adjust all sales related processes or risk falling behind as competitors forge ahead.

It's a beginning, not an end. Mobile sales is a new frontier for creating a high-performance sales culture. This approach supports the operational excellence and transformation many sales organizations yearn for but have yet to achieve.

Chapter Nine

Mobilizing Supply Chains

In business, there is limited room for waste or error. Manual data entry errors, delays in accurate inventory counts, and excess paperwork all pose obstacles in the areas of inbound and outbound supply chain management (SCM) — materials handling, warehousing, transportation, and distribution. Mobile applications are rapidly reshaping key functions of SCM and helping organizations improve their operations around the clock. In this chapter, we highlight various supply chain process scenarios that are being mobilized using three best-practice case studies: C&H Sugar, Volkswagen, and UPS.

Introduction

Supply chains are, by definition, a complex chain of processes comprising manufacturing, warehousing, inventory control, planning, shipping, and transportation. That's just the internal processes! Supply chains also encompass relationships with suppliers and partners, and, on the front end, a growing dependence on the input of customers.

Managing the supply chain and logistics means managing a wide range of activities spread over vast geographical regions. Under these circumstances, the sequential flow of information from activity to activity no longer keeps up with the increasingly rapid pace of business. In response, companies are redirecting the flow of information to an alternate path: adaptive networks that provide timely asset visibility into the global logistics pipeline, whether in storage or in transit.

Dell, Toyota, Dow Chemical, and FedEx are market leaders who are proof that supply chains are evolving from fixed "static" models to become extremely fluid "dynamic" models, upping the demand for a constant stream of accurate, real-time information to achieve supply chain success. Mobile technology is the weapon of choice to control and maintain this flow of data. Robust and intuitive, mobile devices are employed today in all areas of supply chain management, from planning and production, to warehousing and transportation. By incorporating vehicle-mount computers, PDAs, scanning and data collection equipment, and handheld computers integrated with back-end information systems, companies can extend the power of enterprise computing to new processes, people, and places.

As the affordability, reliability and bandwidth of mobile technology improves every year, mobile applications' role in supporting fast-moving supply chains is unmistakable. With real-time mobile access to SCM applications, companies can capture important supply chain data, increase "driver and cargo" visibility, manage time-definite delivery "within minutes," and monitor critical supply chain processes, which ensures that decisions do not have to be revised after tasks have been executed.

The quantitative and qualitative value is clear: faster processes, fewer errors, and quicker responses. No matter where they are, supply chain professionals can pull up accurate information on the movement of goods and related events. With simplified checking and monitoring tasks, as well as up-to-date information on process status, the entire supply chain organization can react swiftly to unforeseen events before they cause costly disruptions.

While the vision and value may be clear, how to systematically execute this "mobilizing supply chains" vision is less apparent. In this chapter, we present an overview of the mobile applications in the supply chain. We then dig deeper into the areas that are adopting mobility the fastest: warehouse management, transportation, and distribution management.

We end the chapter with a case study of United Parcel Service (UPS), which has completely integrated mobile applications into different parts of its upstream (pickup) and downstream (delivery) business. It would be safe to say that without mobile applications, UPS would not be the powerhouse it currently is.

To illustrate the current state of many supply chains and warehouses, we open with a case study of a major North American lighting manufacturer that we call American Lighting. See if you can find parallels to this scenario in your own organization.

A Typical Supply Chain Scenario: Warehouse Chaos

American Lighting is one of the world's largest manufacturers of lighting equipment for commercial, industrial, outdoor, and residential applications. It operates 20 manufacturing facilities in the United States, Canada, and Mexico and maintains five distribution centers and a North American network of regional warehouses.

The manufacturer views on-time delivery as its overarching customer service goal. As orders come from the salesforce and customers, they are assigned a ship-by-promise date. The date is critical for construction companies because they use it to schedule expensive, busy electricians at building sites.

Delivery timing is critical. The fixtures cannot arrive too early or too late. Delivery must occur within a very narrow window of the promised date. Early deliveries cause unnecessary storage expenses for the contractor. Late deliveries can threaten building delay because electricians and installers don't wait; they move to the next available job.

The Current State of Warehouse Order Fulfillment

American Lighting's legacy-based, paper-driven system for managing warehouse order fulfillment was sadly outdated. The system was aging and suffered from much inefficiency that mobile technology could address. The legacy system process involved two parts: a putaway process and a picking process.

As stock arrived from the manufacturing facilities, forklift operators would unload the truck and search for open racks within a stadium-sized distribution center. Once the operator found an open location, he would remove a portion of the pallet ticket and handwrite the location. These handwritten "put" tickets were periodically given to a dispatch clerk who would manually enter the location information into a legacy order management system.

Problems with Warehouse Order Fulfillment

The information integrity of this process was poor. Tickets were lost, the location incorrectly entered or written, and even if everything worked correctly, the warehouse was filled randomly. This seriously affected the order fulfillment, or picking, process.

The picking process began when a bill of lading was printed and physically handed to a forklift operator. On the bill of lading was the rack information for each fixture in the order. The operator would then fulfill the order line by line, traveling to each rack location on the forklift.

Because the putting process was random, the distance traveled to fulfill an order was quite large. It was common for operators to traverse the length of the distribution center for any given order. Once there, operators often found that the rack contained the wrong fixtures. The operator would then radio a dispatch operator who would manually search the information system for an alternate location.

Sherlock Holmes to the Rescue

Hard to believe, but this system worked. A handful of colorful specialists who could troubleshoot the process quite well kept the system intact.

In fact, one gentleman, a 25-year veteran at one of the company's largest distribution centers, was simply known by the nickname "Sherlock Holmes." It seems that Sherlock had found his niche in life by being able to remember the locations of fixtures throughout the dynamically changing warehouse space.

When fixtures were reported missing, Sherlock was called over the radio to assist in locating them. With amazing speed and accuracy, he would locate the fixtures thanks largely to his photographic memory. On any given day, you could see Sherlock racing around the warehouse in his golf cart solving mystery after mystery. The days when Sherlock called in sick, the entire operation came to a standstill, and panic ensued.

Organizing the Chaos with Mobile Warehouse Management

After careful review, management decided that a mobile solution was the answer to improving the haphazard process.

The company decided to outfit each forklift with specialized computers with extensible bar code readers. These computers connect to a back-end information system in a client/server type of arrangement. Operators unloading inbound trucks are directed to the nearest open rack where they use their bar code readers to record the putaway. Location information accuracy and latency have improved astonishingly.

What's more, the warehouse layout can now be optimized for the order fulfillment process because higher velocity items can be placed closer together and thereby reduce travel time. Order fulfillment operators now receive their next order electronically on their mounted mobile device. The line items are arranged sequentially to further minimize the distance traveled to complete the order.

The bottom line: Mobile solutions increased the throughput of American Lighting's warehouse operations enormously. The company has gained a more predictable process for managing warehouse operations.

Mobile Supply Chain Scenarios

Core supply chain functions — planning, warehousing, and exception management — are emerging as targets of improvement for several reasons. First, these functions are the central moneymaking processes for many businesses. Second, they handle paperwork documenting service delivery or change of ownership. Third, they remain relatively untouched by standards-based solutions, in contrast to IT and productivity improvements within the four walls of the enterprise.

The following sections describe some of the ways mobility helps companies create and manage sophisticated supply chains.

Mobile Warehouse Management

Mobile warehouse management enables direct, synchronous communication between handheld mobile units and back-end systems.

At General Motors' Cadillac and Buick assembly plants, forklifts with mounted wireless computers are sighted frequently on the factory and warehouse floors. The computers allow drivers to wirelessly collect and transmit data from their vehicles. The forklift operators can receive work instructions and updates without leaving their vehicles. By enabling this capability, forklift traffic declined by an estimated 400 miles each day. After nine months of usage, operators averaged 60 to 70 deliveries a day, double the number of deliveries they were making before mobile warehouse management entered the picture.[1]

Using radio frequency devices, warehouse personnel can carry out receiving, storage, and shipping tasks more effectively. Accurate, paperless data entry saves time and effort, while real-time inventory controls enable synchronous online monitoring of all stock movements, which maximizes transparency and minimizes error rates.

Mobile warehouse management solutions support tasks such as:

- Unloading, receiving, and putaway,

- Physical inventory and material inquiry,

- Picking, packing, and repacking,

- Shipment loading and goods issue, and

- Mobile printing (for example, pallet labels).

Instantly available information on inventory levels, storage bins, and other critical supply chain resources enables better coordination and reduces flow times.

Mobile Manufacturing

Mobile manufacturing makes sure that shop-floor and top-floor employees can view work instructions on their handhelds anywhere on the factory floor. Users can confirm task completion and collect data, such as output quantities, containers, or batches, with a bar code scanner. Supervisors can monitor production line behavior on the spot by calling up data from process control systems on handheld devices.

With emerging event management and activity monitoring applications, mobile data entries can trigger alerts, notifications, and follow-on activities to keep production rolling. Mobile reporting tools enable factory managers to remotely access the latest production information and make effective management decisions based on real-time data.

Best-in-class manufacturing companies tend to enjoy an advantage of at least 20%–30% over competitors in four key areas: order fill rate and accuracy, work-in-process inventory accuracy, inbound logistics flow through, and compliance with internal company standards. Improvement in these areas drives up production efficiency, which in turn drives customer retention.

Best-in-class companies are using mobile technology to monitor activities, enabling plant managers to spot potential bottlenecks quickly. Mobile process monitoring shows exactly which resources are being used to capacity and which are underutilized. A factory monitoring application can recognize periods of inactivity, determining whether orders have been completed within a set time frame and quickly identifying exceptional situations before they cause supply chain logjams.

Mobile Yard and Transportation Management

Mobile technology can significantly improve onsite verification processes, in-gate access, and out-gate control. It can eliminate time-consuming paper invoices and better match trailers to tractors and drivers.

For instance, with mobile transportation management (MTM), security guards posted at the factory gate can use mobile devices to call up data on incoming vehicles, drivers, weights, and so on. All data on the transportation job, such as loading time and arrival time, can be collected as it occurs and stored directly in SCM applications. The loading time can be recorded by scanning outbound goods as they are placed on trucks. Other information, such as arrival time at an international border or a customer site, can be entered by the forwarder and transmitted via the Internet from an onboard computer or even a cell phone.

MTM also encapsulates fleet management. Take, for instance, trucking company TRL, which is equipping its entire fleet of 600 trucks with wireless tracking and messaging. The company decided to upgrade to a system that automatically switches between land-based and satellite communications without driver or dispatcher intervention. Today, one-third of the companies in the transportation industry use wireless technology, especially fleet-tracking devices.[2]

Mobile Proof of Delivery

This application streamlines the proof-of-delivery process (POD), helping companies manage discrepancies between shipped and received goods and automating the invoice adjustment process. Electronic signature capture provides uncontested proof of shipment acceptance.

Data collected at the point of receiving or shipping increases inventory accuracy and integrity. This is true for both business models: TL — truck load carriers (long haul with few stops) — and LTL — less than load carriers (short haul with multiple stops).

With mobile POD, third-party logistics providers (3PLs) and transport carriers can verify for the supplier that the goods have arrived at the receiving location. They can enter verification dates along with the reasons for any discrepancies. Mobile confirmation functionality adds to the visibility of the entire shipping process and minimizes the need for the shipping and receiving parties to communicate offline.

Mobile Order Tracking

A highly transparent supply network can help companies set themselves apart from competitors through value-added services, such as order tracking and status checking.

Where is my delivery? When will it arrive? With mobile order tracking, all parties in the extended supply chain can see what is happening and respond quickly to contingencies, thereby increasing efficiency and minimizing delays. For instance, real-time transaction data can be used to verify location information.

The detailed data mobile devices gather sheds light on activities across the supply chain. This data can enhance analysis and make it far easier to pinpoint and act on the root cause of delays, bottlenecks, and other glitches. Discovering the root causes of problems helps companies continuously improve logistics processes.

Mobile Warehouse Management Solutions

Today, you easily can separate the best-practice firms from the rest. Simply look at their warehouses. If they don't have wireless warehouse solutions deployed, chances are that they are running an inefficient warehouse and distribution operation.

Every well-run warehouse (or distribution center) is leveraging the power of wireless mobile solutions (rugged handheld and vehicle-mount computers) to meet the needs of fast-moving supply chains, allowing employees to gather, enter, and share data at the point of work.

Wireless warehouse solutions are seen in three areas:

- **Inbound operations.** Inbound operations initiate the inventory handling process (receiving, order management, and putaway).

- **In-plant operations.** Material movement throughout the warehouse, yard, or plant floor is a source of inventory errors. As every movement of material is a potential source of error, a material handling system that improves inventory accuracy is critical.

- **Outbound operations.** Outbound operations such as wave planning, picking, sorting, and replenishment vary widely depending on the type of items selected and shipped.

In all three areas, the goal is simple: A wireless warehouse solution puts real-time order and inventory information at employees' fingertips, from receiving to order selection, picking, loading, and shipping. The objective is to meet delivery demands while reducing operating costs.

For warehouse automation to be effective, it is necessary to integrate the new wireless systems with an existing or new warehouse management application or ERP system, including seamless SAP R/3 integration.

Wireless Warehouse Management at Eli Lilly

Consider the example of Eli Lilly, the pharmaceutical giant. From its Scarborough, Ontario, distribution center, Eli Lilly ships pharmaceuticals and medical devices to 200 wholesale locations and key accounts across Canada. Operating in a highly regulated industry, Eli Lilly sought to replace its inefficient paper-based system with a warehouse management solution integrated with a wireless data communication system.[3]

Eli Lily had specific requirements. It wanted to ensure lot traceability, improve inventory record accuracy, and enhance customer service, while eliminating time-consuming paper procedures. The company wanted a system that provided order fulfillment associates with real-time, online tracking of all products and that met Health Canada's standards.

To implement the solution, Eli Lilly chose a wireless warehouse management solution from SAP's partner Psion Teklogix that delivered increased picking accuracy, higher inventory accuracy, real-time lot tracking, and enhanced customer service.

C & H Sugar: Managing Sugar Production with SAP's Help

C & H Sugar of California processes about 700,000 tons of cane sugar yearly. Its products for the U.S. market include packaged consumer sugars, as well as packaged, liquid, and bulk granulated industrial-use cane sugars. The company, originally the California and Hawaiian Sugar Refining Company, will be celebrating its 100th anniversary in 2006.

C&H Sugar makes more than 250 types, grades, and package configurations of sugar for consumer, food service, and industrial consumption. The company operates a 1,400,000-square-foot refinery and distribution center in Crockett, California, to accommodate its multiple product lines. This facility accounts for roughly 10% of the refined sugar produced annually in the United States.

To manage sugar production more efficiently, C & H Sugar decided to convert its ERP legacy system to SAP ERP in early 2003. It began extending its functionality to include SAP WM later that same year. In the multilevel warehouse, C&H wanted a wireless data collection solution that could improve inventory control and accuracy. The company also intended to transition from a Cobol-based warehouse management system to SAP WM with SAPConsole. Its legacy system provided very little visibility, and many of its business processes were manual.[4]

To execute the transition, the company turned to Catalyst International, a leading supplier of supply chain execution solutions for help.[5] Catalyst used SAPConsole (SAP's native character-based radio frequency (RF) solution designed to translate SAP's GUI screens into character-based screens) to deliver a solution that included:

- Twenty RF-enabled custom data collection transactions such as goods receipt by purchase order, process order confirmation, and pick by shipment, delivery, or group.

- Handheld devices, tethered scanners for forklift operations, and RF data collection devices from Intermec.

- A dual 802.11b wireless infrastructure with 38 access points throughout the warehouse for indoor and outdoor coverage.

- Integration with SAP WM to manage 400 types of finished goods.

C&H's new operation provides up-to-the-minute inventory information for better decision making. Its long-term goal is to use mobile technology to increase visibility and inventory accuracy, reduce errors and re-work, and simplify the materials routing processes.

Many companies are following C&H Sugar's example and are using SAPConsole depicted in Figure 9.1 to get real-time connectivity to SAP functionality without purchasing additional middleware.[6]

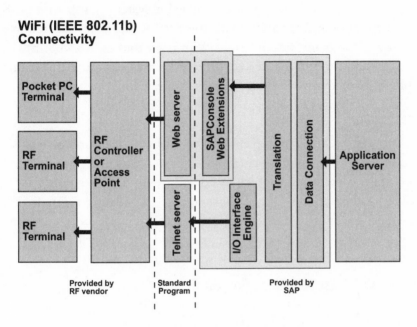

Figure 9.1: Architecture of SAPConsole

Mobilizing Volkswagen's Original Parts Center

Since cars invariably break down at some inconvenient point in their lifetimes, fast, efficient service is critical to keeping drivers happy. Volkswagen's Original Parts Center (OPC) in Kassel, Germany, Europe's largest spare parts logistics center, makes fast, efficient service possible by processing requests for up to 45,000 ordered items and distributing them to regional depots and dealers worldwide.

Volkswagen stores approximately 60,000 of the frequently needed spare parts in this 130,000-square-meter facility. The automaker spreads an additional 270,000 different parts over various adjacent warehouses.[7]

Business Requirements for Mobilizing the Original Parts Center

Volkswagen had specific requirements as it moved through its mobilizing SAP journey. First, the company wanted better inventory management.

It also yearned for a warehouse system that could track the real-time progress of every order through the various divisions of the OPC.

In order to be apprised of its current stock throughout internal and external logistics centers, Volkswagen also needed a system that would enable users to communicate online with the SAP R/3 system located in its Wolfsburg, Germany, headquarters. With numerous local and distributed warehousing operations across Germany, it is essential that central applications know where every part is at any time.

The Solution

Volkswagen picked Psion Teklogix to mobilize its warehouse. Psion Teklogix provided rugged handheld terminals with integrated scanners for mobile workers and for forklift drivers, truck-mounted terminals with locally attached printers for label generation. In addition, Psion Teklogix deployed its TekRF interface software to facilitate communication between the data collection terminals and the central R/3 servers, extending SAP functionality to all wireless users.

This is the largest RF integration project for Psion Teklogix in Europe. The system comprises more than 1,050 Psion Teklogix vehicle and handheld terminals and TekRF middleware software.

According to Stefan Boshold, Volkswagen logistic specialist, the two reasons Volkswagen liked Psion Teklogix were 1) TekRF's user-friendly system interface and 2) the robust terminals. "In our fast-paced environment, a handheld terminal will sometimes get dropped, so a rugged device is essential. At the same time, it is also important that the terminal keys are large and easy to use because some of our employees wear gloves when handling parts." Boshold points out that VW employees quickly accepted the Psion Teklogix solution thanks to the intuitive system operation and the ergonomic terminal design.

The Benefit: Increased Warehousing Efficiency

Most of the 1,000-plus handheld and vehicle-mount terminals were installed at the OPC in Kassel where they are used to scan, track, and process more than 900 tons of spare parts daily. SAP directs and controls all workflow through the Psion Teklogix RF terminals.

To process a specific order, users are directed to select a container. By scanning the container's bar code, it then becomes associated with that specific order. A vehicle-mounted terminal displays location data and directs the warehouse worker to pick designated quantities, with each instruction confirmed when the user scans the bar code of the part.

If one or more of the parts at a storage location is damaged, the employee can use the RF terminal to report the damaged amounts to R/3. The system is optimized to select the shortest distance between part storage locations so that the heaviest parts are loaded into the container first.

As stocking locations are depleted, the central R/3 system is updated and restocking is initiated if necessary. For each part picked, a printer attached to the terminal creates a label with the relevant order data, which is then securely attached to the corresponding packaging.

When the order is complete, the container is taken to the shipping dock. From there the delivery goes to one of nine part depots throughout Germany to be forwarded to the more than 2,800 local dealer showrooms or to any of the 170 importers throughout the world.

Volkswagen's Next Steps

In the most recent expansion, Volkswagen has added more than 200 RF terminals and an additional 30,000 square meters of warehouse space specifically designed to facilitate the processing of urgent orders for delivery within 24 hours. Additional rail connections and 39 heavy transport vehicle-docking stations improved the outward connection.

Based on the success of the Psion Teklogix RF solution integrated with SAP R/3, VW envisages that some 98% of all original parts supplied worldwide will come from Kassel, and it is already thinking about expanding the system again.

Mobile Transportation and Delivery Solutions

Transportation companies are confronting numerous information collection and distribution problems as they attempt to reduce operating costs while synchronizing operations with customers' production, shipment, and delivery requirements. Transportation related processes must balance a series of constraints including:

- Smaller, more frequent lot size, time-definite deliveries, as dictated by customers' just-in-time (JIT) processes,

- Optimal productivity through accurate pickup and delivery scheduling,

- Asset utilization and maintenance schedules, and

- Safety, environmental, and homeland security regulatory issues.

To address these constraints, transportation, delivery, and distribution companies are rapidly adopting end-to-end mobile data solutions. Table 9.1 illustrates the five key ways mobile technology is affecting the transportation industry.

Transportation Process Activities	Specific Task Requirements
Mobile dispatch	• Routing and scheduling • In-transit shipment visibility • Exception alerting • Cross docking • Messaging
Fleet management and compliance	• Vehicle and fleet management • Vehicle tracking (AVL) • Department of Transportation reporting • Fuel tax reporting
Mobile pickup and delivery	• Pickup and delivery • Package tracking • Proof of delivery (POD) • Messaging
Yard management	• Yard management
Third-party warehouse management services	• Warehouse management • Inventory management and integration

Table 9.1: Five Ways Mobile Is Influencing the Transportation Industry

Elements of Mobile Transportation Solutions

Mobile transportation solutions can help retailers, wholesale distributors, railroads, manufacturers, long-haul trucking and third-party logistics (3PL) companies manage their fleets more effectively and synchronize with their trading partners. Typically, these solutions come equipped with the capabilities that follow.

Streamline Loading and Unloading

Mobile computing solutions shorten cycle times and increase efficiency at hub facilities and distribution centers. Handheld computers capture pickup and delivery information and transmit it to the central computer so that inventory is assigned to the appropriate transportation asset.

At the outbound dock, workers use the host-based delivery data to quickly and accurately schedule and load trucks for their next delivery. Delivery schedules can be downloaded directly to driver terminals. When the driver is ready to go, so is his day's schedule.

Manage Mobile Assets

Before trucks leave the terminal, dispatchers download automated route planning to identify the most cost-efficient routes. On the road, drivers and onboard systems collect data as they travel their routes. Efficiency increases through automated data collection that allows drivers to:

- Quickly scan shipping manifests and other documents,

- Reduce paperwork handling at the loading dock,

- Load and deliver inbound and outbound shipments faster,

- Capture and transmit signatures electronically to headquarters, and

- Obtain electronic proof of delivery instantly.

Print on the Spot

This capability allows drivers to print delivery confirmation slips for customers at the point of delivery, send data messages such as service completions, or receive new assignments. For even more efficiency, companies can augment onboard systems with keyboards, global positioning systems, radio modems, and uninterruptible power supply. The components fit in a ruggedized unit that mounts securely in the cab.

Telematics-Based Vehicle Monitoring and Management

The management of vehicles, trucks, trailers, railroad cars, and other mobile resources is complex. Monitoring and tracking the physical movement of fleet assets is critical to companies seeking to minimize resource requirements while maximizing their profitability.

E-Business Strategies, a technology research firm, estimates that there were approximately 25 million cars and trucks in commercial and fleet use in 2004. The U.S. Department of Transportation reports 4.4 million commercial trailers in the same year.

In the past, many businesses used inefficient systems such as wireless telephones and pagers to manage mobile resources. Few businesses used systems based on proprietary technologies that required substantial, ongoing investments in information technology and hardware.

Today, with point-of-activity systems onboard, vehicles are transformed into mobile data centers. In-vehicle systems capture and transmit a constant stream of real-time information on driver performance, routes taken, and hours worked. Companies can study the data to monitor time-sensitive loads, reduce mileage, improve fuel economy, and boost productivity across the board. When you know what your fleet is doing in real time, you can reduce delivery turnarounds, match customer time windows, improve equipment usage, and eliminate aborted deliveries.

Case Study: UPS

We close this chapter with a detailed case study of UPS, the package delivery giant. UPS is a market leader in supply chain management and spends more than $1 billion annually on information technology.[8]

Corporate Overview

UPS is the world's largest package delivery company and a global leader in supply chain services, offering extensive options for synchronizing the movement of goods, information, and funds.

UPS is a unique case study of a firm that has embraced wireless technology extensively throughout its business. The logic behind its adoption of mobility: If you made your living delivering 13 million packages daily to more than 200 countries, chances are you would be interested in how the real-time benefits of mobile technology could help you make your operation more efficient and integrated.

UPS has experimented with ways to improve its core business of time-dependent dispatch, pickup, and delivery via technology for as long as the company has been around. Since the early 1990s, the company has leveraged mobile technology to provide its customers unparalleled capability in tracking and distribution intelligence.

Mobile Technology in Pickup and Delivery

Back in 1991, forward-thinking UPS saw the potential mobile technology had to improve supply chain visibility — the real-time capability to view the movement of documents, packages, and goods as they move through the supply chain. To improve visibility, UPS started supplying its drivers with handheld PCs to improve the flow of package information.

Since 1991, these handhelds, or DIADs (delivery information acquisition devices) as UPS calls them, have evolved considerably. Table 9.2 illustrates the characteristics of each generation of the DIAD device.[9] In one of the largest deployments of mobile devices in history, UPS anticipates having 10,000 DIAD IVs deployed in Europe in 2005 and more than 70,000 worldwide by year-end 2007.[10]

Before we examine UPS's mobile initiatives in package pickup and delivery, we should explain how handhelds became the cornerstone of the package delivery industry. In 1979, Frederick Smith, the founder of FedEx, stated, "The information about a package is as important as the package itself." This was true then, and it is even truer today.

The ability to have real-time visibility into customer shipment status makes the delivery process transparent and gives companies the power to soothe anxious customers and anticipate problems. Hence, collecting and supplying tracking information has become a necessity for transportation and logistics providers.

DIAD I (1990)	▪ Electronically captured delivery information, including signatures ▪ Delivery information uploaded at end of day ▪ Scanned bar codes ▪ Programmed route and maintained timecard information ▪ Tallied CODs (cash on delivery) ▪ 0.75 megabytes of memory
DIAD II (1993)	▪ Delivery information uploaded in real time through in-vehicle cellular service ▪ Conduit for two-way communications in vehicle ▪ Better design and ease of use ▪ Smaller and lighter ▪ Backlit keyboard ▪ 1.5 megabytes of memory (100% more memory)
DIAD III (1999)	▪ First device in industry to capture and transmit real-time delivery information ▪ Enables two-way communication away from vehicle ▪ Three ways to transmit real-time delivery information: internal packet data radio, in-vehicle cellular service, and built-in dialer for traditional telephone transmission ▪ Faster processor, with memory increased more than four times that of the DIAD II (6.5 megabytes) ▪ Keyboard glows in the dark ▪ Modular architecture enables upgrading of components
DIAD IV (2004)	▪ First device in industry to use personal area (Bluetooth) local area (WiFi) and wide area wireless (GPRS or CDMA) connectivity options ▪ Introduces GPS to handheld computer market ▪ Color screen easier to read and facilitates color-coded messages to drivers ▪ Acoustical modem facilitates dial-up access if necessary ▪ Expanded memory (128 megabytes) positions for future services ▪ Continued ergonomic improvement with driver input, (lighter, curved design)

Table 9.2: The Evolution of the UPS DIAD

Standardization and Integration — Key Business Drivers

The DIAD originated from UPS's need for standardization and better information integration. Both are important in the ongoing quest to improve customer service and maintain operational excellence.

All of UPS's technology endeavors have been for better customer service. Since the introduction of the DIAD in 1991, its goal — to quickly provide customers with accurate tracking information — has not changed, but UPS's structure and methodology have. Its technology platform to achieve the mission of customer-centric process integration has evolved every three years. When the new DIAD IV was developed, it was designed to migrate to a standards-based wireless platform named the UPS Standard Terminal Platform (SteP) within five years.

Mobile technology integration is a hot topic these days, especially in companies that have multiple generations of mobile solutions. Companies have begun to realize the impact that disconnected mobile business processes and applications have on the bottom line. While just-in-time delivery players such as UPS, FedEx, and Deutsche Post have always prided themselves on being on the cutting edge of technology, they, too, could be better integrated.

At UPS, SteP is considered to be the solution to the company's mobile integration struggles. Despite implementing technological solutions regularly, the company never standardized any of them in the past. In the 1990s, it wound up with 200,000 terminals of 18 different models made by 13 separate vendors.[11] Supporting the variations was a nightmare and inhibited data flow inside and outside of UPS. With SteP, integrating the flow of information should translate into the customer having access to track-and-trace information that much sooner.

The Mobile Solution: The DIAD IV

The DIAD IV is a compact handheld PC that runs on Windows CE .Net. It is equipped with built-in wireless LAN and Bluetooth short-range wireless systems, a global positioning system (GPS) receiver, a bar code scanner, and a color screen. The main selling point of the DIAD IV is that it helps gather signature capture, proof of delivery, and pickup information to be transmitted to the mainframe in real time, as opposed to the delayed information that customers would receive when drivers used the DIAD III. UPS is set to roll it out to 70,000 drivers worldwide.

The DIAD IV allows drivers to access the UPS worldwide network onsite from customer locations, which means they do not have to walk back to their truck to connect it to a wireless WAN. It also captures delivery information almost instantly. Drivers scan the package bar code with the DIAD scanner, the recipient signs electronically, the driver inputs the last name of the receiver, and then hits a button to finish the transaction and transmit the data to the UPS network. At this point, anyone curious about the status of the package could log on to the UPS Web site and view its tracking information within seconds.

The GPS receiver is another new feature on the DIAD. It should help UPS streamline its European operations where the company more frequently responds to random calls for pickup, as opposed to the United States where scheduled pickups are more often the case. The receiver tracks the vehicle as it travels, which allows dispatchers to send the UPS vehicle closest to the call for pickup.

The DIAD IV also has twenty times more memory than the DIAD III. In the future, maps used together with the GPS receiver may claim some of this memory. Lastly, the DIAD IV runs on the Windows CE operating system, which supports XML messaging. This last characteristic will make it easier for back-end application integration.

The Infrastructure Behind the DIAD IV

The DIAD IV relies on the following:

- Symbol Technologies provides the handheld device, incorporating built-in wireless LAN and Bluetooth short-range wireless systems.

- Microsoft Windows CE operating system that supports XML messaging.

- Major wireless providers, such as Cingular, for its GPRS networks.

- In areas where GPRS is not available, the DIAD IV will turn to wireless providers, such as Verizon, for its CDMA networks.

You might be wondering what FedEx is doing to compete against the DIAD IV. FedEx has an equivalent device called PowerPad designed to capture accurate information about package pickup and delivery operations in real time. PowerPad uses WiFi and Bluetooth to send information scanned during pickup and frees the courier from docking the handheld in order to activate the data transfer, estimated to shave off about 10 seconds per stop.[12]

Mobile Technology at UPS's Sorting Facility

The DIAD IV is aimed at taking package pickup, delivery, and tracking processes to another level. In parallel, a significant mobilization effort is also under way in the warehouses, sorting facilities, and hubs through which packages travel.

Even a small facility, such as the UPS sorting facility in Richmond, California, is a stadium-size building with a maze of belts and funnels that packages move through as they are unloaded from trucks and trains onto other trucks and trains for transshipment. Needless to say, optimizing sorting operations is critical. Even mission-critical.

The business challenge for UPS is to reduce the cost of sorting. UPS is innovating with the deployment of finger-mounted scanners, small pager-sized Bluetooth scanners worn on the middle finger, that send package tracking data to small WiFi (802.11b) terminals worn on the waist by package sorters. The WiFi devices then send the tracking data to UPS's computer network, where customers can access it.[13]

The new global scanning enterprise-wide deployment is expected to be completed in 2007. By then, UPS will have streamlined and standardized more than 55,000 ring scanners in 118 countries; integrated a number of UPS scanning applications into one, improved information flow, and decreased the cost of ownership. As part of the global deployment, UPS will install as many as 12,000 WiFi access points in 2,000 facilities. The resulting WiFi network should be one of the largest in the world.

The Value and ROI of Mobile Technology at UPS

The mobile applications in the UPS supply chain deliver value by minimizing inventory through the chain. Maintaining high inventory levels is costly. In order to keep inventory levels low, manufacturers and distributors depend on just-in-time delivery companies to act as their supply chains. As a result, tracking inventory throughout the supply chain is critical.

More accurate, readily available tracking information from UPS helps customers manage their entire supply chain and deliver better customer service. Thus, the DIADs and the scanners in the sorting facilities are a necessity if UPS plans to remain competitive in its delivery niche.

The productivity improvements from wireless scanning are impressive. By eliminating the cables that connect the ring scanners to the wearable terminals, UPS expects a 30% decrease in equipment and repair costs, as well as a 35% reduction in downtime and another 35% reduction in the amount of spare equipment needed.

For UPS, FedEx, DHL, USPS, Canada Post, and others wireless technology has improved operational speed and accuracy. These firms have shown that in an age of intense competition, supply chain efficiency using mobile technology isn't just a requirement for success but a necessity for survival.

Summary

"That's an amazing invention, but who would ever want to use one of them?"

— U.S. President Rutherford B. Hayes,
after experimenting with a telephone in 1876

Mobile applications are revolutionizing supply chains. It is hard to find a company — retail, chemical, pharmaceutical, or industrial — that is not focused on four variables that drive costs: time, labor, quality, and materials. The nonstop challenge for every organization is to eliminate as much cost as possible, while making demonstrable gains in production and warehousing efficiency, product quality, and distribution.

Mobile supply chains play a critical role in all the cost drivers. The efficiency demands placed on warehouse, distribution, and transportation operations are greater than ever. Companies now view an efficient end-to-end supply chain as a necessary competitive advantage and are requiring greater accuracy, visibility, and velocity.

We expect mobile supply chains to be a key investment area in the coming years. To get started, assess the "needs" of your business. A solution must fit with your business model and philosophy. A wireless or mobile solution is meant to enhance your operations. Solid processes must be in place before any sort of solution will have an impact.

The bottom line: Eliminating paper and time from supply chain operations is critical. Increasingly, the focus is on time since it is a perishable not renewable resource. As we illustrated in this chapter, one of the key strategies for time waste management is deploying mobile applications. By capturing the information, moving it to the point of activity or decision making, and managing the overall business process, significant ROI is possible.

Chapter Ten

Mobilizing Employee-Facing Processes and Portals

What defines a top-performing company? Strong growth. Good processes. These basics only tell part of the story. Maintaining momentum requires productive employees even when they are out of the office. Keeping the millions of employees who work outside typical office settings productive is the goal of a new generation of mobile employee solutions, which facilitate time-sensitive, real-time interactions and transactions. This chapter examines how companies are mobilizing different employee-facing processes like time and travel applications and enterprise portals.

Introduction

Mobilizing employee-facing applications is a growing trend — a question of "when," not "if." The sales representatives, consultants, managers, and many other employees who log millions of hours on the road each year are the people responsible for this trend forming.

For these road warriors, a critical requirement when it comes to the office is the ability to take it with you. It's getting easier all the time. Mobile office applications connect remote blue-collar and white-collar employees seamlessly through the corporate firewall to personal information management systems, corporate data, human resource systems, collaboration services, and business intelligence applications.

At a top consulting firm, managing partners are constantly on the move. Consequently, decision making is slow, and simple issues take months to resolve. To solve this problem, the firm is developing an "information at your fingertips" engine to deliver a complete desktop-on-the-road to its traveling managers. The application provides access to e-mail, calendars, and pertinent applications such as profitability analysis, time tracking, and customer data. More sophisticated features such as real-time conferencing and project management are planned for the second phase of the project.

Employee demand for multi-channel information access is increasing and shifting from desktops to alternative devices. Their demands are forcing companies to pursue mobile employee applications for three primary reasons:

1. **Business.** Companies realize that employee time is a limited, costly resource. As a result, they have to fulfill each employee's information needs while keeping costs as low as possible.

2. **Technology.** Always-on mobile networks with continuous data connections are becoming more reliable. Mobile devices are also becoming less expensive and richer in functionality, and more employees are becoming comfortable using them.

3. **Financial.** The payback for a company's investment is quantifiable in the form of cost reduction, quality, and speed.

Who are your mobile employees? How many do you have? The numbers would probably surprise you. By some estimates, more than 30%–40% of workers travel for a variety of business reasons. As the roster of road warriors grows, so does the call for new mobile applications to keep businesses running smoothly.

Connected Employees: New Tools for New Times

Mobile relationships are the centerpiece of a new employee customization trend. Employee customization means responding to employee needs efficiently and specifically. Employee focused solutions, such as corporate portals, have been widely acknowledged as being vital to business success. Their success is notable considering IT's limited ability to improve the productivity of white-collar, so-called knowledge workers over the past two decades.

Peter Drucker attributed the failure of technology to improve knowledge worker productivity to the following: "The first thing we have learned

— and it came as a rude shock — is about what does not work [in knowledge work]. Capital cannot be substituted for labor. Nor will new technology by itself generate higher productivity."[1]

So it is unrealistic to think mobile technology will succeed where other "silver bullet" technologies have failed. Mobility alone will not magically increase productivity, but it can enhance existing investments in enterprise resource planning (ERP), customer relationship management (CRM), and other system frameworks. A mobile infrastructure complements these solutions but is not a substitute for them.

Corporations must learn to use mobile technology in conjunction with existing technology investments to address three knowledge management problems:

- Increasing the usability of enterprise applications,

- Improving the speed and accuracy of decision support, and

- Spreading information and data visibility.

Increasing the Usability of Enterprise Applications

Current enterprise applications are sophisticated at capturing and managing transaction data. Given their heritage, however, they tend to suffer from a serious lack of usability. Although functionally rich, their standardized design ignores the custom needs of business users in unique work roles. For instance, if I am a manufacturing manager, do I care about marketing information in the enterprise portal? Give employees information relevant to their jobs.

Over the years, critics have complained that enterprise applications have been engineered to the point of being almost unusable. Call it the "all the features that you may ever want but will probably never use" syndrome. Whatever you call it, companies are left with inaccessible repositories with no effective tools for their employees to quickly manipulate or retrieve information. Mobility's value in this context is to solve two problems: provide the information needed in a simple form and do so when and where the employee requests it.

Improving the Speed and Accuracy of Decision Support

Companies operate based on decisions, thousands daily from the office of the chairperson on down to the shop floor. To enable superior decision support, companies have to empower workers. The first step is creating a data-access infrastructure to support decision quality and responsiveness, a step that many have yet to take.

While the vision centers on empowering workers, the reality is far removed. Despite spending millions of dollars, most companies have been blocked when they tried to create an application foundation to support the movement of information across company boundaries. The idea goes against every principle of modern organizational theory. To realize its full potential, mobile technology must integrate with large-scale process changes to break down the barriers to information access and to help, rather than hinder, information visibility.

Spreading Information and Data Visibility

To be useful, real-time process and transaction data must be both accurate and visible to mobile employees and managers. Quick decisions based on inaccurate data cause more problems than they solve.

Information visibility tests many firms. Much of a company's most useful information remains unreachable in the "information silos" that often characterize large enterprises. These silos typically result from political or turf conflicts where knowledge and information often equal power, status, and job security whether for senior management or line staff. These information barriers fragment enterprise-wide processes.

The problem grows when two large companies with wholly different cultures and application frameworks merge. Usually, the balance sheets get integrated, but the firm's business processes and knowledge bases don't, so enterprise data capture and integration is the pivotal first step of mobile enablement.

Information visibility and process integration issues worsen in an outsourcing business model. Companies worldwide have forged alliances, decentralized, and downsized based on an outsourcing strategy. Those who argue for outsourcing do so in the name of flexibility and the freedom to focus on core competencies. Outsourcing may be a common practice, but the resulting intricate information flows are not well understood.

Companies are looking for new ways to solve existing problems. Most enterprises are facing relentless pressure to do three things: reduce the cost structure, improve quality, and increase the speed of processes.

Imagine trying to provide mobile access in a typical Fortune 500 company that operates on four continents, with as many as 100,000 employees, 200 applications, and 5,000 servers. Clearly, the challenge is not simply creating new solutions but solutions that can scale effectively.

One thing is apparent: Implementing mobile technology in many companies is going to take some unnatural acts of process integration.

Mobile Employee Applications Framework

The objective of business-to-employee (B2E) applications is to provide employees in real-time enterprises with control over the various forms of communications they deal with every day. This means having access to the corporate data needed to do their jobs effectively and efficiently, regardless of the employees' location or the type of device they are using.

Another objective is to eliminate paper-based processes. For most employee-facing activities today, the default mode of interaction is pen and paper. The problem with paper is that it's slow and prone to errors. Moving from a paper solution to a mobile solution means more accurate, current information.

Companies are beginning to deploy a variety of applications to facilitate mobile transactions. A review of different business-to-employee applications illuminates how mobility can improve employee efficiency. The following scenarios illustrate the different ways mobile access could benefit corporations:

- **Mobile office and messaging.** Company A, a large conglomerate, has more than 10,000 sales employees who work in teams to sell and deliver products and consulting solutions. These representatives need real-time access to e-mail and instant messaging capabilities.

- **Real-time business intelligence.** Company B has 500 factories worldwide with divisional managers who constantly travel. To optimize production line scheduling, these managers need to monitor key performance indicators, inventory data, production bottlenecks, and incoming customer "expedite" requests.

- **Time and travel.** Company C has 100,000 employees worldwide who need access to internal applications for expense tracking and time accounting applications. These on-the-go professionals want to use mobile devices to support job-specific tasks and manage workflows in the context of projects.

- **Mobile inspection and workflow solutions.** Company D is a government organization with several thousand inspectors who inspect food and lodging establishments. These field employees need access to form-based applications that allow them to fill out compliance paperwork.

Let's examine each of these mobile applications in detail.

Mobile Office and Messaging Applications

Handheld devices can change the way employees organize their work, manage their tasks, and communicate with co-workers, suppliers, and customers. As enterprise users discover and leverage the benefits of personal information management (PIM) applications, such as contact, address, and schedule management, they quickly come to expect even more PIM functionality and applications.

Users are requesting quick access to dynamic info on demand; the capability to send and receive messages interactively; and the ability to be reached in near real time. Manufacturers such as Palm and Microsoft realized they needed to extend their platform functionality to include:

- Access to corporate e-mail communications such as Microsoft Exchange and Lotus Notes,

- Peer-to-peer instant messaging, and

- Unified or mixed-mode messaging.

In the near term, e-mail will drive mobile adoption more quickly than any other application. Employees want to access e-mail at work, at home, while out of the office on business, and even on vacation. Mobile e-mail applications are not only driving the purchase of handheld devices; they are laying the technological foundation for an expanded set of enterprise handheld applications.

Mobile and Wireless E-Mail

Real-time access to e-mail is the current killer app for the wireless market. Wireless e-mail is the transfer of data received or sent from a wireless device to or from a network. Wireless e-mail is just gaining traction in many corporations. It is beyond the early adopter phase of market adoption and has entered the early majority phase.

The de facto standard of wireless e-mail in the corporate segment is Research in Motion's (RIM's) BlackBerry.[2] Introduced in 1999, a BlackBerry handheld device is the wireless extension of the corporate e-mail account that allows users to send, receive, forward, and reply to messages at their convenience. BlackBerry devices are ergonomically designed with a small keyboard optimized for thumb operation. It integrates seamlessly with the existing enterprise e-mail account or personal e-mail account and provides a continuous connection to the user's enterprise e-mail via a nationwide data network.

From a connectivity standpoint, BlackBerry is considered always-on, always connected. It works using over-the-air, push technology so you don't need to retrieve your e-mail. Your e-mail finds you. No dialing in. No initiating connections. No effort required. BlackBerry devices are designed to remain on and continuously connected to the wireless network, allowing you to be discreetly notified as new e-mail arrives. BlackBerry connects the mobile workforce to the office at all times. It allows employees to access the critical e-mail and filter the rest.

While RIM possesses a first-mover advantage in the wireless e-mail market, it's by no means the only one. The Palm Treo is a close competitor to the BlackBerry with similar features and functionality. Good Technology is another competitor. What is interesting in the wireless e-mail trend is that increasing adoption of mobile devices provides the "installed base" for new enterprise applications. Sort of a Trojan horse method of deploying new business applications.

Unified and Mixed-Mode Instant Messaging

Today's employees are mixing the modes or channels of modern telecommunications — voice, e-mail, telematics, and location-based services. The following example illustrates how mixed-mode communication works.

Barb has dropped off her son, Joey, at soccer practice. Practice ends early, so Joey takes out his cell phone and calls his mom. "Mom," he says, "practice is over. Please come and get me." However, Barb, a senior vice president at a Fortune 50 firm, is sitting in a meeting with her notebook PC opened in front of her. It's wirelessly enabled, and her cell phone is on meeting mode. Barb wants messages received during meetings to be handled in a unified-messaging "store and forward" fashion. Using a speech-to-text translation feature, she gets an instant message from Joey on her laptop. She looks at it and thinks I can't deal with this right now. She forwards it to her husband and writes, "Jim, I can't get Joey for another two hours. Can you please pick him up?" Jim is driving home from work in a car equipped with telematics capability. He gets the message from Barb on the dashboard with an attachment (message from Joey) and the soccer practice location. Jim clicks on the location link and gets the navigational information he needs to pick up his son.

A variety of complex technologies supports the above scenario including unified messaging, wireless instant messaging, text-to-speech, speech-to-text, VoIP (voice over Internet protocol) and location-based services.[3] However, the most critical component of each of these scenarios is the context. The context tailors all communication to the needs of a specific individual, device, location, and situation. Context requires the technology to know who a person is, what role they are in, how many mobile devices they carry, which devices are on, and how and from whom they prefer to receive their communications. To meet these contextual requirements, a sophisticated infrastructure is a must-have.

While mixed-mode messaging may sound futuristic, several solutions that represent the convergence of channels are already widely used. One such application is the BlackBerry we discussed, which has nearly achieved cult status by offering very usable integrated e-mail solutions.

Alerts and Notification-Based Solutions

Mobile technology is tailor-made to support notification scenarios. In today's 24x7 real-time economy, it is not an exaggeration to ask, "Isn't everyone on call?" The following scenario illustrates what being on call means today compared to only a few years ago.

A physician is on call and is paged by an application built into her pocket PC. The physician opens her handheld, clicks on the patient identifier, and pulls up the pertinent patient information by accessing the health maintenance organization's (HMO's) secure portal. The portal, accessible to authorized users only, consolidates information from a variety of sources, including patient information files, correspondence, schedules, and clinical information.

Some notification-based scenarios are appropriate for jobs across many industries, such as new customer requests for field service or when internal assistance is required of roaming maintenance personnel. Table 10.1 lists some examples of mission-critical events in different industries that may require immediate attention.

Vertical Market	Examples of Important Notifications for a Mobile Workforce
Utility	A rupture has occurred in a pipeline, a generator is running low on fuel, a transformer is malfunctioning.
Homeland Security	The Homeland Security alert status level has changed, new warrants for someone's arrest have been issued, or an incident has been reported.
Healthcare	In a hospital environment, this could be a patient emergency, a lab test result becomes available (especially if it is out of the normal bounds for the test), or a prescription has expired that requires a refill.
Pharmaceuticals	A participant in a drug trial needs to be notified it is time to take their medication or fill out a form.
Financial Investments	Market changes have reached a level for purchasing or selling certain securities or financial instruments.
Real Estate	New properties have come on the market, typically through a multiple listing service, that match a client's specifications.
Emergency Management	System that sends alerts of bridges that need inspecting due to flood and other weather conditions or due to accident damage.

Table 10.1: Important Notifications for Mobile Workers in Different Verticals

Enterprise Portals -> Mobile Portals

In recent years, enterprise information portals, or corporate portals, have evolved from the concept of the intranet. Corporate portals pull together disparate types of information, including business transactions, customer leads, and inventory information. For example, from a personalized portal, sales representatives can access and manage customer information, view product catalogs, check inventory availability, place orders, and communicate with co-workers, partners, or customers.

The business rationale behind the corporate portal marketplace is to provide personalized destination sites containing a variety of useful applications. These applications try to make it easier for employees to locate the specific information they need in what is often a highly fragmented information environment. Faster access to quality information enhances and speeds decision making. For example, say a portal application links to an ERP system. The link allows managers to view receipts, invoices, and payment data. Corporate portals seek to provide a single point of access to structured and unstructured information by mimicking the approach pioneered by consumer portal sites such as Yahoo!

As competition for customers mounts and the speed of response to customer requests becomes more critical, sorting through file cabinets or performing tedious database queries is an unacceptably slow means of information acquisition. Consequently, major companies are investing billions in developing corporate portals. The challenge these firms face is how to extend corporate portal functionality to a mobile device. The issue is not whether such extension is technically feasible; it is understanding the business scenarios in which it makes sense to do so.

Tethered enterprise portal models of the early 2000s are evolving into mobile portals. Let's look at three mobile portal scenarios: business intelligence (BI), financial portals, and human resource (HR) portals.

Mobile Business Intelligence Applications

Some businesses monitor daily certain milestones and metrics that provide employees with a view into how well the business is operating. Someone needs to be notified when these data points fall outside the acceptable operating range for the business or when a change happens to the organization. The longer the delay in responding to these issues, the higher the potential cost to the business.

Given the speed of modern business, IT groups must determine their strategy for providing their decision makers with real-time BI applications. The information and knowledge base resulting from the use of such applications will be critical to successful business performance.

For example, Sears Home Services implemented a mobile BI application developed by the software company River Run. The application provides 12,500 mobile technicians with wireless dispatch, parts query, and invoicing capabilities. The goal of the application is to enable Sears to deliver superior customer service, reduce costs, and increase its business volume. The application also allows the mobile technicians' managers to monitor the technicians' work activities by tracking performance metrics such as the time it takes to close a ticket, the number of stops per day, the dollar amount per visit, and the cross-sell ratio.

Mobile performance monitoring and measurement applications supply managers with important process information as to how well operations are functioning. Performance monitoring measurement is not only critical to increasing quality and service; it is the bridge between a firm's operations and its strategy. By using key performance indicators linked to a scorecard, companies can continuously monitor actual performance against the strategic targets. For example, one trend in manufacturing, especially in Six Sigma organizations, is to increase real-time performance monitoring in order to correct problems as they occur.

Companies are under increasing pressure to develop effective BI strategies as customer expectations increase and the pace of business accelerates. Today's managers are expected to do more in less time with fewer resources. Gone are the days when large teams of analysts supported major business units within an organization.

Rather than a business specialty, analysis has become every manager's responsibility and may soon be the responsibility of everyone in the firm. In such a tense, fast-paced environment, managers need consistent access to relevant business process information and analytic tools tailored to their specific needs. To meet this need, products like Microsoft's SQL

Server database provide alert services that send out SMS text messages when internal database triggers have been activated.

In short, BI solutions must enable decision makers to:

- Minimize the time required to collect all relevant business information,

- Automate the assimilation of the information into personalized intelligence, and

- Provide analysis tools for making comparisons and intelligent decisions.

With accurate, real-time data, managers can correct potential problems before they escalate. It is also vital for companies that wish to capitalize on new business opportunities quickly or adapt when the customer response to a promotion exceeds expectations.

Vertical Market	Examples of Business Intelligence Scenarios
Engineering	An elevator, farm machinery, large household appliance, or other pieces of equipment need to be serviced or warranty deadlines are approaching.
Insurance	Policies are coming up for renewal or fraudulent claims need to be investigated further.
Manufacturing	The raw materials on hand are not enough to satisfy the current order rate, a piece of equipment or cell controller in the manufacturing process has stopped functioning, or a supplier is unable to deliver its product on time. Alerts can also be sent when machinery or vehicles are scheduled for regular maintenance, reach a warranty replacement date, or are scheduled for obsolescence.
Hospitality	A manager of multiple hotel properties needs to know occupancy rates to determine advertising levels and promotions on a continual basis.
Retail	Inventory is low and needs to be restocked at a retail outlet or a vending machine.
Financial Services	Notification when a customer executes a trade or opens a new account. Based on the account, the financial advisor could then contact customers and be proactive in understanding their investment needs.

Table 10.2: Examples of Business Intelligence Scenarios in Different Verticals

Mobile Financial Portals

In the early 1990s, GE and Motorola pioneered delivering consolidated year-end data to their top executives in a matter of days. Since then, the fast financial close has attracted considerable attention from finance departments worldwide. Today, the fast close is becoming faster and virtual. Cisco's financial systems can close the company's books within a few hours' notice.

An automated notification-driven portal approach can simplify financial administrative tasks. At many typical companies, managers were given thick paper reports. Out of all the raw data provided, they only reviewed a few key numbers, and infrequently action was required. Reviewing the reports in this manner while on the road was time-consuming. Now those data points are being tracked in an enterprise system, and alerts are sent to a manager's handheld device only when action needs to be taken.

Mobile financial portals enable the continuous monitoring of sales amounts, cash flow, product margins, and returns. Efficient management of a company's financials is critical to successful operation.

A look at the hotel operator Carlson, whose chains include Radisson and Country Inns & Suites, underscores the importance of mobile financial portals. In the hotel industry, managers can oversee many properties and tend to be constantly on the move. Carlson requires its managers to oversee the financial performance of the regions for which they are responsible. The managers must monitor several financial and guest satisfaction metrics. As a result, Carlson deployed a solution called Mobile Access to Carlson Hospitality (MACH) to its regional managers, each of whom oversees between 20 and 80 hotels. Carlson's solution gives managers the power to be out of their offices but still monitor hotel financial operations.[4]

How does it work? Managers configure their mobile units to "subscribe" to different applications. These applications then alert the manager with a tone when important events occur. For example, the device can be programmed to monitor occupancy rates at various hotels. The managers can also check a specific hotel's average daily rates to see if excessive discounting has occurred. Monitoring for fraud in high-employee-turnover industries, such as hospitality, is an internal auditing best practice.

Human Resource Applications

Human resource (HR) portals are employee self-service sites that lead to significant cost savings. The self-service functionality of HR portals reduces administrative costs. These sites are also ideal for cutting the time employees spend making travel arrangements since they can be customized to comply with a company's travel policy. One major application in this category is travel and expense management.

Time and Expense Management

Mobile time and travel solutions let mobile employees manage their working time and travel expense data. The old methods of using Excel spreadsheets tied to SAP R/3 and various third-party systems are no longer efficient, given the amount of manual intervention required.

Take, for instance, consulting companies with thousands of employees onsite at various client locations. For these companies, mobile HR portals are excellent tools for tracking business trips and collecting time and expense accounting data. These portals eliminate the problems associated with paper-based time-sheet systems by allowing team members to record the time they spend on specific projects and submit time sheets in compliance with the company's reporting processes.

Atos Origin, an international IT services company is extending its SAP solution set to link its field force of 45,000 field consultants with back-office operations. The objective behind the project is to enable professionals working remotely to quickly deliver project information and time and travel costs to headquarters. The expected ROI centers on time savings and elimination of paper. By gaining faster, deeper insight into projects and costs across its widespread operations in 45 countries, Atos aims to optimize workforce utilization and customer service while expediting invoice processing and improving profit margins.

IDS Scheer of Germany has also implemented SAP Mobile Time and Travel for its 2,000 employees who support 4,000 customers. Employees make around 50,000 trips annually that have to be allocated to around 1,500 projects going on at any time. After the implementation, IDS Scheer has reported that the end-to-end process from data entry to settlement has improved considerably. The mobile recording of all travel and account assignment data, as well as data transfer to the SAP back end, ensure that costs are quickly and accurately allocated.[5]

With their mobile workforces directly feeding data into the existing ERP environments, Atos Origin and IDS Scheer aim to gain more efficient, paperless invoicing processes to achieve faster recognition of revenues. Compliance checking also is an important benefit. Travel expense guidelines are stored in the mobile application and used to check receipts at the point of entry. This cuts down on the number of errors. In addition, changes to travel policy can be uniformly applied and instantly propagated across the organization.

Figure 10.1 illustrates the typical process flow for the mobile time and travel solution.[6] The individual processes in the overall workflow include travel request, travel planning, travel recording, travel expense services, and settlement. The data from the mobile devices is invaluable in creating global consolidated reports.

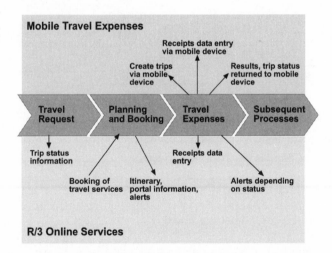

Figure 10.1: Integrating Mobile Processes with Travel Management

Mobile Project Management and Collaboration Portals

Linking mobile workers to project management systems could save companies in the construction and utilities industries considerable time. For example, work could be rescheduled due to a delay, and those affected could be notified. The link could be used to locate a replacement worker when a consultant is unexpectedly unavailable. Each example illustrates how mobile solutions complement Web portal applications.

For instance, mobile project management solutions that can interface with SAP xApps (packaged composite applications) like xRPM (resource and program management) help address companies' need for comprehensive project portfolio management. These types of solutions give senior managers visibility into entire portfolios of enterprise programs and projects, while supporting strategic capacity planning and resource allocation based on up-to-date information on skills and availability.

Specialized Workflow and Forms-Based Applications

The fastest way to identify a business-to-employee mobile solution that has a high potential for a significant, quick ROI is to streamline any process that utilizes pen and paper for data capture.

Paper is an inherently slow, inaccurate tool for collecting data. Paper-based communications are also error-prone and harder to track. Many enterprises that have converted a paper-based process to an electronic form–based application on a mobile device have seen data collection times reduced in the field, more accurate data flowing to central enterprise servers, and faster business reporting.

To provide a sense of the benefits possible from this type of approach, we describe the following instances where enterprises replaced paper with electronic forms on mobile devices:

- Food services inspection and compliance audits;
- Insurance claims adjusters; and
- Field casework in vocational schools, care centers for children and the elderly, and home visit healthcare workers.

Food Services Inspection and Field Audits

In the food industry, there is a growing interest in sophisticated inspection and audit capture systems that help inspectors and food safety workers collect vital data needed to ensure that food facilities are compliant with existing standards.

The interest in these inspection and audit capture systems is generated by concerns over the safety of consumables and a need to ensure that hotel, leisure, and food service operators keep up with changing regulations that influence many things such as shipping requirements, waste-disposal restrictions, hazardous substance control, and product labeling and documentation.

For faster and more accurate job performance, inspectors also require a high-performance mobile data management system that synchronizes easily with corporate databases. The goal is to ensure:

- Consistent flow of information to and from field personnel,

- Data collection and processing times reduced from 8–10 days to as little as 2 days for better customer service,

- Well-presented reports in a unified format to comply with food, premises, and health safety laws,

- Reduced administrative costs due to an auditable process, and

- Document integrity to meet regulatory requirements.

The result of a well-integrated mobile data management system: a more productive mobile workforce focused on information gathering.

Similar to the food industry, other industries are contending with increasing regulatory complexity today, not only for products and processes but also in the area of environment, health, and safety (EH&S). Mobile solutions are becoming a critical part of the compliance process.

Small PDAs can support inspectors for an entire day shift while wirelessly connected, allowing them to handle tasks that are not possible with laptop computers. Automating data capture in this way helps to reduce the overall time it takes to audit facilities. This enables more visits at the same staffing levels while improving overall customer satisfaction.

Mobile Social Workers

Social work is a generic term that comprises many different fields within the social welfare sector. Professional social workers are found in social services offices, elderly and disabled homes, schools, and hospitals, as well as halfway houses and recovery institutions.

Most social casework environments have become more automated in order to make work procedures more efficient. Within social work, high demands on documentation and confidentiality respectively increase the forms workload.

Best-practice social services organizations are beginning to use customized interactive prepopulated forms to input case management data, access case histories and records in the field, then submit forms to headquarters. These forms provide a quality assurance checklist to ensure services are completed as prescribed.

Automating lengthy, tedious tasks like filling in paper forms can result in lower social worker attrition rates, decreased training costs for new employees, and less money spent attracting new talent.

Mobile Insurance Claims Adjusters

Insurance adjusters by definition are mobile. They deal with paper documents every day, whether completing forms to document claims, submitting expense reports to their supervisors, or filling out applications on behalf of customers. In return, they receive more paper documents as follow-up to their requests.

Take for instance, the claims settlement process. In the insurance industry, filing a claim may be the only interaction a customer has with its insurer. The claimant's experience lays the foundation for building customer loyalty. Rapid, responsive service and consistent follow-up help ensure a steadfast clientele. In the case of an unforeseen event, mobile insurance adjusters can easily create prepopulated claim applications complete with customer data and a list of insured property.

Adjusters use their PDAs or notebook computers onsite, complete interactive forms offline, and submit data to the back-end systems when connected. Agents, adjusters, and vendors with role-based access, (ensuring protection of personal or business-sensitive information) are engaged at the right time to ensure rapid settlement. In the insurance business, next to the amount of settlement, it is the claims processing speed that determines customer satisfaction.

Interactive Forms on Mobile Devices

SAP and Adobe are jointly delivering Interactive Forms based on Adobe Software as part of the SAP NetWeaver platform. Interactive Forms on mobile devices has the potential to further automate and streamline manual, error-prone, forms-based processes.

The ability to enable structured, forms-based interaction on mobile devices can revolutionize remote data entry and collection. Since these forms are based on Adobe PDF, they retain the visual appearance of the paper forms they replace. Little or no training is required for employees to fill out the same government tax form for the umpteenth time.

Consider this scenario in homeland security: Customs officials and officers increasingly use mobile handheld devices when inspecting inbound aircraft and sea vessels at more than 300 international air and sea ports of entry. The objective is to use prepopulated forms to make the time officers spend in the field conducting inspections more efficient while increasing the accuracy of data collected. Incorporating mobile handheld devices for homeland security has led to a savings of almost one work week per month and reduced errors.[7]

Based on the wireless connectivity, the digital forms then update the organization's SAP application with new information, eliminating costly and faulty manual data entry. This solution is far superior to the old model of capturing the information in the remote location and then going back to headquarters and rekeying it into the SAP system.

The immediacy of capturing data in the field at the point of activity can be tied back to the SAP back end to reduce the information delay. To succeed, however, interactive forms solutions have to feel the same as working with paper. Content delivered electronically needs to have the same appearance and accessibility of paper documents.

We expect the Adobe-SAP partnership will generate some interesting success stories as mobile technology increases productivity for a variety of scenarios — fire, police, and health inspections; building and construction permit management; and social services case management — by eliminating reliance on paperwork and streamlining business processes.

Summary

"New capabilities emerge just by virtue of having smart people with access to state-of-the-art technology."

— Robert E. Kahn

Tools or toys is the debate raging in companies over employee-facing mobile applications. In a 24x7 environment, companies want employees always available — with access to all the tools and knowledge they need when and where they need them. Equipping mobile workers with e-mail access and critical corporate intranet information and transaction capabilities is now possible with new application extension technologies. (Application extension means expanding the Internet desktop functionality to the mobile device.)

The trend of extending enterprise applications is in its earliest stages. As the business velocity increases, companies will implement new employee-facing solutions to improve their competitiveness and service. Managing and streamlining employee-centric information flows will be central to any firm's ability to compete in the marketplace. By thinking broadly about the work challenges employees face, rather than narrowly about job tasks, companies can usually find ways to not only improve the work process but to make it easier for employees.

Of all the areas of mobility, business-to-employee applications will be adopted the fastest. However, the extension of desktop functionality to mobile devices will be a steady evolution and will most likely take a decade to occur. During this time, companies will experience serious change management issues. Emerging mobile applications will change the nature of white-collar work. Mobile technologies not only affect tasks, activities, and processes, they also transcend the boundary between work and private life.

The challenges of linking mobile employees to real-time transactions aren't just technological; they are social and ethical. Unless these challenges receive as much attention and discussion as the technology has, the mobile economy's tremendous potential will be only minimally realized.

Chapter Eleven

Radio Frequency Identification and Auto-ID Infrastructure

The revolutionary technology radio frequency identification (RFID) is expected to influence many areas of business, particularly "sense-and-respond" supply chain management. This chapter describes RFID and includes an overview of how the technology functions, as well as its benefits, costs, and limitations. We also focus on SAP's Auto-ID Infrastructure, which is part of the multi-channel access layer in SAP's NetWeaver.

Introduction

On November 4, 2003, Wal-Mart's top 100 suppliers convened near Springdale, Arkansas, for what *FORTUNE* described as "a United Nations of Retail." They were there to discuss tactical strategies for attaching RFID tags by January 2005 to most of the product shipments (boxes and pallets) sent to Wal-Mart. Also in attendance were RFID hardware and software providers hoping to get a piece of the action.

Having the merchandise customers want to buy at the moment they want to buy it is one of the drivers behind Wal-Mart's adoption of RFID. Eliminating empty shelves or stockouts requires optimizing the flow of information throughout the supply chain. It's the reason why companies are adopting RFID-enabled pallets and cases. Like the bar code compliance initiative ignited by Wal-Mart in 1984, the push to incorporate RFID is expected to transform the retail industry and result in long-term cost savings and efficiencies for supply chains. This strategic move could also catapult Wal-Mart to the next level of business performance and put a lot of pressure on its competition.

According to Linda Dillman, CIO of Wal-Mart, "It is imperative that we have the merchandise the customer wants to buy when they want to buy it. We believe RFID technology is going to help us do that more often and more efficiently. This will help us increase customer satisfaction in the near term and ultimately play an important role in helping us control costs and continue offering low prices."[1]

In response to Wal-Mart, competitors METRO Group, Target, Albertsons, Tesco, and others have announced RFID mandates for their supplier bases. In retail, RFID will allow supply chain partners to read electronic product codes from tags as product cases or pallets move through distribution centers and into stores. Companies will better understand where products are in the supply chain.

The public sector is not far behind in RFID adoption. The U.S. Department of Defense, U.S. Postal Service, and U.S. Food and Drug Administration have ordered suppliers to use intelligent RFID tags as a complement to the venerable bar code technology. The U.S. Transportation Security Administration estimates that the airline industry will have to spend billions over the next decade to upgrade baggage-screening systems in order to comply with new security laws. Airlines and cargo shipping companies are exploring RFID's ability to improve baggage and cargo sorting to streamline check-in systems.

Companies are also using RFID internally to streamline processes. For instance, Airbus, the aircraft manufacturer, is trying out RFID-enabled enterprise asset management in its tool lease supply chain. Specialized tools are RFID-tagged, providing identification, transportation, and lifecycle information. When the tools require servicing, they are sent to the calibration lab and repair shop. The vital data is written on the RFID tags. This paperless tracking system for tools improves visibility and control at Airbus.[2]

Why are so many organizations smitten by RFID? It drastically shortens the time it takes to track inventory in the supply chain. RFID helps companies figure out the location of their shipments and answers security questions such as which containers contain hazardous materials.

RFID also streamlines information flow in the warehouse. For example, say a truck enters a retail distribution center carrying hundreds of cases of mixed consumer merchandise. With RFID technology, the contents of the truck register immediately in the back-end systems. Questions such as which manufacturers are these cases from or what is in this mixed pallet or does this order correspond with the advance ship notice (ASN) are easily answered.

Since RFID can accurately identify a single item as it moves from the factory to the store shelf and then on to post-sales support, companies no longer have to wonder how long a particular product has been sitting on a shelf or if it's counterfeit.

Lastly, RFID improves the customer experience by making sure that the products they want are stocked on the shelves. Companies can also incorporate RFID into promotions and relationship management.

Large suppliers like Procter & Gamble, Gillette, Hewlett-Packard, International Paper, Black & Decker, VF Corporation, and Michelin are investing heavily in RFID. The investment activity has created a feverish environment around a mobile technology that is just beginning to mature.

Welcome to RFID, a new mobile technology and automated data capture infrastructure that many claim has the potential to transform how business is conducted for both retailers and their suppliers.

At its core, RFID boasts three process benefits: 1) it eliminates errors associated with identification or data collection; 2) it accelerates the checkout process; and 3) it maximizes system flexibility with minimum investment. Decreased labor costs, simplified business processes like returns, better inventory control, and reduced shrinkage number among RFID's business benefits.

Table 11.1 captures the reasons why companies are deploying RFID.

A Brief Primer on RFID

Before we go any further, it would be prudent to define RFID for those readers less familiar with the technology.

What Is Radio Frequency Identification?

RFID refers to a branch of automatic identification technologies in which radio frequencies are used to capture and transmit data.

Broadly speaking, the business press sees RFID as a way to track assets throughout the supply chain. Very small RFID tags containing a unique identifier are placed on assets (pallets, cases, or individual items). When the tags pass near a "reader," the tags activate and their unique product codes are transmitted back to an inventory control system.

RFID tags can be read from distances of 10–30 feet at rates of 1,000 tags per second from any angle, resulting in the ability to collect data automatically without human intervention. Wal-Mart's readers are thought to have an average range of 15 feet. Unlike bar code systems, RFID tags can be read even when hidden from view, a common situation in manufacturing or warehouse operations.

RFID Business Drivers	Industries and Companies Affected
Mandates from major retail and government customers to increase their operational efficiency.	Major suppliers to Wal-Mart and the U.S. Department of Defense
Reducing significant losses due to theft or shrinkage by reducing return fraud and enhancing loss and theft prevention. (Theft is estimated to be a $53 billion problem for consumer packaged goods sector alone.)	Retail, apparel, consumer electronics, and music
Manufacturing requires complex compliance processes that call for strict tracking based on lot, batch, and serial number.	Pharmaceuticals, aerospace, hospitals, and chemicals
Improvement of forward (factory-to-shelf) distribution (recovering misplaced inventory, improving cross-docking, and improving in-transit inventory information).	Distribution, retail direct store delivery, and scan-based trading
Management of distributed assets by more efficiently tracking the vessel of transport (pallet, crate, train, trailer, or truck).	Manufacturers, facilities management, and transportation
Enhancement of consumer experience (ensuring that the right products are stocked; improving checkout experience; and maintaining product freshness).	Retailers
Better plant maintenance (ensuring that frequent inspections are actually conducted; remote diagnostics; and work-in-process asset tracking).	Manufacturers, utilities, and mining and construction

Table 11.1: Drivers of RFID Investments

Currently, the common method of reading tags at close range is termed "inductive coupling," in which the antenna of the reader creates a magnetic field with the coiled antenna of the tag. The tag uses the energy generated by this field to send back waves to the reader, which turns these waves into digital information. The reader then transmits this data to the RFID system middleware, which associates the unique information stored on the particular tag with information about the pallet or product to which the tag is attached. After the middleware processes the information received from the readers, it uploads the data to the company's supply chain execution (SCE) software, which updates its inventory data accordingly. All this can take a few seconds to complete.

Types of RFID Tags

Three main types of RFID tags track assets today:

- **Active RFID tags** are battery powered to communicate with readers, typically track assets over long ranges (100 feet or more), and are priced as much as $20–$150 apiece.

- **Passive RFID tags** are proximity systems primarily used to track assets at the pallet, case, and individual levels, have a general read range of less than three meters (more typically 1–2 feet), and are priced at $0.25–$1.00 apiece.

- **Semi-passive RFID tags** rely on batteries to run the microchip's circuitry (not to power communications with the reader), usually monitor high-value goods, and are priced north of $1.

The microchips contained within RFID tags fall into two categories: 1) read-write (those to which new information can be added or existing information can be written over) or 2) read-only (those which carry information that can never be changed unless the chip is reprogrammed). Read-write chips generally cost more than read-only chips.

The evolution of tags parallels the improvements in integrated circuits technology. During the late 1980s and early 1990s, integrated circuit breakthroughs allowed RFID tags to shrink from a brick-size footprint to a wafer-size miniaturized tag. The circuits had evolved so much that they could extract sufficient energy from the incoming reader signal to drive their own response. This development of going "passive" allowed producers to eliminate batteries that added weight and cost.

Tags have many uses. For instance, in the supply chain, companies depend on RFID tags to track their assets on three levels — pallet, case or carton, and item or unit. Tagging at all three levels allows tracking at various stages in the supply chain. For example, when a pallet passes by a reader the RFID system can identify the pallet and check its location into the software system, while recognizing the corresponding cartons and units that it is carrying.

Level of RFID Tagging	Benefits
Pallet tagging	• Product diversion • Supplier vendor-managed inventory and replenishment • Production planning • Distribution center (DC) and goods receipt • Put-away; inventory control, and storage • Real-time available to promise (ATP) inventory
Case or carton tagging	• Case theft • Demand and supply planning • Subcontracting or re-packer visibility • Pick, pack, and ship • Physical counts and reconciliation • Cycle counts • Consign or hold inventory
Item or unit tagging	• Store level promotions and pricing • Unit or item theft • Pay-on-scan; consumer buying behavior understanding • Product research and design • Work-in-process (WIP) inventory • Routing and assembly • Aging and quality control • Manufacturing resource planning (MRP) and capacity planning • Product assortments • Product recall or warranty process

Table 11.2: Benefits of Tagging Assets

Benefits of RFID versus Bar Coding

In a now-classic IBM television commercial first aired in October 1999, the camera follows a retail customer who wanders from shelf to shelf, stuffing items in his coat pocket. As he prepares to walk out the door, a security guard stops him by saying, "Sir, you forgot your receipt!" The ad's conjecture was that RFID-enabled checkout technology eliminates the need for conventional bar code checkout scanning.

The vision of 1999 is rapidly becoming the reality of today. Many expect RFID tags to replace traditional bar code technology in the next ten years. Some of RFID's advantages over bar codes follow.

No physical contact or line of sight required. Because RFID does not require physical contact or line of sight with the item being tracked, it is generally more efficient than traditional bar coding. For example, a case full of items with individual RFID tags attached can be read by a reader in one step as the items pass by, whereas identifying these items using the traditional bar code method takes longer since each item must be scanned individually.

Increased visibility to supply chain. RFID technology has the ability to track items in real time as they move through the supply chain with more touch points than a conventional bar code scanning solution offers. By tracking items almost in real time, users of RFID technology have a better idea of what is going on in the supply chain. A more transparent supply chain provides opportunities to lower inventory carrying costs and lessens the need for storage warehouses, thereby improving cash flow, boosting productivity, and reducing overhead.

Reduced shrinkage. With the capability to monitor the movement of goods throughout the supply chain, consumer packaged goods (CPG) firms and retailers are counting on RFID to reduce shrinkage (stock loss), including theft. Shrinkage has long plagued supply chains, particularly those with high-volume goods. RFID technology is expected to help pinpoint the specific spot where the problem is occurring, and ultimately aid in prevention.

Tags can withstand harsh conditions. In order to function properly, bar code readers must have clean and clear optics, and the label it is reading must be clean and free of abrasion as well. RFID, on the other hand, enables tag reading from great distances (up to 100 feet for active tags), even in challenging environments such as -30°F.

Bar codes will not disappear from checkout overnight. It will take many years to systematically replace the existing bar code infrastructure with RFID. Let's briefly look at the technology architecture that makes the various RFID applications possible.

RFID Technology Architecture

A basic RFID system includes the following components:

- A tag (also called a label or a transponder) that is embedded with a single microchip and an antenna encased in a protective covering. The antenna can be printed on the tag with carbon-based inks. The tag is an extension of the bar code labels you see in stores today, but with more intelligence. Tags can be programmed to contain identification, serial numbers, history, price, color, or virtually any other characteristic.

- A reader (also called an interrogator) that contains an antenna (much like a wireless LAN radio) that communicates with the tag. The readers (either fixed or handheld) send a radio signal to a tag, which responds with information. In the supply chain, readers are embedded in solutions for dock doors, conveyors, inventory shelves, forklift trucks, and handheld units.

- Middleware (also called savants) that aggregates the electronic product code (EPC) information and events from the various readers and ships them to the back-end SCM or ERP systems. These savants located on the edge of the data collection network act as data smoothing and event reporting engines that report only significant product movement events either to higher-level savants or to enterprise applications.

Behind the scenes, these front-end data capture instruments connect to the integration and workflow layer that helps route the business data and events to the appropriate back-end applications. These applications provide decision support and aid in transaction execution.

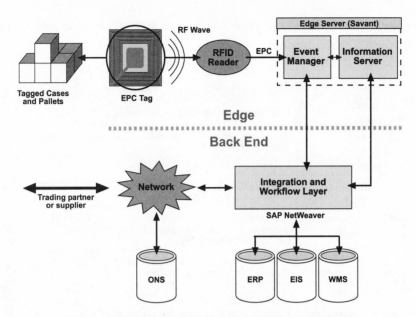

Figure 11.1: A High-Level View of RFID Architecture

The RFID Technology Ecosystem

The RFID market has entered the early stages of maturity with numerous vendors offering different solutions. In Table 11.3 we organized the vendors into categories to help you better grasp who is offering what.

RFID middleware is the growth area today. Many early RFID middleware solutions focused on features like reader integration and coordination, as well as basic data smoothing and filtering capabilities. As the market evolves, we expect middleware platforms will include a deeper set of capabilities: reader and device management, real-time data management, application integration, partner integration, process management and application development, packaged RFID content, and architecture scalability and administration.

However, it is important to note that due to the relative inexperience of suppliers with respect to RFID, most are taking a wait and see approach. They don't want to invest in integrated middleware solutions until things become clearer. Most suppliers are using what is termed a "slap and ship" or "tag at ship" method that enables compliance with the retailer mandates. Slap and ship is the process of putting RFID tags on right before products leave a warehouse and are shipped to a retailer, rather than earlier in the business process.[3]

Type of RFID Vendors	Companies Competing in the Space
Tag vendors	Alien Technology, Matrics, Texas Instruments, Infineon, Intel, and Philips
RFID label printers	Zebra Technologies
Reader vendors	Intermec, Symbol Technologies, Psion Teklogix, SAMSys, Tagsys, and Tyco Sensormatic
Software vendors	SAP, Manhattan Associates, Microsoft, RedPrairie, OAT Systems, Provia Software (viastore systems), and HighJump Software (3M)
Middleware or integration vendors	SAP, TIBCO Software, Microsoft, webMethods, IBM, Sun Microsystems, and GlobeRanger
Data management	IBM, Microsoft, Sybase, and MySQL
Systems integrators	Accenture, IBM, Unisys, and Capgemini

Table 11.3: A Sample of RFID Players

The RFID Market Opportunity

How big is the RFID market? Traditional uses of RFID included tracking heavy, expensive assets such as rail cars, airplanes, and livestock. Now factories can monitor shipments of smaller parts with RFID as the costs of tags and readers come down. In the "new age" of RFID, managers can keep tabs on fixed assets such as construction supplies, dollies on workshop floors, wheelchairs in hospitals, or laptop computers in the office. Other uses of the technology include library checkout and return (Checkpoint Systems) and video rental and return (Tyco Sensormatic).

What has consultants and the press so excited about the technology are recent RFID tag manufacturing improvements, which have led to cost reductions great enough to move the technology from just identifying pallets and truckloads to identifying the individual products.

RFID is somewhat of a holy grail for manufacturers, marketers, and retailers, considering the amount of information that could be contained on any given product. For example, product liability could be better managed. The tire recall situation of 2000 actually generated the very first RFID Tracking and Traceability Standard for Items, a standard developed and published by the Automotive Industry Action Group.[4]

Thanks to the standard, an RFID tag can now track a tire on a Ford Explorer, learning when and where it was manufactured, how it was shipped, where the major stops were, and maybe even track the driving conditions under which it has spent most of its time.

Inventory replenishment and management is also an area that will see significant process improvements. For instance, Cintas, a leading uniform rental company, has been shifting from bar codes to RFID at its garment distribution centers. By eliminating the need to scan a bar code each time the product moves to a different point in the supply chain, the company increases order accuracy and reduces labor costs.

Retailers like RFID because, among other things, when their stores receive boxes of mixed goods, they can quickly scan the items into inventory without manually counting or verifying their contents. Once readers are installed in stores, staff can ensure that each color and size of every style is in stock and locate items when a consumer has returned it to the wrong rack or shelf. The Gap did a trial at one store and found sales rose by more than 5% because in-store availability improved.

Retailers also feel intense pressure to differentiate their in-store experience in ways other than everyday low price. At Prada's store in New York, RFID-enabled dressing rooms are equipped with plasma display screens. When a customer brings a garment into the room, the screen reads the tag and displays information about the designer and choices of fabric and color; it even offers accessory ideas.[5]

The market opportunity for RFID is huge. Some of the projections may prove to be too optimistic, but it bears repeating that we are early in the adoption cycle. It took bar codes almost thirty years to become ubiquitous. We anticipate that RFID will penetrate the market especially in business scenarios where line of site is questionable, where read/write is required, and where unattended scanning, and simultaneous reading and identification of multiple tags is desired.

Typical Applications of RFID

Specific RFID applications have been developed in many areas including material identification, tool handling, automatic guided vehicle control, toll and fee collection, hazardous material identification, meter reading, equipment maintenance, personnel identification, asset location and tracking, animal tagging, and home and security systems.

Let's examine some of the traditional applications that were in place prior to the low-cost RFID tags that companies are piloting.

Security. RFID technology can be utilized for access control to ensure that only authorized personnel can enter restricted areas. Similarly, the technology can identify and locate key personnel and track employees working in critical areas. Airports, buildings, maritime ports, railway stations, and bus terminals find this type of access security useful.

Theft prevention. Because RFID allows an item to be tracked in real time, it can prevent theft. Traditionally, this technology was primarily used for relatively high-priced items. Since the cost of RFID has dropped in the past few years, RFID is being marketed as a means to track inexpensive items such as Gillette's MACH3 razors.

Library use. Given the volume of books that libraries must track as they are checked in and out, RFID was a logical choice. When a book is scanned using RFID technology, the tag identifies the book and then links it to the bibliographic record. As a result, if a book that has not been properly checked out passes through a security gate, an alarm sounds that signals that the item hasn't been checked out and identifies which book it is. Checkpoint offers an RFID system tailored for libraries called Intelligent Library System, which eliminates manual checkout and return in addition to controlling theft.

Electronic toll collection. RFID has begun replacing coins, cash, and tickets for toll collection. One such system is the popular E-ZPass in which drivers prepay tolls and attach a small electronic device (an RFID tag) to the windshield. This tag contains information about the user's account. As E-ZPass customers drive by, an antenna at the toll plaza reads the vehicle and account information contained in the tag, and tolls are automatically debited from prepaid accounts.

Consumer payment systems. Similar to toll collection, gasoline, food, and various types of merchandise can be purchased with RFID technology. Examples of this application include ExxonMobil's Speedpass and Shell's easyPAY system. Speedpass uses an RFID reader located in a gasoline pump to charge purchases to a credit or debit card.

Intermodal rail tags. RFID technology allows rail companies to monitor their rail cars and shipments in real time. Trucking companies and intermodal container carriers are using RFID technology to identify trucks and contents as they pass readers in ports or terminals.

Military applications. Prior to showing interest in low-cost passive RFID, the U.S. Department of Defense (DoD) has tracked major shipments of military supplies with active RFID (and global positioning system, or GPS) technology. Dubbed the Total Asset Visibility (TAV) network, the DoD began using an active RFID system after some logistics problems developed during the first Gulf War. In 1994, the DoD began to install active RFID hardware and software from Savi Technology for item-level tracking on freight containers, consolidated air pallets, and large engine containers shipped around the world.

Tracking prisoners. Prisoners wear wristbands containing tamperproof RFID transmitters that communicate with readers that are installed throughout the prison. Software is used with the RFID technology to determine the location of inmates.

Tracking patients, assets, and medicine. RFID systems are being used to track patients, medicine, blood and specimen bags, and expensive equipment in hospitals. For instance, hospitals can attach RFID tags to the ID bracelets of all patients or just patients requiring special attention, so their location can be monitored continuously.

Baggage tracking. Lost bags pose a recurring problem for airlines. It is estimated that U.S. carriers mishandle about one bag for every 250 pieces of luggage they carry.[6] To solve this problem, major airlines like Delta and United are adding RFID tags to all labels placed on baggage. Readers at check-in counters, on conveyor belts where the bags are sorted, and at aircraft cargo compartments monitor the whereabouts of every bag. RFID tags minimize the problem of misdirected bags because an inventory of the plane's cargo before takeoff determines if the right luggage made it into the hold. If a bag is loaded onto the wrong plane, the airline can locate it quickly without the huge manual labor costs normally incurred when tracking down lost luggage.[7]

Material management and procurement. RFID technology also improves project material tracking, cycle counts, and commodity management. RFID could eliminate 20%–30% of the time spent locating materials and parts during complex construction projects. During installation, large pieces of equipment can require as many as 50 different steps of installation, certification, and inspection. Automating this process with RFID technology could save 1–2 hours per step. Instead of the traditional paperwork that an engineer or inspector stamps, RFID tags and task management software could automate work processes.[8]

Since RFID has been around for a long time, many of the applications we mentioned were developed with proprietary technology. Converting these applications from proprietary models to more standards-based models is where most of the action is today. Global standards must be drafted; otherwise, the RFID landscape will largely maintain its current status quo: proprietary, fragmented, and with vendor specific silos.

The Evolution and Standards of RFID

RFID's roots reach back to World War II and the invention of radar for IFF (Identification Friend or Foe). Its commercial use began in the 1970s with read-only versions for tagging cattle, which don't lend themselves to bar coding. Read-only RFID tags for railroad freight cars and locomotives, chosen partly because they don't require line-of-sight scanning, came next. Then came read-only RFID tags that enabled cars to pass through electronic toll booths. In Florida, a read-write version goes further, instantly telling the motorist his current toll account balance.

In manufacturing, the use of RFID tags started on a fairly large scale in the 1980s (see Table 11.4). The big automakers began using what became known because of their size as RFID "bricks," made by Allen-Bradley and other companies. These big read-only tags were attached to car bodies going through paint shops and are still in use at some automakers' factories. Companies like Intermec, Siemens, Texas Instruments, Philips, and Motorola have since reduced the bricks to the size of a thumbnail.

Although RFID has been around for a while, employing it to track physical objects in the supply chain is a recent development. It was only in the 1990s that people finally recognized RFID's value in expediting supply chain operations. In the late 1990s, the business world came to realize that global RFID standards had to be developed before the technology could be used widely for supply chain execution.

Time Frame	Development and Applications
1940-50	Radar was invented with the help of a major World War II development effort. RFID as we know it was invented in 1948.
1950-60	Early explorations of RFID technology in the laboratory.
1960-70	RFID theory is developed, and some applications are tested in the field. Retailers adopt bar codes.
1970-80	RFID development explodes. Tests of RFID for applications such as animal IDs accelerate. Very early adopters implement RFID.
1980-90	Commercial applications of RFID enter the mainstream Automated toll collection for roads and bridges begins.
1990-2000	RFID standards emerge, and it becomes more widely deployed. Electronic article surveillance in clothing retail outlets is the typical use.
2000-2010	The next century sees Auto-ID standards and RFID-enabled supply chains. The technology is used to protect against theft and manage assets.
2010 and beyond	Sensor networks are introduced. RFID is the first step in integrating physical entities into business processes. The next evolution is expected to be wireless sensor networks and other machine-to-machine (M2M) applications like environmental monitoring.

Table 11.4: RFID Time Line

Retail Industry RFID Standards: Auto-ID and EPCglobal

The continued development of RFID technology hinges on two elements: effective product data standards and an integrated technology infrastructure.

A group called the Auto-ID Center, a consortium of retail, consumer product, and technology companies working with the Massachusetts Institute of Technology (MIT), came together to create an electronic standard of identification called the electronic product code (EPC).

Prior the Auto-ID work, there were too many different product identification and technology standards leading to incompatible, proprietary solutions. The Auto-ID Center for RFID standardization opened at MIT in 1999 and began field tests in 2001. The focus of the Auto-ID effort was primarily North America initially, but as the interest became more widespread, responsibility for the standard has moved to the Uniform Code Council (UCC).

In May 2003, UCC and EAN International spun off a separate organization, EPCglobal, to promote worldwide acceptance of an EPC standard. The Auto-ID Center shut its doors in October 2003, having completed its work and transferred its technology to EPCglobal, which assumed responsibility for completing the transition of the code to a commercial, globally connected, and viable system.

Electronic Product Code

RFID tags in the retail industry are often associated with electronic product codes (EPCs) that are a lot like bar codes. They simply contain information about a product.

Like many current numbering schemes used in commerce, an EPC is divided into a sequence of numbers that identify the manufacturer and product type. An EPC number contains 1) a header, which identifies the length, type, structure, version, and generation of EPC; 2) a manager number, which identifies the company or company entity; 3) the object class, similar to a stock-keeping unit or SKU; and 4) a serial number, which is the specific instance of the object class being tagged.

The value of the EPC lies in its ability to convey detailed information. For instance, unlike bar codes that can tell you that a box contains product ABC, EPCs can differentiate one box of ABC from another box of ABC. They carry detailed lot and product information that can help with monitoring product expiration dates or acting quickly during recalls. EPCs also help suppliers and retailers improve their supply chains so that they send the right products to the right places at the right time.

The biggest benefit of EPCs for retailers will be better merchandise availability. Retailers want to ensure that products are available for purchase when customers need them. Longer term, as the usage of this technology expands, EPC and RFID will help keep costs down, which translates into lower prices at the stores.

EPCglobal Network

The EPCglobal Network is a set of technologies that enable real-time identification and sharing of product information in the supply chain.

The EPCglobal Network comprises five elements:

- The electronic product code (EPC),

- The ID system (EPC tags and readers),

- Object naming service (ONS),

- Physical markup language (PML), and

- Savant data filtering middleware.

The EPC, a code designed to identify and track a specific item in the supply chain, resides on the RFID tag, which communicates its code to a reader. The reader then passes the code to a computer or local application system known as ONS, which tells computer systems where to locate information on the network for objects being tracked.

The common language of the EPCglobal Network, used to define data on physical objects, is PML. The central nervous system of the EPCglobal Network is savant software, which manages readers, filters data, and moves information to the target execution system.[9]

EPCGlobal Network in Action

We'll follow the hypothetical example of a razor blade moving through the supply chain to illustrate what each element of the EPCglobal Network does.

Identifying products. At the point of manufacture, ABC Corporation, the manufacturer, adds an RFID tag to every package of razor blades it produces. Each tag contains a unique EPC that is stored in the tag's microchip, along with a tiny radio antenna. Where appropriate, the EPC will incorporate an existing EAN.UCC identifier (a globally unique number) for the product.

Identifying cases. These tags allow the package of razor blades to be identified, counted, and tracked in a completely automated, cost-effective fashion. The razor blade packages are packed into cases, which feature their own RFID tags, and loaded onto tagged pallets.

Reading tags. As the pallets of razor blades leave the manufacturer, RFID readers positioned above the loading dock door hit the tags with radio waves powering them. The tags "wake up" and start broadcasting their individual EPCs to the readers, which read each tag only once.

Savants at work. The reader is wired to a computer system running savant software. It sends savant the EPCs it has collected, and savant goes to work. The system sends a query over the Internet to an object naming service (ONS) database, which acts like a reverse telephone directory — it receives a number and produces an address.

ONS at work. The ONS server matches the EPC number (the only data stored on the RFID tag) to the address of a server, which has extensive information about the product. This data is available to and can be modified by savant systems around the world.

PML at work. This second server uses PML, or physical markup language, to store comprehensive data about manufacturers' products. It recognizes the incoming EPCs as belonging to the tagged razors from ABC Corp. The server knows the location of the reader that sent the information, so the system now also knows which plant produced the razor blades. If an incident involving a defect or tampering arose, this information would make it easy to track the source of the problem and recall the products in question.

Distribution efficiency. The pallets arrive at the shipping service's distribution center. Thanks to RFID readers in the unloading area, there's no need to open packages and examine their contents. Savant supplies a description of the cargo, and the razor blades are quickly routed to the appropriate truck.

Inventory efficiency. The delivery arrives at RetailWorld, which has been tracking the shipment thanks to its own savant connection. RetailWorld also has loading dock readers. As soon as the razor blades arrive, the retailer's systems are automatically updated to include every package of razor blades that arrived. In this manner, RetailWorld can locate its entire inventory automatically, accurately, and in real time.[10]

Eliminating overstocking. RetailWorld could also feature integrated shelf readers so that when the packages of razors are stocked, the shelves "understand" what's being put in them. When a customer grabs a pack of razor blades, the diminished shelf will route a message to the retailer's automated replenishment systems, which will order more razor blades from the supplier. With such a system, the need to maintain costly safety levels of product in remote warehouses is eliminated.

Checkout convenience. Tags also make the customers' lives easier. In the future, customers can simply walk out the door with their purchases. Readers built into the door will recognize the items in customers' carts by their individual EPCs; with a swipe of the debit or credit card customers are on their way.

The above scenario illustrates the new value created by sharing product information among the various players in the supply chain. Let's now look at different elements of SAP's RFID solution.

SAP's RFID Solution

With the bulk of consumer goods manufacturers and the majority of suppliers to Wal-Mart, METRO, and Tesco already using SAP, it was natural for the SAP supply chain management group to take a lead in creating an RFID infrastructure to support its customers.

The history of RFID at SAP is a storied one. According to Dr. Peter Zencke, executive board member of SAP AG:

> SAP has a long history in the area of RFID technologies, including research that started in 1999 in SAP Labs Tokyo. The Japanese technologists were quite advanced in their work on this type of mini-IT solutions, so SAP has been aware of this technology since then. In 2000, our first prototype RFID solutions were released for our logistics software. We saw interest in this technology, but people thought it was something way off in the future. Then in 2002, we released our first pilot for RFID. Based on the pilot and real-world evaluation of the technology,

we were able to hold a customer meeting in March 2003 to determine which business applications should be affected. There was a lot of interest, mainly in retail, to use it for their adaptive supply chain in stores.[11]

Things started to accelerate in late 2003 and early 2004. To support the suppliers of Wal-Mart and others doing business with the Department of Defense, SAP began offering its RFID solutions in early 2004. The solutions consist of middleware called "Auto-ID Infrastructure," a supply chain event management tool, and an enterprise portal, which is built upon the NetWeaver platform.

Elements of SAP's RFID Solution

The SAP RFID solution package comprises:

- **Auto-ID Infrastructure:** connectivity with readers, tags, and other devices; integration with back-end business processes.

- **SAP Event Management:** full tracking and tracing of EPCs; distribution of EPC-related data to business partners; ONS (object naming service).

- **ERP Adaptors:** integration into existing R/3 supply chain execution processes.

The RFID solution package is linked with the supply chain execution layer, the warehouse management layer, and the event management part of the supply chain solution. The solution's objective is to improve planning and execution throughout the demand and supply chain.

SAP's Auto-ID Infrastructure, developed on a fully Java-based system, is designed to manage data capture from readers to back-end enterprise applications. The solution is considered stand-alone. It does not require the use of SAP's ERP system in order to operate.

METRO Group: An RFID Leader in Europe

Eliminating out-of-stock situations and making shopping more convenient is a goal shared by retailers. Taking the lead in making this vision a reality is METRO Group, one of the world's top five retailers, with annual sales of more than €53 billion. METRO operates more than 2,300 stores mainly in Germany and the rest of Europe.

Through the Future Store Initiative, METRO Group is promoting innovations in retailing on an international level. Its model store in Rheinberg, Germany, demonstrates how technology can benefit retailing operations from inventory to point of sale.

METRO is moving aggressively to compete against Wal-Mart's RFID strategy (see Table 11.5). METRO has assembled a consortium of more than 40 partners from the IT, consumer goods, and service industries. The group develops and tests systems in an actual retail setting to help set retailing standards that can be implemented internationally.

Wal-Mart's RFID Strategy	Wal-Mart's Execution Strategy
Pallet and case tagging for top 100-plus suppliers by January 2005	• "Keep it simple"
• Pilot ramp-up in 2004	• Collaborate so everyone wins - distribution center and back-of-store visibility via Retail Link
• Regional implementation rollout in Texas region (three distribution centers and 150 stores)	**Key Benefits**
• Direct store delivery and distribution center for all the current Wal-Mart formats including SuperCenters and SAM'S CLUB	• Inventory management
	• Reduce out-of-stocks (OOS) - be proactive about OOS reduction with less labor
• By January 2005, all products flowing through Texas region for top 100-plus	• No significant changes to processes (for example, receiving) until technology evolves
• By year-end 2006, all products from all suppliers in all U.S. regions	

Table 11.5: Wal-Mart's RFID Program[12]

Partners in the Future Store Initiative

The Future Store project is one of the first to showcase RFID applications for logistics and retail shop-floor management. It is one of the first test beds of RFID technology based on international standards.

METRO's partners in the Future Store Initiative include SAP, Intel, IBM, and Intermec. SAP brings to the table its SCM solution with its integrated Auto-ID infrastructure, Intel its wireless knowledge, IBM its WebSphere-based RFID and data management system, and Intermec its RFID inventory tracking system.

The different systems allow retailers to track goods throughout their supply chains, from the initial product order through shipment, delivery, warehousing, shelf stocking, and all the way to the point of sale. This innovative pallet- and case-tracking application is more efficient and accurate than manual tracking. It cuts time spent on administration while providing a thorough inventory report.

How Does the Future Store Initiative Work?

At the manufacturing stage, goods receive an RFID tag that contains a unique number called a global trade identification number (GTIN) and a serial number that allows it to be identified at every point along the supply chain. As the goods leave the factory floor and pass through dock doors, the Intermec readers read the tags on the pallets and cases, identifying all the products and automatically building the manifest.

The tags are read again at the distribution center and warehouse, where arrival is confirmed and the information is sent into the inventory system. To avoid duplicate entries and to guarantee inventory accuracy, the RFID tags on the empty cartons and pallets are read a final time then removed or disabled. Each scan gathers complete, accurate shipment, back-store, and front-store inventory levels.

Lastly, this information is sent to METRO Group's SAP enterprise resource planning system. The RFID readers also provide inventory and expiration date control of cosmetics and food products.

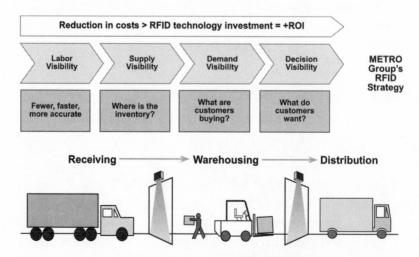

Figure 11.2: METRO Group's RFID Strategy

Expanding the Successful Future Store Initiative

The success of METRO Group's Future Store Initiative has resulted in METRO rolling out RFID company-wide to help control inventory.

METRO is implementing a multistage plan beginning November 2004 that calls for 100 suppliers to outfit all pallets and transport packages with RFID tags in their production facilities for goods bound for ten of METRO Group's central warehouses and for 100 Real and Extra supermarkets, 122 Kaufhof department stores, and 59 METRO Cash & Carry wholesale stores in Germany.

The project is focusing on inventory and supply chain management. Around 20 suppliers will be involved in the first phase of the rollout: pallet level tagging of packaged goods. A second phase will add 80 more suppliers, eight centralized warehouses, and around 270 stores.

The success of innovator METRO Group is being closely watched by many other retailers. These retailers aim to become fast followers once the ROI of RFID investments is better understood.

TransAlta: RFID in the Utilities Industry

The following TransAlta case study illustrates how to capture step change performance improvement through new RFID-enabled best practices and a proactive, action-based culture to achieve improved field operator-driven reliability.

These improvements are supported by a combination of wireless handheld computers, process improvement software, and RFID asset tagging. The ROI and payback have been significant and evident in the reduced de-rates and outages of assets such as boilers, turbines, generators, and electrical systems.[13]

Background

TransAlta Corporation is one of Canada's largest non-regulated power generation and marketing companies, with operations in Canada, Mexico, Australia, and the United States. The company has more than 10,000 megawatts of capacity in operation, under construction, or in development, making it one of the world's leading energy companies.

Its portfolio of generation assets includes coal-fired, gas-fired, hydro, geothermal, and wind-powered plants.

The company's mission is to supply safe, reliable electricity to customers while achieving top-tier performance. The corporate vision is to be the most respected and competitive generator and wholesaler of electricity while creating sustainable value for stakeholders. Strategically, TransAlta concentrates on four key activities: 1) achieving operational excellence, 2) maintaining a strong balance sheet, 3) managing disciplined growth, and 4) effectively managing its key risk factors.

Forces of Change: The Business Drivers

TransAlta management was convinced that it could enhance its competitiveness and profitability by improving its operations, squeezing more out of its diverse existing facilities, and streamlining its business practices to manage costs better.

Operational excellence by itself was not enough. The corporation decided that it needed to take a broader view of its business practices. One manager summed it up saying, "Operational excellence is well and good, but the way you make money is selling the power into the market." Consequently, operational excellence was considered a means to enhance market competitiveness and overall corporate profitability.

TransAlta narrowed its vision for operational excellence to three areas:

- **Intelligence.** Before the new RFID solutions, the company had limited ability to see equipment trends, key performance indicators (KPIs), and production performance on a fleetwide basis, as well as a limited capacity to detect market shifts. The desired state was to have real-time visibility across the fleet and markets. Executives also wanted a better view into real-time production information, costs (including the cost of the next incremental megawatt), and KPIs. Finally, plant personnel wanted to monitor equipment health to predict issues or problems at the plant level.

- **Optimization.** The previous state at TransAlta had been one where it felt it could not respond quickly enough to market supply and demand shifts. It also could not effectively manage fuel blending in response to market price fluctuations. The desired state was to have real-time optimization of market and forced outage plans to better respond to external conditions. Improved management of fuel blending with production planning in response to changing market prices was also necessary.

- **Productivity.** TransAlta wanted to eliminate or streamline inefficiency, duplication, and manual and paper processes within its walls. These processes inhibited TransAlta's ability to perform business analysis, such as evaluating longer-term trends. The company sought to improve the real-time quality of data to increase employee wrench time and reduce production losses, as well as boost record keeping, workplace security, safety, and environmental performance.

Productivity Improvements via Mobile Technology

TransAlta's management team began seriously investigating wireless technologies in 2003. Some members of the management team intuitively thought wireless technology would be disruptive for employees, vendors, and customers; however, they also believed that in every problem lies an opportunity if they could just look closely enough and extract the key value by identifying payback areas across the enterprise.

The first question TransAlta answered concerned the disruptive nature of wireless. TransAlta concluded that the impact from wireless technology was primarily because workflow for mobile workers radically differs from stationary or desktop bound workflow. Mobile workflow requires "store and forward" data because mobile workers are not bound to desks or always connected to a network.

TransAlta's investigation revealed that radio frequency (RF) technologies such as WiFi, Bluetooth, and RFID allow data to exist in areas and on devices where it never existed before. The mobile worker could interact with these new data stores and knowledge bases in new ways, for example, validate events that occurred, access more data, ensure better accuracy of data, take predictive action at the point of incident based on focused advice, and accelerate collaboration.

Early trials of wireless data-driven technology with TransAlta executives yielded positive results. Using RIM BlackBerries, TransAlta's management team quickly determined that it could make better and faster decisions and facilitate near real-time collaboration on demand.

An epiphany occurred. If TransAlta's executives could benefit from better and faster real time decision making, what could mobile wireless technology do for the field workforce? In 2003, TransAlta commissioned a task group to answer that question.

After a comprehensive analysis, the task group concluded that TransAlta could potentially capture significant benefits annually if it deployed wireless technology to the field operators and maintenance technicians at its power generation plants, which generate over 10,000 megawatts of production capacity. TransAlta decided it was time to invest in a front-line defense to improve operating efficiencies and reduce work order maintenance costs across these assets.

TransAlta's vision was then set. The company sought to equip operating personnel with wireless tools and training to achieve the following complementary goals:

- Augment asset availability,

- Cut operating expenses,

- Raise operating personnel productivity,

- Reduce errors while improving safety,

- Increase management review of collected data, and

- Enact proactive maintenance.

No Change, No Gain — Why Process Improvements Come First

TransAlta started looking for cases where mobile investments seemed justified. The due diligence showed that most vendors and most technical approaches couldn't prove that the effort to use wireless technology was warranted. Many vendors and consultants were not knowledgeable enough about applications or TransAlta's business and industry to be able to meet the strict value justification goals the project team had.

A few companies did stand out. One company, SAT Corporation (an SAP partner), emphasized that if TransAlta was not interested in improving field worker processes, "the meeting was over." The company also stated its process improvement support software for field workers was "useless" unless TransAlta was committed to changing field worker processes. SAT's vision fit well with what TransAlta wanted to achieve, and a dialogue ensued. The two companies began to collaborate on areas where field worker process improvements could be made.

Soon TransAlta was looking at its operational KPIs, and, based on SAT's success with improving field worker processes in the refining and chemicals industry, the companies developed a simple framework to estimate what those savings could mean to power generation plants.

From there, the study team was expanded to include members who could provide evidence to support the positive impacts on these KPIs and vouch that TransAlta was likely to achieve the savings seen in other industries. The team found that a three- to six-month payback on the project was likely.

Several process improvements were discussed and rejected before the project team settled on an operator-driven reliability (ODR) initiative. Such a project, accelerated and sustained by SAT's IntelaTrac field worker process improvement support software, could deliver a significant hard dollar payback by doing the following:

- Reducing downtime associated with mechanical equipment failure,

- Trimming total maintenance work order costs by eliminating many secondary equipment failures through predictive maintenance at the point of incident, and

- Realizing some labor savings associated with a reduction in overtime.

The team concluded that the ODR project could yield a step change improvement for better plant operational performance, so it recommended it to management. The project was approved and executed in under six months.

Implementing the Operator-Driven Reliability Project

As part of the project scope TransAlta decided to use RFID tags to track assets and enable ODR and equipment health monitoring (EHM) process improvements.[14] TransAlta selected SAT's IntelaTrac for the mobile infrastructure.

Texas Instruments' 134 kilohertz (kHz) RFID tags were installed on process plant equipment to verify process location for improved data integrity and to help with regulatory requirements and equipment and safety inspections. Mechanical equipment types included pumps, motors, valves, seals, and safety equipment, which can now be tracked throughout the process plant equipment lifecycle. In addition, TransAlta is using the low frequency 134 kHz multi-page RFID tags to confirm operators properly perform procedures and verify that operators are at the correct piece of equipment while collecting data.

With the RFID tags installed, field operators make scheduled plant inspections to collect process and mechanical data about equipment using rugged handhelds.[15] Once operators complete inspections, the data is uploaded and synchronized with the IntelaTrac mobile infrastructure. The next step is the integration of the data with the plant's process historian database and enterprise asset management system (SAP PM).[16]

Using approximately 20 Symbol handheld computers and hundreds of RFID tags, TransAlta is now able to collect ten times more field data with the same resources. By deploying the RFID tags for equipment verification, the company estimates that data is being collected with 40% more accuracy than with previous manual data collection methods.

Show Me the Loonies!

A loonie is a Canadian dollar coin. Every TransAlta project is expected to generate a lot of loonies. The ODR project delivered a solid payback in less than 6 months on a several hundred-thousand-dollar investment (including all external and internal costs) through the benefits listed in Table 11.6.

A project is not successful until the stakeholders accept the process improvements. TransAlta's ODR project has gained acceptance across the stakeholders, from executive management to middle management to the field workers.

Next Steps for TransAlta

Based on the success of the ODR project, TransAlta is exploring different areas for leveraging RFID and mobile technology, including substation and transformer maintenance; line distribution and operations; regulatory compliance reporting; condition monitoring; line and plant security; and customer service.

Overall Benefit for TransAlta	Tangible and Strategic Benefits
Improved availability (less unplanned mechanical downtime)	■ Reduction in de-rates (more than one save per month since process improvement, mostly pending feeder failures) ■ Increased production from faster start-ups through use of IntelaTrac best-practice procedures on critical start-up of equipment ■ Lowered risk of massive production loss (for example, cold reheat start-up procedures validated)
Reduction in total work order maintenance costs	■ Elimination of many secondary failures altogether and overall decrease in repair time of mechanical assets ■ Decrease in costs of primary failures (for example, reduction in annual pump repair costs and motor repair costs) ■ Reduced operator overtime, and overall productivity has increased
Improvement in training and knowledge management	■ Field workers and supervisors understand the KPIs affected (the value to TransAlta), as well as the process improvements and supporting technology

Table 11.6: Benefits from the ODR Project

Making a Business Case for Investing in RFID

How can you plan, develop, and implement RFID solutions with optimum business benefits? The first step of prioritization of RFID opportunities should be based on value proposition and on an understanding of what is currently feasible.

Once you have identified that RFID is right for your organization, you need to answer a series of questions (see Table 11.7). The objective of this exercise is to make sure that you have looked at all the factors needed for a successful implementation. If you are not careful, you may end up implementing an infrastructure characterized by the following:

- It's very expensive to integrate with your existing applications.

- It requires excessive coding and data management workarounds.

- It's hostile to current business processes requiring significant process retooling.

- It interrupts as opposed to streamlines your physical operations.

Before you start, make sure that you clearly understand what you are trying to accomplish, what problem you are trying to fix, and how you will determine if the project is a success. Too many RFID trials have failed because users piloted RFID without directions for implementation.

Moving from Strategy to Implementation

Where do you start? Due to the rapidly changing RFID market, companies are facing the challenge of selecting, integrating, and deploying a heterogeneous collection of RFID hardware and software components, so picking the right partners is an important first step.

Strategic	How can RFID complement our overall strategic vision?
	Should we be a leader or a fast follower?
	Which trading partners should we pilot with and when?
	How will we operate in a world of dual processes? For how long?
Financial	What is the expected return on our RFID investment?
	Which specific RFID applications can drive value (increase revenues, reduce operating costs, enhance safety, improve quality control) for us?
	What is a realistic adoption rate of RFID, and how will that influence our business case?
Technological	What are our technology requirements for an RFID implementation?
	What is the architecture that best delivers on our strategic technology plan?
	How will an RFID implementation affect our current applications?
Organizational	What are the change management implications?
	What are the risks involved in an RFID implementation?

Table 11.7: Questions to Answer in Creating an RFID Business Case

RFID experience is best gathered through action. Once you have completed the analysis phase, the only way to learn RFID's true value is to start testing the technology in your desired application. Running field pilots is an excellent way of understanding the applicability of the existing technology and what benefits are achievable.

Some basic steps in the RFID pilot implementation journey include:

- **Understanding your supply chain requirements:** What items do you want to read? Where? How often? From what distance?

- **Querying other end users about recommendations for trials:** What to do? How to do it? Recommended technologies? Many experienced end users are willing to share their learning experiences.

- **Moving into the action phase in a real-world setting:** Pilot early and often, and reapply what you learn through successive iterations. Put tags on objects and set up readers at the points you seek enhanced visibility.

- **Evaluating technical performance:** Do you get reliable reads? What is the accuracy of the data capture? Are your applications being properly updated?

- **Assess the economic benefits:** Is it better than what you are currently doing? What are the real costs and benefits versus the anticipated ones?

- **Determine RFID's impact** on business processes and integration issues with enterprise systems.

- **Make a decision:** If the pilot is successful, move forward with a larger-scale implementation, refine the trial (different processes, technologies, items or read points), or cease activities.

Sooner or later, mainstream supply chains will fully adopt RFID. It is inevitable. One key to achieving success with RFID is disciplined implementation — knowing the capabilities and limitations of the technology and adjusting them to fit your operation.

Gaining experience with RFID is important. Only those companies with firsthand knowledge of this powerful mobile technology will be able to maximize its impact on their supply chains.

Summary

"Creativity is thinking up new things. Innovation is doing new things."

— Theodore Levitt

As this chapter shows, both creativity and innovation are evident in the RFID ecosystem. RFID is a next-generation data capture technology utilizing active tags that emit radio signals or passive tags that respond when illuminated. These tags, attached to products or assets, remotely read information relevant to the asset, similar to the data contained in a bar code. Because RFID does not require physical contact between the reader and the tag, or even a line of sight, it acquires more data more efficiently and is useful in areas such as supply chain management, asset tracking, and security.

RFID looms as a crucial technology for competitiveness in the twenty-first century. The electronic tracking and management of inventory — from containers or pallets to components — offers substantial benefits in new business flexibility and cost structure that will rapidly differentiate a company from its competitors.

As we highlighted, translating the vision of RFID into reality is a major project for managers. Key issues involve the timing of the investment (When will this revolution sweep the industry?) and the nature of the investment (What infrastructure is needed? What vendor will prevail?).

It's important to reiterate that RFID must be deployed as part of a complete system that allows organizations to capture, move, and manage information to and from the point of business activity. Treating it as a stand-alone technology, disconnected from other business processes, will result in negative ROI.

Chapter Twelve

Creating and Implementing
Your Mobile Solution

Despite the tough IT environment, mobilizing SAP applications is a trend that continues to gather momentum. However, as is always the case with corporate change initiatives, successfully moving from the realm of technology's possibilities to the realm of concrete strategy requires considerable analysis, planning, and discipline. We anticipate that a mobile business strategy will not just be a nice-to-have but a need-to-have in the coming years, so in this chapter, we provide a disciplined methodology for developing a mobile solution strategy.

Introduction

Mobile field service, mobile asset management, direct store delivery, mobile sales, mobile employee-facing processes, and RFID — we covered a lot of ground in the previous section. We presented numerous case studies to highlight what is possible and what some best-practice firms have achieved.

We also illustrated through various examples that the days of the best-of-breed solution are numbered. Specialized mobile capabilities stitched together from niche providers are beginning to fuse into integrated, enterprise-wide infrastructure platforms. The most sophisticated mobile users and providers like SAP, in fact, are already thinking in these terms.

Now it's time to for you to ask: What mobile solutions and infrastructure am I going to implement in my company? How do I justify an investment? How do I execute?

In the current environment of cautious IT spending, dramatic productivity gains are becoming increasingly rare. Mobile applications have emerged as a strong exception, with the potential to drive substantial increases in worker productivity. To build and deploy these applications you need a well-articulated strategy.

Developing a mobile solution strategy is a detailed, intricate process. Formulating one involves assessing mobile worker and employee needs, drafting a mobile blueprint based on those needs, and using the blueprint to prepare a comprehensive business case for gathering the resources — capital, labor, and talent — required to make the strategy a reality.

Envisioning how mobile technology can improve company performance is far easier than executing the strategy in a way that ensures profit. What makes execution difficult is often the process understanding and behavioral change needed among the employees or customers.

Mobile solution strategies invariably fail when they are conceived as handheld devices being slapped in front of some process rather than a new way of doing things. Remember, first-generation e-commerce conceived of a Web site as an "Internet strategy." The current generation of mobile solutions does not need to repeat this mistake. Underestimating the change effort required to deploy a mobile strategy wastes time and resources over the long term.

Figure 12.1 illustrates the different elements — user role, mobile business processes, mobile infrastructure (SAP MI), integration infrastructure (SAP NetWeaver), and back-end applications (ERP, CRM, and SCM) — that must be considered when crafting an effective mobile solution. As you can see from the figure, the mobile applications and the infrastructure are heavily interdependent. The quality of the infrastructure significantly influences the capabilities of the application.

Let's look at the steps involved in the creation of a mobile solution.

From Strategy to Implementation — A Roadmap

Mobile is a way of doing business, not a technology. Incorporating mobile into an organization involves four key elements: the solution strategy, business process evaluation, solution blueprint formulation, and tactical execution.

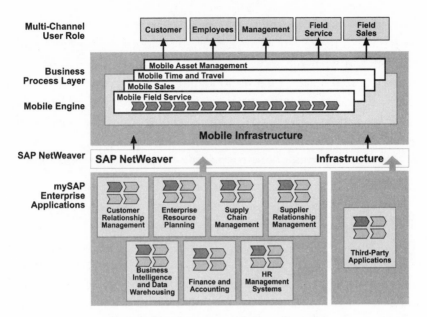

Figure 12.1: Elements of Mobilizing SAP

Mobile business will work only if it provides a complete solution to a problem. All too often, mobile is simply novel technology in search of a business problem. The first step of any solution strategy is to find and structure the business problem. Simply paving the cow path is not enough. You need to find something that can't be done the old way. In established companies, this is most often done by studying the customers in their natural environment to determine gaps between existing solutions and customer needs. For instance, mobile salesforce solutions solve the problem of providing remote users almost instant information, a capability unavailable through any other means.

Creating a solution strategy is a four-phase process.

Phase one: Based on a solid needs assessment, the first step of a solution strategy is to formulate an approach for meeting the business needs and structuring the problem that mobilizing a process is going to solve. The solution strategy clearly identifies why the company is pursuing a mobile strategy and what value it will provide the end users (for example, the service technicians or the salesforce).

Phase two: Once companies articulate and structure their problem, the next step is to figure out what the current state of the business process looks like and what the future state is going to be. The nature of field operations often makes it harder to identify what needs to be changed or fixed. A disciplined process analysis effort can overcome this problem. The process analysis feeds into a high-level blueprint. The Socratic adage "know thyself" is vitally important when structuring any initiative. So, don't underestimate the need for process analysis and evaluation.

Phase three: The solution blueprint is a statement of the strategic, operational, and technical issues the company must address before its mobile strategy can succeed. Why is a blueprint necessary? No sane person would think of building a house without an architectural plan. Yet many corporations attempt to build large-scale mobile applications without a blueprint. The high-level blueprint lays out how the solution strategy is to be implemented and what technology infrastructure is needed to make it happen.

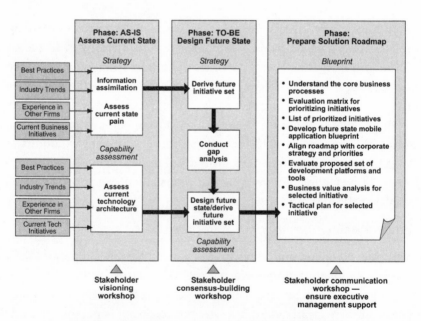

Figure 12.2: Steps in Creating a Mobile Solution

Phase four: Lastly, tactical execution is the implementation front lines, where strategy is converted into action. Here usability experts design the user experience, business analysts create detailed use cases, and programmers create the applications and integrate the front-end user interface with the company's back-end infrastructure. This phase also focuses on how the mobile applications and devices will work with a firm's existing systems.

The next section discusses each of these four phases at length.

Phase One: Creating a Mobile Solution Strategy

In this phase, a team and its sponsors agree on what the mobile project is and what it should accomplish.

Formulating a mobile solution strategy requires taking the general concept of mobility and turning it into a viable business initiative. The outcome of this phase should be a concise statement of which users are affected, what their needs are, how the current processes fail to meet their needs, and how the company's mobile solution will solve the problem. The ability to articulate the strategy crisply demonstrates that the business concept has been thought through with care and thoroughness.

The following questions help define the end goal:

- After our firm implements its mobile solution, the employee is going to do _____.

- After our firm implements its mobile solution, the organization is going to be _____.

A clear statement of the destination is critical to formulating a successful mobile strategy. As with any corporate initiative, defined goals minimize the risk of a project deviating from its original strategy. Not only must the destination be clearly defined, it must also be measurable. In other words, the company and its employees must have a tangible, verifiable sense for knowing "we've arrived."

Specifying a quantifiable destination requires significant background work and analysis. Companies are often tempted to select a destination quickly, to pick one that has been widely written about or talked about. Such "momentum strategies" are similar to momentum investing in the stock market. They reflect a company's unwillingness to focus on its own internal issues, unique characteristics, and customer needs when shaping its mobile strategy. Formulating a strategy takes patience and focus — both rare commodities in the time-deprived world of instant everything.

The first step in developing any mobile strategy is determining the unmet needs of the mobile worker and knowing what the workforce seeks that is novel or unique. The second step is honestly assessing the company's capability for meeting these workforce needs and preferences. A capability assessment identifies the skills and resources the firm currently has and identifies how to acquire the ones it doesn't have. Formulating any solution strategy requires a company to be conscious of its own abilities and limitations. Mobile business is no different.

What Is the Need or Pain?

Any serious attempt to map mobile solution strategy must start with the end user — his pain, his needs, his expectations, and his values. Hardly a new insight. Every manager knows that companies should assess the current state of their end users before introducing something new and unproven. Most business processes have inefficiencies that are best identified by listening to end-user unhappiness with existing processes. Removing the sources of dissatisfaction or offering end users a breakthrough on performance can result in mobile opportunities.

As we stated in the previous chapters, one relatively quick way to identify a mobile solution that has a high potential for a significant, quick ROI is by looking for any process that utilizes paper for data capture. Paper is an inherently slow, inaccurate tool for collecting data. Paper processes are often coupled with key data transmitted through conversations that are also error-prone and harder to track.

Many enterprises that have converted a paper-based process to an electronic form-based application on a mobile device have seen data collection times reduced in the field, more accurate data flowing to central enterprise servers, and faster business reporting. The very small size of PDAs available in different form factors, along with internal battery power that can support mobile workers for an entire day shift while wirelessly connected, makes them capable of handling tasks that are not possible with notebook computers.

Automating data capture in this way helps to reduce the overall time it takes to provide customer services. Automation enables more business transactions at the same staffing levels while improving overall customer satisfaction. Errors can be very costly, so in some cases error avoidance can be the vehicle for achieving a rapid return on one's mobile solution investment.

The bottom line for mobile solution strategy: Opportunities often come from viewing the world differently and from simple insights, but awareness of service and business process gaps is not enough. You must also understand how to address them using mobile technology.

The five critical steps in creating a mobile strategy include:

1. List the really painful process areas and prioritize,

2. Identify the potential payback from solving each pain,

3. Validate the pain by collecting some primary data,

4. Estimate the ROI and reprioritize, and

5. If ROI is significant, develop a preliminary business case to present to management.

Now you are ready for phase two.

Phase Two: Evaluating Business Processes

Even the most well-intentioned business strategies are often visionary, abstract, and qualitative. They remain at the 20,000-foot level, never becoming pragmatic, concrete, or quantifiable.

To pluck a vision out of the ethereal realm and ground it in everyday reality, a business must analyze its objectives, process structure, process limitations, and constraints. Most firms ignore this critical step when initiating a company project, believing that their business processes are well known. The reality is that most large firms know very little about themselves in terms of concrete tasks, skills, abilities, and resources.

The Difficulty of Process Analysis

Suppose you asked ten people who perform the same task to walk you through what they do. The odds of getting the same description from each person are slim. You would probably end up with ten variants of the same process.

So the question is: How do you improve and mobilize a process that is really ten different ones in reality? The lack of a standard, well-documented process model is one of the many reasons why mobilizing business processes can be particularly challenging. Filling that gap is a critical point in the process analysis phases because doing it well will significantly reduce downstream rework.

This is easier said than done. We have found that far too often corporate executives embrace a business vision but are incapable of staying focused on the next step. For example, a Fortune 50 company wanted to develop a consistent field sales experience across different business units. Everyone at the firm came to accept this vision during a two-day workshop. Their acceptance, however, was only philosophical, and they left the workshop wondering what to do next.

Luckily, this firm had a strong leader who stepped in to show the way. Over the next quarter, a mobile task force was set up to drill into the business process specifics. The task force took the time to understand salesperson' needs and preferences, the current AS-IS process, and how mobilizing the process could create value.

A good process analysis effort involves focusing on the company's internal operations and on how to extend them to implement the new mobile strategies. In this phase, the company is assessing whether or not it can achieve the mobile vision it has said it wants. It must honestly look at its current organization, business processes, and people to support the new vision. It must determine what changes need to be made to ensure success. Lastly, a process evaluation prioritizes each mobility project according to the "burning need" and the value the project brings.

Future State Process Design

Once the capabilities are evaluated and linked to the broad strategy, various opportunities or scenarios begin to emerge. At this time, it is essential for companies to select a scenario based on what they know is right for them.

A capably executed strategy delivers better results than a seemingly more elegant one that does not reflect an organization's strengths. It makes sense to choose a sound strategy that meets financial goals and provides the best fit with the abilities of the organization.

When determining a company's "TO-BE" strategy, it is crucial to assess its strengths and weaknesses. Such an assessment can challenge long-held beliefs. However, strength and weakness are both relative concepts — relative to the competition and to customers' expectations. Yesterday's strengths may have become today's weaknesses without anyone in management noticing. A corporate self-examination clarifies a company's readiness in the existing business environment, given the vulnerabilities and risks to which it is open.

It is also important to uncover and address any differences between the philosophies of the various lines of businesses, the technology group, and that of the leadership. Often these differences are reflected in a business organized around application "stovepipes" resulting from political conflicts. Companies in which the application infrastructure isn't aligned with customer-facing or employee-facing business objectives must clean house before they can embark on a mobile strategy. As a result, top management commitment will be crucial in going forward.

What New Capabilities Do We Need?

Once a strategic scenario is chosen, capability assessments identify what the company must acquire, improve, learn, or build in order to make its mobile strategy a reality. The assessment step requires having a fully developed statement of the effort's scope and focus. The next step is to structure a firm's capability assessment and ensure that its vision and capabilities are clearly aligned, leading to the creation of a business case.

The assessment will reveal gaps in the company's current capabilities. These gaps have to be filled by either acquiring, hiring, or contracting, or through strategic partnering. If these missing capabilities are ignored, the company risks "mobilizing" its existing inefficiencies. In other words, it automates a mess. Despite the investments, the root causes of historical company problems remain, putting the project at risk.

A significant part of the assessment is evaluating application and information infrastructure readiness. Mobile infrastructure can either accelerate or impede an organization's ability to adapt to changing business conditions. The infrastructure design must be flexible enough to integrate emerging technologies without compromising the existing enterprise architecture. The ability to fully meet new business requirements is revealed during the infrastructure assessment.

The capabilities assessment phase should also factor in the change management requirements. It must assess the cultural willingness to change and whether the initiative is something the employees approve of or whether it is mandated by management. Never underestimate the changes required in culture, business practices, and operations when undertaking a company project.

The change plan should carefully phase in mobile initiatives with the company's overall strategy. A thorough plan details how the current business operations will be performed while transitioning to the new way of doing business. The plan should provide a sense of stability and security as the firm moves from its current to its future state.

Creating a Detailed Process Transition Roadmap

This step links a company's mobile "TO-BE" strategy with its current "AS-IS" capabilities. It describes the unique combination of capabilities, processes, partnerships, and funding needed to support a strategy.

Determining the appropriate structure for a new initiative means addressing a variety of issues, including creating transition models for bridging the old and new, developing a strategy to motivate employee adoption, and designing incentives to overcome employee inertia.

Employee inertia is a response to living and working in environments of constant change. It is essentially "innovation fatigue," and it creates a vicious spiral in which the pressure to perform leads to accelerated burnout. Employees become exhausted, with little energy for new innovation, and this stalls the change process. The result is greater disruption to the company's social structure.

When adopting any innovation, the transition should occur in a way that minimizes disruption. Capability configuration helps define a high-level structure for making explicit exactly how the transition will take place and who will be responsible for making it happen. The structure and transition plan are documented in the business case.

The business case helps the executive team to fully understand the mobile business efforts and objectives. It relates the project's objectives to each executive's functional area and informs executives of the project's impact. It defines the scope, specific milestones, deliverables, activities, and critical success factors for each function.

Phase Three: Formulating a Solution Blueprint

A business case leads to a solution blueprint. The solution blueprint explores different alternatives for executing the mobile strategy.

Developing the blueprint forces management to consider all the aspects involved in creating the mobile solution. A blueprint ties together all activities on a project. A strategy may be well conceived, the business case carefully drawn up, the project adequately financed, the technology very sophisticated, and the consultants brilliant, but if the efforts of all participants are not coordinated and skillfully managed, the project may fail to meet the schedule, overrun the budget, or fall short of expectations. The larger and more complex the project, the more critical the overall solution blueprint is.

In preparing the blueprint, the firm must analyze the project's potential ramifications for existing technology, operations, and customer service strategies. The blueprint also outlines the human, physical, and financial resources the project requires. Further, the blueprint grounds the strategy in practical reality and saves time, energy, and resources that would have been consumed through trial and error. On a typical project, novel and puzzling problems have a way of cropping up constantly. The ability to respond to these challenges and creatively resolve conflicts can spell the difference between success and failure.

In more mature organizations, solution blueprint planning links the strategy, applications, and infrastructure together in an iterative design. Figure 12.3 shows a multitier model of the different elements of a solution blueprint. The challenge in solution blueprint planning is to try to preserve viable legacy assets, to replace outmoded assets, and to add new ones — all in the context of a broader infrastructure (SAP NetWeaver) that links them coherently.

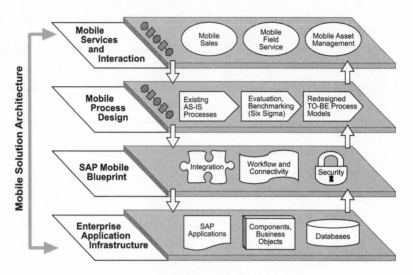

Figure 12.3: Mobile Solution Blueprint

When reviewing your blueprint priorities, be practical and balance expectations with reality. The mobile Internet is supposed to link applications and users effortlessly, ushering in an era of frictionless commerce. In this vision, the role of traditional infrastructure elements — legacy systems, applications, databases, and networks — would be supplanted, enhanced, or bypassed with more efficient technology. Barriers to information would go down, even as the complexity increases.

We have seen these scenarios before. Instead of falling prey to "visionary" rip-and-replace efforts, traditional infrastructure elements have maintained their presence in the corporation. Most companies get 99% of their information from existing applications. Bypassing the existing systems is a fantasy, so spend time thinking through how to integrate and leverage existing applications. That is the hard part of mobile solution blueprints — designing the right integration points.

In our experience, most "great strategies" have failed in linking the new with the old. Laying new mobile processes on top of the existing infrastructure often creates unforeseen problems. Today's typical corporate infrastructure comprises a diverse mixture of application packages, legacy systems, and functional processes. Integrating them is often the most difficult part of any solution blueprint.

The solution blueprint evolves continuously. It requires considerable discipline to develop one that will survive over the course of the next decade as problems with device usability and slow Web access are overcome. A clearly thought-out and adhered-to blueprint plan helps to ground a company's mobile strategy in the realities of a business environment in flux. It is a living document able to adapt to business and technological innovations that will occur in the near future.

Phase Four: Tactical Execution

Given the relative novelty of mobile business, we recommend companies start with a pilot to test their assumptions and understand the terrain.

Mobile business may require different approaches in design, development, and implementation of applications due to the inherent characteristics of wireless networks and mobile devices. Whenever a new period of innovation begins, software architects, programmers, and managers strain their intuition hoping to gain an understanding of the applications most likely to work.

Mobile business implementations may be quite different from those of e-business. Corporations that want to gain a first-mover edge, whether by being the first to launch new channels, know how much they depend on new application architecture to achieve their objectives.

Usually, the architecture is a mix of costly and aging applications, hardware systems, and networks. Far from making it possible to achieve mobile application goals, it can make a mockery of them.

We often recommend that companies, especially large ones, refrain from leaping headfirst into the unknown, but rather prototype to understand the ROI, integration pitfalls, change management issues, and customer adoption patterns.

Only hard-won experience in the trenches will give companies this knowledge. As Theodore Roosevelt once said:

> It is not the critic that counts, not the man who points
> out how the strong man stumbled...The credit belongs

to the man who is actually in the arena...who strives valiantly, who errs, and often comes up short again and again...if he fails, at least he fails while daring greatly so that his soul shall never be with those cold and timid ones who know neither victory nor defeat.

Step-by-Step Guide to Mobilizing Processes

RFID, wireless data, wireless Internet, wireless Web, pervasive computing, mobile computing, mobile commerce, mobile business — all point to the same thing: process change. Every mobile solution is at its core a systematic business process change management effort. You are changing the old ways of doing certain things and replacing them with newer, automated ways.

Like every change initiative, a mobile solution does not just happen; it must be designed with the users in mind and implemented systematically. In other words, certain existing processes (for example, field service) have to be literally disassembled into their fundamentals and reassembled to meet new objectives.

Disassembling paper-based processes and reassembling them as mobile processes is the theme of this section. To undertake this effort, you have to understand the current process inefficiencies that cause time, resources, and money to be wasted. Eliminating waste and creating new value implies a willingness to redesign the current way of doing things.

To bring about effective change, you must first understand the unique situation. The rest of this section guides you through the steps necessary to create and implement an optimum mobility-driven process change strategy. We use an iterative yet simple model to guide you in this process. The Six Sigma DMAIC process — define, measure, analyze, implement, and control — should help you to channel these mobile change management efforts.

If you already have picked a business process to be mobilized, then it is time to get your hands dirty.

Define the Problem — The Strategy

Always start with the users (the buzzword for this is customer centricity). Figure out what they want and how to better satisfy them. Take a 50,000-foot view to identify the key output variables (the buzzword for this is critical-to-quality) and list what is important to customers. Do you understand your customer's pain?

Defining the problem means collecting, defining, and communicating all the background information on the current product, process, work environment, and customer or end user. The detailed steps for defining your problem follow.

Clearly state the business context. Define the scope of the business context. Delineate your boundaries clearly (Who are the customers? What are the outputs? Who are the suppliers? What are the inputs? What are the expected outcomes?). The output of this step is a project charter (What do we want to accomplish?). For instance, in a project involving digitizing field service, the project charter is to reduce end-to-end problem-to-invoice process cycle time from an average of 3 days to an average of 24 hours.

Be the customer (or user). Take a moment and look at your organization from the customers' perspective. What do they see? Mobilizing any process requires you to look at the processes from the customers' perspective, not yours. In other words, study processes from the outside in. By understanding the transaction lifecycle with customer needs in mind, you can discover what they are seeing and feeling.

Voice of the customer (VOC), a customer interview and analysis technique, is a useful method for gathering firsthand information about what the customer is looking for. With this knowledge, you can identify areas where you can add value or improve from their perspective.

Map the current process. What broad steps (composite processes) are needed to serve a customer? Assess and map the high-level flows of products, programs, services, information, and payments as appropriate and based on the end-to-end services. Without knowing how you or customers complete an activity at least at the high level, you will never know how to change it for the better.

Figure 12.4 illustrates the yawning gap between expectation and reality. Why does the gap exist? After several years of evolution, process flows tend to get complicated as time progresses. Companies buy other companies; they sell off some companies. They grow from 100 to 10,000 employees. Workflows become convoluted. The challenge usually is to think of new ways to simplify those flows.

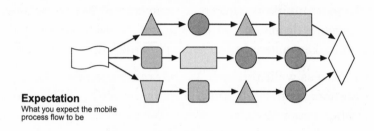

Expectation
What you expect the mobile
process flow to be

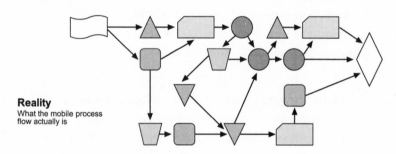

Reality
What the mobile process
flow actually is

Figure 12.4: Process Expectation versus Reality

Measure — Process Analysis

After you finish defining the high-level process, you must begin studying the details. Developing the detailed process decomposition is the foundation of mobilization. It keeps efforts grounded in reality.

The detailed steps include:

Draw an AS-IS map. Start with current state and validate boundaries, values, company outcomes, vision, and mission. Adjust the initial assumptions as necessary to reflect reality. The output summarizes current reality in a visual map that allows the whole organization to see the opportunity. Understanding the assumptions behind a process is extremely important. Certain processes are the way they are for a reason. Not understanding these reasons will create problems downstream.

Drill down. Take each portion of the current state and drill down one layer to the next level of processes, flows, components, or influences. Drilling down one layer makes the interaction of the various flows more apparent and allows more data to be gathered and analyzed. Drill down is a long, tedious process and often the step where firms begin to lose interest. Extracting details of the different ways tasks are being done in the real world takes quite a bit of detective work.

Conduct a process walk-through. What is causing the process to break down or be inefficient? What causes variations? Variation is what you encounter when you walk up to the counter and get great service once and lousy service another. Variability is the enemy of consistency and customer satisfaction. Overlay the soft stuff (workforce issues) with the hard stuff (technical components) of the flow not already captured and mapped. Validate the existence of the connections and the decision points of the process decomposition structure.

Perform linkage analysis. Capture relevant data that is measured in terms defined by the company and understood consistently (to prevent data comparison flaws). That is, capture the metrics or information available for each piece and analyze the behaviors that each generates. Conduct assessments to capture other data elements and to create a comprehensive view.

Talk to the people who actually perform the work that you are studying as they are the most knowledgeable about how to improve the workflow and eliminate variation. Then start measuring and refining. Remember to measure current customer satisfaction constantly because that is your ultimate measure of success.

Analyze and Improve — Solution Blueprint

The next action is to develop a practical TO-BE map for what you would like to achieve in the near future. To reach this point, you have to change your processes to maximize customer satisfaction and identify performance gaps and improvement objectives. This often involves slicing and dicing the AS-IS data to understand the existing process conditions and problems that create customer dissatisfaction.

The detailed steps include the following:

Conduct a process analysis. Analyze and capture bottlenecks, flow, value inhibitors (whether social or technical), costs, risks to flow, and risks to success criteria. Group these findings into priorities and analyze them to understand how they affect service and wait time, resources, and money. Prioritize the list of changes into short term and long term and assess the impact of each proposed process change.

Create an ideal state. The ideal state should include process, technical, and social elements. Perfection is impossible, but reaching for it stimulates breakthrough thinking and analysis that will create a more robust future state.

Develop a version map. Take your ideal state and work backwards. Create a TO-BE version map achievable in a relatively short-term window (six to nine months) based upon that ideal state. Versioning is a commonly used method of moving towards an ideal state.

Conduct a feasibility analysis. Assess and analyze the gaps in the ability to achieve the next version. Create a balanced set of metrics for success and confirm behaviors generated conform to the future state directives.

Simply tweaking the old work processes may not be enough to implement these changes. You may have to invent new ones.

Implement — Tactical Execution

Customer-centric design is consistently giving the customer what they want, when they want it. Once the root causes of problems are determined, the goal is to implement solutions that minimize, reduce, or eliminate them altogether. The detailed steps follow.

Design the mobile platform. Establish and implement actions, programs, or events to create value and eliminate inefficiency in order to achieve the future state.

Develop project management structure. Create necessary project management infrastructure (including organizational structure) to ensure leadership, integration, course corrections, validation, and accountability for the changes. Analyze risks, change management issues, and other inhibitors of successful implementation.

Control and Learn — Versioning

A critical part of execution is the ability to evaluate and learn. In this step, the firm analyzes before and after data, monitors the overall project, and documents the overall user acceptance. The detailed steps include:

Manage change. Establish a change management program to get adoption. Simply implementing the applications and taking a "build it and they will come" approach usually fails. People tend to resist imposed change; thus, overcoming it requires a deliberate strategy. Create a marketing and communication plan to ensure stakeholder enrollment, ownership and accountability for all actions and ongoing analysis.

Analyze the return on investment. What value did your efforts yield? Quantifying the ROI is a great way of forcing everyone involved to understand that there is a financial goal that anchors process mobilization. Based on the ROI, decide on a renewal period to revisit and adjust the future state (a continuous versioning view) on the path to the next state. To make this happen, you need to collect detailed data on mobile process performance.

Learn. Repeat the entire process for the next version, but reflect first. Usually, managers have little or no time for reflection. This important step helps articulate various dysfunctional underlying dynamics that are causing problems.

In summary, designing a mobile solution requires making choices in seven areas. It requires specifying *what outcomes* are to be produced and deciding *who* should perform the tasks, *where* they should be performed, and *when*. It also involves determining under which circumstances *(whether)* each of the tasks in the field should be synchronized with the back end, *what information* should be available to users, and *how thoroughly* each task needs to be performed.

Summary

"People who get on in this world are the people who get up and look for the circumstances they want, and, if they can't find them, make them."

— George Bernard Shaw

Why is it that when you have two companies with the same capital assets and a similar number of employees one struggles and the other grows steadily? The difference in operational performance comes from how work gets done: how companies do what they do, how they operate using mobile technology. The quality of the mobile strategy and its execution are the difference between success and failure.

The answers to five questions — why, what, when, where, and who — form the foundation of mobile solution strategy. A constantly changing business environment makes mobile strategy more, not less, important to business success. Yet we can safely predict that many organizations will fail to create effective mobile business strategies. As a result, these firms risk investing valuable resources in poorly conceived initiatives that will at best return mediocre results.

Established firms must decide for themselves whether to spend time and money carefully defining a mobile strategy. If they decide to do so, the time has come for their management to understand the potential of new mobile applications and begin the necessary planning to integrate them into their business processes. If they choose not to pursue a mobile initiative, competition and new entrants most likely will.

Finally, when creating a mobile solution strategy, a company must plan as though it is confronting a moving target. Hence, what matters is the ability to adapt the plan to market and customer reactions rapidly and smoothly. Flexibility is thus a cardinal principle of mobile solutions, but it will be of benefit only if it is bound by a rigid disciplinary framework. Flexibility and discipline, however, are not easy to combine. In many cases, they can be achieved only at each other's expense. The next decade promises to be a very interesting one.

Endnotes

Chapter One

1. For more details on first-generation mobile solutions, see Ravi Kalakota and Marcia Robinson, *M-Business: The Race to Mobility* (New York: McGraw-Hill, 2001).

Chapter Two

1. Eric S. Rabkin, "SciFi: Novel Inspiration," *BusinessWeek*, October 11, 2004.
2. Aisha M. Williams, "Doing Business Without Wires: PDAs," InformationWeek.com News, January 15, 2001.

Chapter Three

1. For a fascinating 20-year retrospective on the personal computer, see the video "Triumph of the Nerds" by Robert X. Cringley. Also see Jim Carlton's article, "It Seems Like Yesterday," (*The Wall Street Journal*, November 16, 1998) for some insightful commentary on the PC industry.
2. Yankee Group's report "Europe, Middle East, and Africa to Remain the World's Largest Regional Wireless Market," June 2004.
3. According to IDC, annual worldwide sales of handheld devices are projected to increase to an estimated 16.5 million units in 2007, from approximately 10.1 million units in 2000.
4. IDC projects annual worldwide sales of these converged handheld devices to grow to an estimated 80.6 million in 2007 from approximately 409,000 in 2000.
5. May Wong, "Sharp to Stop Selling PDA in U.S.," Associated Press, October 21, 2004.
6. The Palm Treo 650 has a high-resolution 320 x 320 pixel thin-film-transistor, 65,000 color screen, and a faster Intel 312MHz processor. The Treo 650 includes a built-in MP3 player and allows video capture and playback. Bluetooth technology is built into the Treo 650.
7. Source: http://www.embedded-linux.org/
8. Java 2, Micro Edition (J2ME) technology is an optimized runtime Java environment designed to enable Java applications to run on small computing devices. Recognizing that small devices vary greatly in their nature and application, J2ME defines standard subsets of APIs that target specific classifications of small computing devices.

9.   For more technical information, see Agilent Technologies' feature story "Next-generation wireless: Far more than phones," available at http://www.agilent.com/Feature/English/archive/E014.html as of October 2004.

10. Sam Diaz and Dean Takahashi, "Taking WiFi to the Max," *San Jose Mercury News*, October 4, 2004.

11. Bluetooth was the name given to Harald Blatand, a tenth-century Danish Viking king who united and controlled Denmark and Norway. The name symbolizes the specification's ability to unify the telecommunications and computing industries using wireless technology.

12. UWB is potentially suitable for high data rate, short-range links — a "better" Bluetooth. For more information, see www.uwb.org.

13. For more information, see www.zigbee.org

14. Jaye Scholl, "The Chips Are Down," *Barron's*, March 12, 2001.

15. NTT DoCoMo, "NTT DoCoMo Develops Prototype Micro Fuel Cell for FOMA Handsets," September 30, 2004, press release.

16. For more detailed information on how telematics works, see www.telematics.motorola.com.

Chapter Four

1.   According to Webopedia, there are many different middleware categories. A typical example is one where a middleware product links a database system to a Web server. This allows users to request data from the database using forms displayed on a Web browser, and it enables the Web server to return dynamic Web pages based on the user's requests and profile. See Webopedia's site www.webopedia.com for more detail.

2.   WAP is a standard for data transfer between mobile handsets with minimal screen display and the Internet. WAP strips all graphics before displaying data on small screens, such as mobile phones. WAP was an initiative started in 1997 by Unwired Planet (now Openwave), Motorola, Nokia, and Ericsson to develop a standard for wireless content delivery based on the next generation of mobile communicators.

3.   With the integration into NetWeaver, the former product SAP Mobile Engine has been rebranded SAP Mobile Infrastructure.

4.   This figure was adapted with SAP's permission from the company's marketing presentations.

5.   From a historical perspective, SAP Mobile Infrastructure extends the SAP Mobile Engine (SAP ME), which was a Java-based runtime and development environment.

6.   Source: SAP Developer's Network (www.sdn.sap.com). If you want the most current information on SAP NetWeaver Mobile, this Web site is a good one to visit.

7.   This figure was adapted with SAP's permission from the company's technical presentations.

8.   Ibid.

9.   Ibid.

10. This information came from an interview E-Business Strategies conducted with Fernando Alvarez on September 20, 2004.

Chapter Five

1.   Sears chose to use River Run software, Itronix hardware, and the BellSouth Intelligent Wireless Network to meet the needs of its field force.

2.   This section is adapted with permission from an SAP mobile business case study on Messer Griesheim GmbH.

Chapter Six

1.   David Leonhardt, "U.S. Economy in Worst Hiring Slump in 20 Years," *The New York Times*, February 6, 2003.

2. Leading players in the asset management software industry include SAP, Indus, Datastream, and MRO Software.

3. Source: Düsseldorf Airport Fire, www.geocities.com/framemethod/report5E.html.

4. The content of this case study is adapted from an SAP AG case study and various presentations. See also Chapter 14 of Ulrich Kipper's *Real-Time Case Study: Fire Safety at Frankfurt Airport*, published by SAP as a tribute to one of its founders, Hasso Plattner.

5. The size and shape of the shutters depend on their location. They can range in size between 350 square centimeters and 2 square meters.

6. The content of this case study is adapted from an SAP AG case study written in collaboration with IDS Scheer. The case study is reproduced with permission.

7. The content of this case study is based on an SAP Mobile Business success story about Wesertal GmbH. The case study is reproduced with permission.

8. Wesertal was using SAP's industry solution for the utility sector, mySAP Utilities, to manage its business.

9. Wesertal worked with both SAP and consulting partner IBM to implement the solution.

10. The IFD used by SBC technicians is the Panasonic Toughbook, equipped with an integrated Sierra Wireless modem. For more information on this initiative, see Sierra Wireless's November 29, 2001, press release "SBC Communications Inc-Accenture, Panasonic, and Sierra Wireless Win Top Honors at the Moby Awards."

Chapter Seven

1. According to the Global Commerce Initiative's Direct Store Delivery Working Group, the textbook definition of DSD is "a business process that is based on the direct delivery of products from supplier to retail store, bypassing the retailer's warehouse. This practice is primarily used for products that have high turnover, are perishable (such as snack foods, beer, carbonated beverages, and bread), or fragile. Among the benefits reported by DSD companies are timely shelf replenishment, improved inventory management, reduced costs, and enhanced product availability for the consumer."

2. In the context of DSD, a brand owner refers to the entity that owns the brand; a distributor is the party responsible for moving the product from the brand owner to the retail store; a retail store is defined as an individual store; and, lastly, the term "retailer" indicates a decision maker usually from headquarters with some level of authority over local, individual stores.

3. Source: Grocery Manufacturers of America (www.gmabrands.com).

4. "E-Commerce Opportunities for Direct Store Delivery," a 2002 white paper by the Direct Store Delivery Committee of Grocery Manufacturers of America available for purchase on www.gmabrands.com.

5. For more information about Symbol's handhelds and the MC9000 in particular, visit the company's site, www.symbol.com.

6. For more details on the DSD processes, see the GMA white paper sourced in note 4.

7. SAP AG, "Coca-Cola Enterprises Joins SAP in Direct Store Delivery Initiative to Enhance Sales, Logistics, Service and Mobile Applications," February 2004 press release.

8. For more information see Robert Puric and Bob Schreib's article, "PepsiAmericas taps rugged, mobile computers for timely, accurate deliveries," published on www.planetpdamag.com on September 4, 2002.

9. This case study is based on ongoing research at E-Business Strategies into mobile DSD strategies.

10. Source: Frito-Lay's Web site, www.fritolay.com/faq.html.

11. Source: Frito-Lay's Web site, www.fritolay.com/edi/pages/impl_dex/steps.html#benefits.

12. This case study is based on ongoing research at E-Business Strategies that examines mobile DSD strategies.

13. Sara Lee, "Sara Lee Corporation to Acquire Earthgrains for $2.8 Billion; Becomes Number-Two Player in Fresh Bread Category," July 2, 2001, press release.

14. The top bread vendors include Interstate Bakeries, George Weston Bakeries, Flowers Bakeries, Pepperidge Farm, United States Bakery, Grupo Bimbo, Stroehmann Bakeries, and Bestfoods.

15. Source: the Symbol Technologies' site http://www.symbol.com/solutions/retail/food_drug_scan-based_trading.html.

Chapter Eight

1. Palm Inc., "Palm Tungsten T Handhelds Used as Data Collection and Reporting Tools," March 3, 2003, press release.

2. Customer scoring combines multiple aspects of the customer into a coherent evaluation, which enables the salesperson to understand quickly the customer's relevance for business success.

3. Mobile detailing complements other methods — direct-to-consumer advertising (in North America), e-detailing, and direct mail campaigns — used to influence physicians.

4. This case study is adapted from a TÜV Nord case study written by SAP. This content is used with permission.

5. This case study was developed by Capgemini under the supervision of Cindy Warner, vice president, Americas SAP CRM. This content is used with permission. PharmaCo, the global pharmaceutical company, asked that its identity not be disclosed.

Chapter Nine

1. Source: Symbol Technologies, www.symbol.com.

2. Stacy Collett, "Wireless Gets Down to Business," *Computerworld*, May 5, 2003.

3. Source: Psion Teklogix, www.psionteklogix.com.

4. "C&H Sugar implements SAP Console," case study written by Catalyst International.

5. Catalyst International, "Catalyst SAPConsole Data Collection Solution Set Improves Inventory Control at C & H Sugar," April 8, 2004, press release.

6. This figure was adapted with SAP's permission from the company's technical presentations.

7. Source: Psion Teklogix, www.psionteklogix.com.

8. Source: UPS's 2003 annual report.

9. This information came from a UPS fact sheet titled "The Evolution of the UPS Delivery Information Acquisition Device (DIAD)," available at www.pressroom.ups.com as of October 2004.

10. Source: http://www.pressroom.ups.com/

11. Dan Farber, "UPS Takes Wireless to the Next Level," www.zdnet.com ("Wireless that Works" series), April 28, 2003.

12. Galen Gruman, "UPS Versus FedEx: Head-to-Head on Wireless," *CIO*, June 1, 2004.

13. UPS "UPS Starts European Deployment of Its Latest Wireless Technology," June 22, 2004, press release.

Chapter Ten

1. Ravi Kalakota and Marcia Robinson, *M-Business: The Race to Mobility*, (New York: McGraw-Hill, 2001).

2. Founded in 1984 and based in Waterloo, Canada, RIM is a leading designer, manufacturer, and marketer of wireless solutions. RIM's product portfolio includes the RIM Wireless Handheld product line, the BlackBerry wireless data solutions, OEM radio modems, and related software development tool kits. RIM also licenses its enterprise server applications, solutions, and hardware reference designs to third-party OEMs.

3.   VoIP (voice over Internet protocol) is the basic transmission of voice in a packet form. Voice and data traffic share the same "one pipe," but there is little in the way of business-grade voice applications. IP telephony is related to VoIP and is an application suite for voice communications. IP telephony applications are based on open standards. A common architecture makes it easier and more cost-effective to integrate voice and data applications.

4.   For a detailed case study on Carlson Hotels Worldwide, see the following Hewlett-Packard Web site: www.hp.com/hpinfo/newsroom/feature_stories/2002/mobile02.html.

5.   Thomas Feld and Marc Vietor, "Easy Travel Expense Recording," *SAP INFO*, October 2004.

6.   This figure was adapted with SAP's permission from the company's technical presentations.

7.   For more detailed case studies on Adobe Interactive Forms, see www.adobe.com.

Chapter Eleven

1.   Wal-Mart, "Wal-Mart Begins Roll-Out of Electronic Product Codes in Dallas/Fort Worth Area," April 30, 2004, press release available on www.walmart.com.

2.   "SAP Drives RFID Adoption," *SAP INFO*, May 13, 2004. Also see LogicaCMG's case study "Airbus takes RFID into the spare parts supply chain" available on www.logicacmg.com.

3.   Elena Malykhina, "Campbell Uses 'Slap-And-Ship' Approach to RFID," *InformationWeek*, September 30, 2004.

4.   On September 30, 2004, AIAG and EPCglobal announced a revision to the AIAG B-11: Tire and Wheel Label and Radio Frequency Identification (RFID) standard that now conforms to automotive and retail requirements. The standard allows retail information, such as the manufacturer, product, and serial number, to be included on the RFID tag.

5.   Stacy Collett, "Wireless Gets Down to Business," *Computerworld*, May 5, 2003.

6.   Philip Alling, Edward M. Wolfe, and Scott D. Brown, "Supply-Chain Giants Drive Early Adoption of RFID," Bear Stearns, January 2004.

7.   Also see Bob Brewin's article, "Delta begins second RFID bag tag test," in *Computerworld* on April 1, 2004.

8.   For more applications of RFID in the construction industry, see the Web site www.construction-institute.org.

9.   Source: www.epcglobalinc.org.

10. It is important to note that this same visibility can be technically achieved with some newer bar code standards that support serialization. However, it is not cost-feasible to read bar codes throughout the supply chain as they require line of sight, which is often not reliable in high-volume supply chains.

11. Source: Dr. Peter Zencke's executive blog entry, December 2003. Dr. Zencke's blog, along with the blogs of other SAP executives, can be found at the following Web site: http://www.sap.com/community/pub/blogs.aspx?logonStatusCheck=0 as of October 2004.

12. Source: www.walmart.com.

13. This case study was developed by Charles Mohrmann at SAT Corporation in conjunction with Paul Kurchina at TransAlta.

14. TransAlta's deployment of SAT Corporation's IntelaTrac field worker process improvement support software supports RFID asset tracking.

15. These rugged handheld computers are Symbol 8146 color RFID/barcode handheld PPC computers (ruggedized, Class 1 Div. 2 non-incendiary hazardous use certification, 256MB CompacFlash).

16. The tags attached to the assets use SAT Corporation's patented Universal Tag Formatting Protocol and Active X Controls to manage data storage and data compression on the RFID tags.

Index

2.5G (wireless technology between the second and third generations) 31, 57, 61–62
2G (second generation of wireless technology) 31, 57, 62, 64
2Roam 22
3-D graphics 58
3G (third generation of wireless technology) 5, 27, 29, 31, 34, 57, 61–64, 67, 69, 71, 78, 83, 172, 196
3M (company) 250
4G (fourth generation of wireless technology) 31, 61–62, 64
724 Solutions 22
802.11 61, 64–66. See also WiFi

A

Abaco Mobile 96–97
Accenture 250
Adobe Interactive Forms 181
Advance ship notice (ASN) 243
Aether Systems 22
Agassi, Shai vii, viii
Airbus 242
Albertsons 242
Alien Technology 250
Allen-Bradley (company) 254
Allscripts 5
Altair 8800 47
Alvarez, Fernando 97
Always-on 3, 61, 63–64, 83, 195, 222, 227
Amazon.com 36
Anheuser-Busch 166
AOL (America Online) 34
Apple Computer 36, 69
Application enablers 32, 34, 55
Application execution environment 58–59
Application infrastructure 29, 32–33, 35, 44, 77, 84–86, 98, 100, 281
Application programming interface (API) 58, 96
AT&T (American Telephone & Telegraph) 38
Atos Origin 234–235
Auto-ID Center 255–256

Auto-ID infrastructure 241, 260–261. See also SAP RFID solution
Automation 2–3, 5, 22, 24, 37–38, 41, 77, 101, 105–107, 123, 126, 142–143, 145, 207, 279
Automotive Industry Action Group 251
AvantGo 22

B

B2E (business to employee) 78, 225
Bannister, Roger 1
Bar codes 11–12, 41, 53, 89, 97, 108, 113, 115–116, 138, 140, 144, 147, 202, 204, 211, 217, 241–242, 244, 247–248, 251, 272
BASF 127
Bell Canada 13–14
BI (business intelligence) 78, 112, 221, 225, 230–232
Black & Decker 243
BlackBerry 25, 27, 35, 42, 83, 85, 96, 227, 228. See also Research in Motion
Bluetooth 51, 55, 61, 66, 68–69, 75, 91–92, 217–219. See also personal area network
Boingo Wireless 34
Boom-bust cycle 21–22
Bopack Systems 11
Boshold, Stefan 210
Brience 22
Broadband 38, 62, 67, 83
Business case 17, 97–98, 119, 142–144, 147, 274, 279, 281, 283
Business process management 5
Business-to-employee 78, 225, 236, 240

C

C & H Sugar Company 207–208
C++ 58
Camera phones 74
Campbell Taggart 166
Canada Post 220
Capgemini 190, 250
Carlson Hospitality Worldwide 233

Index 299

Catalyst International 208
CDMA (code division multiple access) 51, 64, 218
Change management 240, 282, 285–286, 291
Channel synchronization 35, 37
Checkpoint Systems 250
ChevronTexaco 127
Cingular Wireless 34, 218
Cintas 251
Client-side execution 59–60
Cobol 208
Coca-Cola Company, the 86, 157–158
Colgate-Palmolive 12
Colorado MicroDisplay 71
CompactFlash card 72
Consumer-facing applications and portals 4
Consumer packaged goods (CPG) industry 13, 153, 171, 173, 175, 180, 244, 247
Contract management 106, 132, 135, 149
Country Inns & Suites 233. See Carlson Hospitality Worldwide
Covigo 22. See Symbol Technologies
CRM (customer relationship management) 4, 9, 11, 12, 58, 77–79, 83, 85–88, 100, 105, 108, 110, 113, 155–156, 223, 274
Crossing the Chasm 16–18. See also Geoffrey Moore
Current state (AS-IS) 148, 280, 282, 284, 286, 288, 290
Customer Interaction Center (CIC) 190

D

Delta Air Lines 253
Deregulation 103
Deutsche Post 217
DIAD (delivery information acquisition device) 3, 215–218. See also UPS
Dial-up 83, 103
Diffusion of Innovations 16. See also Everett Rogers
Dillman, Linda 242
Direct EXchange Commerce System (DEX) 164–165, 172
Direct store delivery (DSD) 13, 151–176, 244
DMAIC (define, measure, analyze, improve, and control) 286
Doolin, Elmer 162
Dow Chemical Company, the 127, 199
DSL (digital subscriber line) 65, 67

E

E-Business Strategies 105, 125, 214

E-commerce 7, 22
E-ZPass 252
E.ON Group 145
EAN International 256
EAN.UCC identifier 257
Early adopters 17–18, 21, 25, 103
Early majority 17
Earthgrains 151, 162, 165–167. See also Sara Lee
easyPAY system 253. See also Royal Dutch/Shell Group
Eli Lilly 207
Employee applications 42, 225
Enterprise applications 1–2, 4, 6, 9, 15, 19–20, 22–25, 223, 227, 240, 248, 260
Environment, health, and safety (EH&S) 141, 237
Envoy (device) 51. See Motorola
EO Personal Communicator 50. See AT&T
EPC (electronic product code) 248, 255–257
EPCglobal Network 255–257
Equipment health monitoring (EHM) 267
Ericsson 31, 55, 63
ERP (enterprise resource planning) 4, 9, 12, 25, 45, 77–79, 87, 100, 207–208, 248, 260, 262
Executive dashboards 15
ExxonMobil 253

F

FedEx Corporation 41, 199, 215, 217–218, 220
Field force automation (FFA) 37–38
Field sales 9, 11–12, 26–27, 33, 37, 39, 75, 80, 89, 177, 179–185, 187–195, 198, 273
Field service 1, 9–10, 12, 26, 101–126, 177–198
Financial portals 233
First generation of mobile 7
FLASH-OFDM 64
Flat-panel display 71
Food services industry 236
Ford RESCU 73
FORTUNE 77, 174, 225, 228, 241
Fraport AG 127, 135–140
Frequency hop synchronization packet (FHS) 68
Frito-Lay 3, 151, 162–164, 170
Fujitsu 71
Fulfillment and delivery management 39, 41
Future state (TO-BE) 148, 281–282, 284, 286, 289–290
Future Store Initiative 261–263. See also METRO Group

G

Gap Inc. 251
GE (General Electric) 106, 233
Gillette Company, the 243
GIS (geographic information system) 75
GlobeRanger 250
GM (General Motors) 73
GoAmerica 34
Good Technology 227
Google 36
GPRS (general packet radio service) 7, 19,
   51, 61–62, 64, 78, 83, 91, 94, 172, 218
GPS (global positioning system) 52, 75,
   124, 217–218, 253
Grocery Manufacturers of America (GMA)
   153, 169
Gross, Al 49
GSM (global system for mobile communica-
   tion) 7, 19, 31, 51, 64, 94
GUI (graphical user interface) 89

H

Hardin, Garrett 21
Hardware and device trends 49
Hardware platforms, requirements for 53
HDTV (high-definition television) 1
Healthcare industry 2, 41, 82, 182, 236
Heavy equipment industry 181
Hewlett-Packard 243
HighJump Software 250. See also 3M
High Speed Downlink Packet Access
   (HSDPA) 64
Hings, Donald 49
Hitachi 71
Home Depot, the 106
Home repair and installation services 106
Homeland security 75, 212, 239
Hotspot 32, 64–65. See also WiFi
HotSync 51. See also Palm
HR (human resources) 14, 79, 221, 230,
   234
HTML (Hypertext Markup Language) 36
HTTP (Hypertext Transfer Protocol) 92, 94
HTTPS (secure sockets layer) 92

I

IBM (International Business Machines) 85,
   247, 250, 261
IDS Scheer 234–235
IEEE (Institute of Electrical and Electronics
   Engineers) 64–65, 67
IFF (Identification Friend or Foe) 254
In-vehicle information system (IVIS) 73

Inductive coupling 245
Industrial products industry 177, 180–181
Infineon Technologies AG 250
Information silos 224
Infrared ports 92
Infraserv 127, 141–145
Infrastructure 5, 18, 22–26, 29, 32, 44, 62,
   76–79, 82–84, 87–100, 144, 146, 173,
   195, 223, 267–268, 274, 282
Innovation curve 19
Innovation fatigue 282
Insurance industry 2, 5, 74, 106, 109–110,
   236, 238
Intel Corporation 67, 250, 261
IntelaTrac 267–268. See SAT Corporation
Intelligent field devices (IFDs) 149
Intelligent Library System 252. See
   Checkpoint Systems
Intelligent Transportation System (ITS) 73
Intellisync 34
Intermec 31, 41, 53, 61, 208, 254, 261–262
International Paper 243
Interrogator 248. See also reader
Inventory management 25, 78, 102, 132,
   134, 209
Isovia 22

J

J-Phone 74. See Vodafone
Java 31–32, 55, 58–60, 70, 78, 88, 90–92,
   260
Java 2 Platform, Micro Edition (J2ME)
   31–32, 58–60, 91
JavaServer Pages (JSP) 91
Java Virtual Machine (JVM) 70
JetBlue Airways 42–43
JIT (just-in-time) delivery 212

K

KDDI Corporation 71
Kopin (company) 71
KPIs (key performance indicators) 226,
   231, 264
Kyocera 31, 55

L

Laggards 17
LAN (local area network) 2–3, 42, 64, 68,
   94, 116, 217–218, 248
Late majority 17
Lay, Herman 163
Legacy application extension models 42
Life sciences industry 180, 182

Linux 27, 31–32, 55–56, 58
Litzinger, Joachim 143
Lobbe, Klaus Peter 127
Location-based services (LBS) 58, 60, 75, 228
Loonie 268
Lotus Domino 79, 85
Lotus Notes 42, 226
Lowe's 106
Lucent Technologies 63

M

M-banking 37
M-commerce 35–37
M-shopping 36
M-ticketing 36
M-trading 37
Manhattan Associates 250
Manufacturing message service (MMS) 57–58
MATRICs Group 250
McKesson Corporation 41
Mean time to repair (MTTR) 130
Menzel, Burkhard 146
Mercedes-Benz 73
Messaging and office applications 42, 226
Messer Griesheim GmbH 113–119
Metropolitan area network (MAN) 62
METRO Group 242, 260–261, 263
Metrowerks 56
Michelin 243
Microdisk 72
Micro-fuel cells 71
Microsoft 32, 42, 51, 54, 250
Middleware 5, 21, 26, 34, 43, 77–84, 93–94, 98, 209–210, 245, 248–249, 257, 260
Military Standard 810E 52. See also U.S. Department of Defense
Miniaturization 51, 69–70
MIT (Massachusetts Institute of Technology) 255–256
Mobile adoption cycle 15
Mobile asset management (MAM) 9–10, 26–27, 39–40, 78, 80, 89, 95, 106, 110, 127–129, 131–133, 135–136, 139–140, 145–150, 242, 268, 273
Mobile chasm 17
Mobile innovation curve 19
Mobile Internet 4, 7, 14, 19, 30–32, 34, 61, 284
Mobile Internet service provider (MISP) 34
Mobile Java 88
Mobile Linux 31–32, 56, 58, 179
Mobile portals 230

Mobile supplier curve 19–20
Mobilizing processes, step-by-step guide 286–291
Moblogging 74
Mobog 74
MontaVista Software 56
Moore, Geoffrey 16
Moore's Law 48
Motorola 27, 31, 54–55, 233, 254
MP3 51
MRP (material requirements planning) 143
MS-DOS 155
MSN 34. See also Microsoft
Multi-channel customer focus 30, 35
MultiMediaCard (MMC) 51
mySAP Business Suite 87, 108, 187–189
MySQL 250

N

NetMorf 22
Netpad 140. See Psion Teklogix
Newton MessagePad 51. See Apple Computer
Nextel 34
Nokia 31, 55, 63
Nortel Networks 63
Notification management 132–133
Notification-based solutions 229
NTT DoCoMo 71

O

OATSystems 250
Olson, Ken 47
OmniSky 34
ONS (object naming service) 257–258, 260. See also EPCglobal Network
OnStar 73. See also GM
Openwave 32
Operator-driven reliability (ODR) 263, 267–269
Operating systems 54, 56–57
Order management 78, 108, 132–133, 185, 201, 206
OSHA (Occupational Health and Safety Administration) 130
Outsourcing 42, 129, 131–132, 224
Overall equipment effectiveness (OEE) 150

P

PalmOne 7, 29, 31–32, 34, 41–42, 55, 85, 177, 179, 226–227
PalmSource 32, 55, 58
Panasonic 53, 55, 144
PCMCIA card slots 72

PDA (personal digital assistant) 2, 50–52,
    54–55, 58, 74, 78, 83, 113, 140, 146, 179
Peer-to-peer messaging 226
PepsiCo 39, 158, 163
Peripherals 32, 68, 70, 74, 92, 96–97. *See
    also* camera phones, scanners, and Web
    cameras.
Personal area network (PAN) 68–69
Personal information management (PIM) 42,
    52, 221, 226
Pharmaceutical industry 143, 177, 182–183,
    189, 193, 198, 207, 220, 244
PIOS (peripheral input-output services)
    96–97. See Abaco
PLM (product lifecycle management) 4, 9,
    45, 77, 79, 110, 147
PML (Physical Markup Language) 257–258.
    See also EPCglobal Network
Pocket PC 54–55, 61, 155, 179, 229
POP3 (Post Office Protocol) 79.
Popular Electronics 47
Portable data terminal (PDT) 41–42
Portals 4, 14–15, 30, 42–43, 59, 221–222,
    230, 233–235
PowerPad 218. See FedEx
Prada 251
Price/performance ratios 8
Process models 49, 148, 156, 194, 280
Process monitoring 204
Process-centric mobile solutions 8
Procter & Gamble (P&G) 243
Procurement 13–14
Productivity multipliers 14
Progressive Corporation 5
Proof of delivery (proof of delivery) 41,
    205–206
Provia Software 250
Psion PLC 31, 35, 55, 140, 207, 210–211,
    250

Q

QUALCOMM 31–32, 63

R

Radisson 233. See Carlson Hospitality
    Worldwide
Reader 138–140, 155, 244–249, 253,
    257–258, 272. *See also* RFID
RedPrairie 250
Reliability centered maintenance (RCM) 150
Research In Motion (RIM) 32, 83, 85, 179,
    227, 265
RFID (radio frequency identification) 5, 27,
    53, 97, 115, 139–140, 241–273, 286

River Run Software 231
Rogers, Everett 16
ROI (return on investment) 4, 6, 9–10, 15,
    17, 20, 26, 28, 46, 104–105, 118, 123,
    140, 144, 147, 165, 170, 174, 179–180,
    182–183, 192, 196, 219–220, 234, 236,
    263, 272, 278–279, 285, 291
Route accounting 13, 151, 169, 172, 175
Royal Dutch/Shell Group 253
Royal Philips Electronics 254
Rugged handheld devices 52–53, 77, 102,
    105, 213

S

Sales analytics 187
Sales portals 42
Salesforce automation (SFA) 179–180, 188
Samsung 55, 64
SamSys 250
SAPConsole 89–90, 208–209
SAP Labs Tokyo 259
SAP Mobile Application Studio 96
SAP Mobile Business 44
SAP Mobile Client 86, 95
SAP Mobile Development Kit 95
SAP Mobile Infrastructure (SAP MI) 29, 32,
    44, 77, 79, 87–94, 97, 98, 100, 146, 274
SAP Mobile Time and Travel 234
SAP NetWeaver 19, 23, 44, 77, 79, 82, 87,
    88–89, 92, 98, 100, 116, 239, 241, 260,
    274, 284; mySAP Enterprise Portal and
    94
SAP Plant Maintenance (SAP PM) 137, 139,
    145–146, 268
SAP RFID solution 259–260
SAP Warehouse Management (SAP WM)
    208
SAP xApps 79, 236
Sara Lee 166, 170
SAT Corporation 266
Savant 257–258. *See also* EPCglobal
    Network
Savi Technology 253
Scan-based trading 165, 167–169, 244
Scanners 5, 31, 41, 68, 89, 92, 97, 108,
    116, 155, 173
SCE (supply chain execution) 39, 245
Schmidt, Jochen 141
SCM (supply chain management) 4, 9, 13,
    45, 77, 79, 89, 155–56, 180, 241, 248,
    259, 261, 263, 272, 274
Screen scraping 81
Sears 77, 101–102, 106, 231
Second generation of mobile 8, 27, 109
Secure digital/multimedia card (SD/MMC) 51

Security 18, 32–34, 39, 42, 54, 58, 67, 74–75, 92, 130, 140, 224, 239, 242, 247, 252, 265, 269, 272, 282
Semiconductor industry 2
Server-side execution 59
Sharp (company) 51, 55
Siemens 254
Six Sigma 286
SKU (stock-keeping unit) 174, 256
Slope of hype 19–20. See also mobile supplier curve
Slope of ROI 20. See also mobile supplier curve
Smart phones 29, 31–32, 45, 79, 91, 179
Smith, Frederick 215
SMS (simple message service) 7, 232
SOAP (Simple Object Access Protocol) 91
Social workers 237
Solution blueprint formulation 274
Speedpass 253. See ExxonMobil
Sprint PCS 34
SRM (supplier relationship management) 79
Standardization 153, 256
Strategy 29–30, 35–36, 102, 105, 120, 125, 136, 145, 163, 170; creation and 275–286
Sun Microsystems 32, 250
Sybase 34, 250
Symbian Ltd. 31–32, 55, 58
Symbol Technologies 146, 218
System-on-a-chip 70

T

T1 line 65
Tablet PC 52
Tagsys 250
Target Corporation 242
Task-centric mobile applications 7
Technical object management 132, 134
Technology adoption lifecycle 16
Technology platforms 29, 31
Telecom industry 13, 102–104
Telematics 70, 72–74, 214, 228
Telematics communications unit (TCU) 73
Tesco 242, 259
Texas Instruments 250, 254
Textamerica 74
Thaden, Gunnar 188
Third generation of mobile 62
TIBCO Software 250
Time, expense, and travel management 187, 234–235
Time division duplex (TDD) 64

Toffler, Alvin 69
Torvalds, Linus 55
Toshiba 51, 71
Total Asset Visibility (TAV) Network 253. See also the U.S. Department of Defense
Total cost of ownership (TCO) 84, 100
Total productive maintenance (TPM) 150
Tragedy of the commons 20–21. See also Garrett Hardin
TransAlta 40, 263–268
Transponder 138–140, 248. See also RFID
Transportation and delivery solutions 211–212
Transportation and logistics industry 3, 106, 108–109, 215
Transportation management 205
Treo 52, 227
TÜV Nord Group 177, 187, 188, 198
Tyco Sensormatic 250

U

U.S. Department of Defense (DoD) 242, 244, 253
U.S. Department of Transportation (DOT) 214
U.S. Food and Drug Administration (FDA) 130, 242
U.S. Postal Service (USPS) 242
U.S. Transportation Security Administration (TSA) 242
Ultrawideband (UWB). See also personal area network 68–69
UMTS (universal mobile telecommunications system) 31
Uniform Code Council (UCC) 256–257
Unisys 250
University of California 21
Unix 31
UPS (United Parcel Service) 3–5, 17, 41, 199–200, 214–220; Standard Terminal Platform (SteP) and 217
Utilities industry 102–104, 263

V

VeriSign 34
Verizon Communications 32, 34, 79, 218
VF Corporation 243
Viastore systems 250
VMI (vendor-managed inventory) 13, 167, 246
Vodafone 32, 34, 79
Voice of the customer (VOC) 287
Volkswagen 199, 209–211

W

Wal-Mart 5, 152, 157, 241, 242, 244, 259,
  260
Walkie-talkie 49
WAN (wide area network) 57, 61, 217
Warehouse order fulfillment 201
Warehouse management 202–204, 206
Web cameras 70, 74
WebMethods 250
WebSAPConsole 90
WebSphere 261. See IBM
WEP (Wired Equivalent Privacy) 67
WESCO Distribution 40
Wesertal GmbH 127, 145–147
WiFi (wireless fidelity) 5–6, 27, 29, 31–32,
  34, 51, 55, 64–65, 67, 69, 83–84, 155,
  218–219, 265
WiFi Alliance 67
WiFi Protected Access (WPA) standard 67
WiMax forum, the 67
Windows Mobile 27, 29, 31–32, 54, 58, 60,
  78, 155
Wireless application gateway (WAG) 21
Wireless Application Protocol (WAP) 7, 59,
  81
Wireless Markup Language (WML) 36
WLAN (wireless local area network) 2, 42,
  61, 64, 94, 116–117, 172, 217–218, 248
Workforce automation (WFA) 105, 107
Workforce management 110, 112

X

XML (Extensible Markup Language) 218

Y

Yafro 74
Yahoo! 36, 230

Z

Zebra Technologies 250
Zencke, Peter 259
ZigBee 68–69. See also personal area
  network

About the Authors

Ravi Kalakota, Ph.D., is the CEO of E-Business Strategies. Dr. Kalakota holds the distinction of having co-authored the bestsellers *e-Business: Roadmap for Success* and *Frontiers of Electronic Commerce*. He has consulted extensively with Fortune 1000 companies such as SAP, Sun Microsystems, Intel, Guidant, and AT&T, and is a sought-after speaker. Previously, Dr. Kalakota has held the Georgia Research Alliance Chair in E-commerce at Georgia State University, the Xerox Chair in Information Systems at the Simon Graduate School of Business, University of Rochester, and also taught at the University of Texas at Austin.

Ravi Kalakota can be contacted by e-mail at *ravi@ebstrategy.com*

Paul Kurchina is regarded as an SAP visionary and a leader in exploiting SAP technologies. Currently, Kurchina is driving Process/Application Architecture and the Mobile/RFID program for TransAlta, a global electrical generation and marketing company. Since joining the Americas' SAP Users' Group (ASUG) in 1993, he has held multiple leadership positions in enterprise portals, plant maintenance, utilities, production strategies, and enterprise architecture. He is currently leading an SAP NetWeaver Mobile Influence Council within the SAP user community. Kurchina became actively involved in the SAP world in 1993 through previous positions at Ontario Hydro and PricewaterhouseCoopers in which he developed and launched large-scale IT initiatives.

Paul Kurchina can be contacted by e-mail at *paul@kurchina.com*

MivarPress

Mivar Press books are available at special
quantity discounts for bulk purchases.

For corporate customers, Mivar Press can
custom-design books or provide book excerpts.

E-mail Mivar Press for details.

contact@mivarpress.com

www.mivarpress.com